JUANA INÉS DE LA CRUZ
AND THE THEOLOGY OF BEAUTY

Juana Inés de la Cruz and the Theology of Beauty:

The First Mexican Theology

George H. Tavard

University of Notre Dame Press
Notre Dame   London

Library of Congress Cataloging-in-Publication Data

Tavard, George H. (George Henry), 1922–
    Juana Inés de la Cruz and the theology of beauty : the first
Mexican theology / George H. Tavard.
        p.   cm.
    Includes bibliographical references and index.
    ISBN 0-268-01206-7
    1. Juana Inés de la Cruz, Sister, 1651–1695—Criticism and
interpretation. 2. Christianity in literature. 3. Theology,
Doctrinal—Mexico—History—17th century. 4. Catholic
Church—Doctrines—History—17th century.   I. Title.
PQ7296.J6Z896   1991
861—dc20   90-70857
                                                          CIP

Contents

Introduction

Three remarkable women wrote extensively in the North American colonies of the seventeenth century. Each wrote respectively in one of the three colonial languages, English, French, and Spanish; one lived in New England, one in New France, one in New Spain. Anne Bradstreet (1612–1672), whose father and husband were governors of the colony of Massachusetts, was born in England; she became a delicate poet, called, in the first publication of her poems, "the Tenth Muse, Lately Sprung Up in America" (London, 1650). Marie de l'Incarnation (1599–1672), recently canonized by Pope John Paul II, was born in France, married, was widowed, became an Ursuline sister, lived and died in Québec. She is acknowledged as one of the great mystics of the Catholic Church. On account of obedience to her spiritual director and a concern to offer maternal spiritual care for the son of her early marriage, she wrote several *Relations* of her experience of God. The third of these women, Inés Ramírez de Asbaje (1648–1695), is known by her religious name, Sor Juana Inés de la Cruz. The only one of the three born on North American soil, in Mexico, she was, like Anne Bradstreet, celebrated as "the Tenth Muse" by her first publishers. Sor Juana is the subject of the present study.

Well known in her native Mexico and in the generality of the Spanish-speaking world, Juana Inés de la Cruz has remained largely unknown to the educated public of English-speaking North America, in spite of the fact that good scholarly investigations of her life and works have been done in the United States. Even American Catholicism, which could well use the help of Latin America as a critical counterpoint to its self-image, has ignored her. Undoubtedly, the disregard of a major literary figure from south of the Rio Grande proceeds in part from the traditional indifference of the English-speaking populations of North America to speakers of the Spanish language, from misunderstandings between Anglos and Hispanics

1

that have been inherited from past wars, from the estrangement between the dominant Puritan culture of the original English colonies and the Catholic culture of the vice-royalty of New Spain, from the militant economic imperialism of the North, and possibly from a modern dislike for, or rather ignorance of, the baroque art and writings of the seventeenth century. Yet this cloistered nun of the seventeenth century not only was a great poet, but she also anticipated in her writings some aspects of the current movement for women's liberation.

Juana's life, her poetry, her talent as a playwright, her defense of women, the religious dimension of her writings, even her psychology (with the hazards of an attempted modern psychoanalysis) have been carefully studied, chiefly by scholars in the Hispanic world. One aspect of her work, however, has not been investigated: there has been no systematic study of her theology.

After she entered the convent, Sor Juana placed her gifts for writing, which had presumably been tested before, at the disposal of members of the vice-royal nobility, of her friends and acquaintances in the Church and at court, of several bishops, and of sundry monasteries. This led her to compose numerous occasional works, pieces of a somewhat ephemeral nature that were written to celebrate many an event, secular or religious, in the official public life of her native land. Her familiarity with the vicereines, which seems to have reached rare levels of friendship with the marchioness de la Laguna, inspired a plethora of lyrical poems in their honor. Her passion for learning, her deep conviction of the rights of women to learn as much as they could in all areas of literature, science, philosophy, and theology, and her indignation at men's mistreatment of women of the middle or the lower classes came to be expressed eloquently and movingly in both poetry and prose.

Through much of this, Juana formulated certain theological ideas. Indeed, the controversy of her later years, to which most authors trace back her renunciation of further writing, was occasioned by a theological piece. Spanish-speaking theologians, who until Vatican II were excessively bound by scholastic forms and methods, have generally neglected her. The notes of Alfonso Méndez Plancarte in the standard edition of Juana's works[1] contain a number of theological remarks. So do several of the books devoted to Juana Inés de la Cruz: Maria Esther Perez has included some theological references in her investigation of Juana's dramatic works; Marie-Cécile Bénassy's major study, in French, of Juana's religious conceptions naturally touches on her theology. Nevertheless a gap remains that I intend to fill, at least in part, in the present work.

Sor Juana's Career

The birth of Inés Ramírez de Asbaje y Santillana cannot be dated with certainty. The year 1651 has been accepted in the past on the testimony of her early biographers. Yet 12 November 1648 is more likely: the baptismal certificate of a certain Inés, in the parish archives of Chimalhuacán, probably refers to her, given the name, Ramírez, of the two sponsors. At any rate, Juana was born at San Miguel Nepantla, a small ranch some sixty kilometers southeast of Mexico City at the foot of the great volcano, Popocatepetl. Her mother, Isabel Ramírez de Santillana, was herself a Creole, born of Spanish parents in the New World. Her father, Pedro Manuel de Asbaje y Vargas Machuca, was a military officer from Guipuzcoa, in the Basque provinces of Spain. As was not infrequent then at a certain level of Mexican society, her parents were living in concubinage. As was customary in such a situation, the baptismal certificate does not provide the parents' name but instead gives the baby the title, "daughter of the Church." Having fathered three children, Pedro Manuel vanished from their life some two years after Juana's birth. Her mother then followed the only practical course that lay open to her: she found a second companion, who turned out to be more stable, in the person of another soldier, Diego Ruiz Lozano. Altogether, Isabel gave birth to three daughters and three sons.

Juana was not raised at Nepantla but in a village a short distance away, Panoayan, at the home of her maternal grandparents.[2] In 1659, for reasons that according to her testimony were related to her wish to study, she was sent to Mexico City, where she lived with relatives of her mother. In 1664, at the age of thirteen, Juana moved to the residence of the new viceroy, Don Antonio Sebastián de Toledo Molina y Salazar, marquis de Mancera, where she lived under the protection of the marchioness, Doña Leonor Carreto. Such a situation was not unusual. The viceroys were officially expected to help a number of girls and boys acquire a good education and the civilized virtue of urbanity. Presumably Juana took an active part in the social life and festivities of the court of New Spain. The two secular plays that she wrote later may well allude to life at the viceregal court. The girl had a close relationship with the vicereine.

As she explains in her autobiographical piece, the *Respuesta a sor Filotea de la Cruz* (1691), Juana grew into an intelligent and intellectual woman eager to lead a life of scholarship. She felt "a great aversion to matrimony."[3] In 1667 she therefore decided to become a nun. She was accepted as a postulant at the convent of San José, an establishment of the discalced Carmelites, the order of the great St. Teresa of Avila, whom Juana still called years later, "the holy Mother and my mother, Teresa" (p. 835). She left the Carmel, however, three months later. Officially, her health could not bear the rigors of the Carmelite rule, and she was sick for several months after leaving the convent. Yet I suspect that this was less a matter of bodily than of intellectual health. The great desire to study that Juana had felt from the early age of three had guided her toward the choice of a religious vocation. She preferred study to matrimony; but the life of intellectual research to which she aspired could hardly fit the Carmelite tradition and customs, and San José was known for the austerity of its observance.

There were ample possibilities in selecting another convent, for the city of Mexico had in 1650 no fewer than sixteen. Besides Carmelites, there were Poor Clares, Bernardines, Capuchin and Dominican sisters, and, among the least rigorous, Conceptionists (with several monasteries in the capital city) and Hieronymites. The convents largely followed class lines in accepting postulants. One convent of Poor Clares, for example, was reserved to Indian women.

In any case, only a few months passed before Juana, having taken care of her health, entered St. Paula's Convent, established in Mexico City since 1586, of the order of St. Jerome (the Hieronymites). The order was a Spanish foundation, the male branch having been created in 1373; the female branch in 1510. As her admission required a dowry and she was poor, her godfather, Captain Don Pedro Velazquez de la Cadena, donated the money for it.[4] At her profession in February 1669, she took the religious name of Juana Inés de la Cruz.

Juana's life at the monastery is well documented. The Hieronymites were, like most nuns of the time, cloistered. Their rule, however, was somewhat loose; the vow of poverty was interpreted broadly, and some sisters owned extensive possessions, which they administered from behind the convent walls. The office, said or sung in choir, and some manual labor were the sisters' chief and nearly sole common obligations. Even the meals were not taken together. The nuns could have their own slaves and servants. Like the others, Juana Inés lived in her own ample quarters, which she eventually bought from the community. When she entered, Juana was given a young slave by her mother. This was a twelve-year old mulatto girl, Juana de San José. At the age of eighteen or nineteen, the girl became pregnant. Letting her out of the convent so that she could marry, Sor Juana sold the young woman to one of her own sisters, Josefina Maria de Asbaje, who later, in 1684, paid 250 pesos for the girl. Even after this departure, Juana did not live alone in her quarters. She had undertaken to raise two of her young nieces, daughters of her half-brother, Diego Ruiz Lozano: they shared her lodgings, and she supervised their education. As the convent ran a school for girls, there was nothing unusual in this; convents commonly housed a number of *niñas,* who were raised and educated until they were claimed back by their family, often at the time of a prearranged marriage.

Besides the nuns, their slaves and servants, and the children, the population of such a monastery frequently comprised some *donadas,* or oblates, who lived like nuns but did not take vows. They therefore did not share the responsibilities and the prerogatives of the professed sisters. There were also servants employed by the community.

Juana was eventually entrusted with material responsibility, becoming *contadora,* "treasurer," of her convent. For herself, she read intensively, gathering a number of books of literature and science: the estimates vary from some four hundred to four thousand. Being highly interested in science and music, she also collected scientific and musical instruments. Above all, the facility with which she composed poetry brought her in high demand as a writer and poet at the court and in the Church. Most of her poems are occasional pieces prompted by some celebration and commissioned by some organization or person who remunerated her for her work. As there was little difficulty in receiving visitors in the parlors, and some, like the vicereine, in her personal quarters, Juana was in constant touch with the world and, especially, with the court. She was able to keep and develop an extensive network of acquaintances and some deeper friendships. Don Carlos de Sigüenza y Góngora, a priest and former

Jesuit who was a distinguished scientist and writer, was often seen in the parlor.

Juana got to know all the viceroys who presided over New Spain during her life as a nun. The viceroy was usually in office for a renewable three-year period. After the marquis de Mancera (viceroy from 1664 to 1673), there were Pedro Nuño Colón de Portugal, duke de Veragua (who died six days after his inauguration); Don Payo Enríquez de Ribera, archbishop of Mexico, who exercised the temporal power from 1673 to 1680; Tomás Antonio de la Cerda y Aragón, marquis de la Laguna de Camero Viejo (viceroy from 1680 to 1686); Melchor Portocassero Lasso de la Vega, count de Monclova (served from 1686 to 1688); and Gaspar de Sandoval Cerda Silva y Mendoza, count de Galve (reigned from 1688 to 1696). Juana Inés was particularly well acquainted with three of the vicereines: Leonor Carreto, marchioness de Mancera ("Laura" in Juana's poems), under whose protection she had lived at the court; Maria Luisa Manrique de Lara y Gonzaga, who was in her own right countess de Paredes, marchioness de la Laguna by marriage; and Maria Elvira de Toledo, countess de Galve.

Of these three, the marchioness de la Laguna was by far Juana's closest friend. Both the viceroy and his wife belonged to the high aristocracy of Spain. The marchioness, who, in Juana's poems about or addressed to her, becomes "Lysi," "la divina Lysi," "Lisarda," "Filis," was not only rich but also beautiful, intelligent, cultured, and pious. After the viceroy's return to Spain, Maria Luisa had the first edition of Juana's poetry, which was dedicated to the marchioness herself, published in Madrid in 1689. The delicate and ambitious title, *Inundación Castálida,* had presumably been suggested to Maria Luisa by some acquaintance who was knowledgeable in classical lore. (In Greek mythology Castalia was the name of a nymph who drowned herself in a fountain rather than accept Apollo's advances. Her name passed to the fountain, which, located at Delphi, was at the source of the prophetic inspiration of the Sybil.) On the very cover of the book Juana was given highly complimentary titles: "the Unique Poetess, the Tenth Muse."

In the early years of the viceroyalty of the marquis de la Laguna, around 1681–1682, however, the secular topics of much of her poetry, composed at the request of persons at the viceregal court and, often, of the vicereine herself, brought Juana into conflict with her confessor, the Jesuit Antonio Núñez de Miranda (1618–1695), who had been instrumental in guiding her in the choice of her vocation. He ordered her to abandon all writing, and he even complained in public about her unbecoming self-pride.[5] In a letter that has been preserved, she dismissed him as her confessor. She told him that following his injunction was impossible on her part, and that his public criticism of her was both unfair and unworthy of him. She therefore would manage without his services, relying on the Spirit of God and on the viceroy's protection.

The problem, however, did not disappear with Núñez de Miranda. In 1690, Juana was at the height of her talent and her fame. A second volume of her poetry appeared in Spain, and her most theological work, the religious play, *Auto del divino Narciso,* was published in Mexico. But she again became the object of criticism on the part of highly placed clerics. In the same year, one of her occasional visitors, the Spaniard Don Manuel Fernández de Santa Cruz y Sahagún (1637–1699), bishop of Guadalajara in 1675, then of Puebla in 1676, released to the public her theological critique, which she had not intended for publication, of a sermon by a Portuguese Jesuit, Antonio de Vieira (1608–1697). The bishop gave Juana's work the title that has remained: *Carta atenagórica.* Several critics have surmised that this publication was a weapon in a lasting feud between the bishop of Puebla and the archbishop of Mexico, but this is no more than a hypothesis. In his accompanying letter, which he signed "Sor Filotea de la Cruz," the bishop of Puebla invited Juana Inés to devote her talents exclusively to the salvation of her soul and to religious writing, as would be more appropriate to her female sex and her religious vocation than secular poetry and the pursuit of scientific knowledge.

Juana Inés's response, *Respuesta a Sor Filotea de la Cruz* (1691), is cast in autobiographical form. It includes a spirited defense of the right of women to study in both secular and theological matters. The ideas had already been formulated in Juana's letter to her Jesuit confessor, though in a more familiar and less restrained form.

Only one point is clear in the ensuing events: in 1692, at the height of her career, Juana Inés stopped writing. She returned to her former confessor, Núñez de Miranda, to whom she completely entrusted her spiritual life. She also had all her books and instruments sold, and the money was given to the poor. She never wrote another line for the public.

We shall return in more detail to this episode later, but an overview is useful at this point. The more common reconstruction of what happened is this: The archbishop of Mexico, Fray Francisco de Aguiar Seijas y Ulloa (died 1698), was a friend neither of the bishop of Puebla nor of Juana Inés de la Cruz. Known for his austerity, he did not approve of literary-minded sisters. He had been in competition with Fernández de Santa Cruz, who had also been considered for the see of Mexico City. He was an admirer and perhaps a friend of the Portuguese Jesuit, Vieira, who had dedicated to him, in 1675 and 1678, the Spanish translation of two volumes of his sermons. Don Francisco had a passion for helping the poor, and to this purpose he was not loathe to demand monetary gifts from the monasteries and convents of the city.

In these circumstances it has naturally been assumed that the archbishop viewed Sor Juana Inés and her publications with a critical eye. Heavy pressures bore on Juana from him and possibly also from her own community, which may have been eager to please the archbishop and which must have harbored some jealousy. Meanwhile, the current viceroy, count de Galve, and his wife Maria Elvira were too preoccupied with secular politics to involve themselves in the matter and protect Juana from criticism or gossip. They had to cope with social unrest among poor Indians (public buildings were set afire in the riots of June 1692); there were epidemics; English and French buccaneers raided the Atlantic coast; a French army had taken possession of Santo Domingo. No longer shielded by the court, Juana Inés the writer was reduced to silence.

Another reading of the facts allows, however, for a very different interpretation. Juana Inés would simply have been led through her own spiritual growth to abandon worldly interests, to seek for a more spiritual beauty than may be expressed with words, and to pursue holiness more resolutely and exclusively.[6] In any case, three years after entering into silence, on 17 April 1695, Juana Inés de la Cruz died during an epidemic, after having fallen ill while nursing other sick sisters.

Sor Juana's Works

Juana's writings are neither simple nor easy for modern readers. She takes her models, naturally enough, from what was then recent or contemporary Spanish poetry. She admires and imitates the great poets of the previous generation, Luis de Góngora (1561–1627) and Francisco de Quevedo (1580–1645). She shares with them the tastes and aesthetic conceptions of the baroque age. Following the literary theories of the Jesuit Baltasar Gracián (1601–1658), Juana makes considerable use of *conceptism*, a device that uses wit and word play to suggest philosophical conceptions. Largely on the model of Góngora, she loves the procedure that classical rhetoricians call *hyperbaton*: she systematically reverses the syntactic order of words in imitation of the Latin language. Often, she places an adjective at an unexpected distance from the noun it qualifies.

The chief model of Juana's religious theater is the great Calderón de la Barca (1600–1681). Her villancicos are largely inspired by his. For her most important play, *Divino Narciso,* she borrows from him much of the theme.

In addition, Juana has a degree of acquaintance with the advanced science of her time as it was spread in the writings of the German Jesuit, Athanasius Kircher (1601–1680).[7] Kircher was an investigator of physics, the inventor of the magic lantern, and a prolific writer. Knowledgeable in astronomy, he also dabbled in astrology, and he helped to popularize an interest that had grown from early Renaissnce speculations about ancient Egypt: egyptology was taken by many as the key to all sciences. And egyptology made use of mythology. Precisely, Juana multiplies allusions to the classical mythologies of Greece, Rome, and Egypt. She takes for granted that her readers are as familiar with them as they may be with the details of the Old and New Testaments. But what was grasped as an enlightening imagery in the cultured classes of her time is likely to strike the modern mind as a conundrum that requires recourse to specialized dictionaries. A certain amount of arduous spade work is thus necessary before one can truly appreciate Juana's poetry. The effort, however, is well worth making.

Juana Inés's writings fall into several categories. Georgina Sabat de Rivers, the modern editor of her first volume, *Inundación Castálida,* distinguishes, on the basis of literary genres, among four types of works:

1. "personal lyrics": among them the editor places poems with "philosophical themes."
2. *Loas:* originally these were introductions to presentations or plays with a religious theme; those of Juana have often be-

come independent pieces composed on some occasion that
was deemed worthy of commemoration and celebration.

3. *Villancicos:* this old form of Spanish lyric, made for song and
   dance and related to the ballads of other European lan-
   guages, could have many different forms; they were often
   made up of an envoy (*estribillo*) and a number of stanzas
   (*coplas*), which in some cases ended with the same last line.

4. In a class by itself, the composition *Neptuno alegórico:* this
   consists of explanations in prose and poetry destined to
   adorn a triumphal arch erected by the city of Mexico in
   honor of the marquis de la Laguna when he took up his post
   as viceroy of New Spain on 30 November 1680.[8]

A study of Juana's theological views needs to distinguish be-
tween themes rather than between literary genres. I will therefore
propose the following eight categories for Juana's religious works:

1. a strictly personal didactic poem, which falls into no specific
   genre and bears the title *Primero sueño (First Dream)*

2. sonnets, villancicos, and other poems in honor of various
   saints, including a series of poems inspired by St. Bernard
   (1690)

3. religious theater (loas; villancicos; and *autos sacramentales,*
   dramatic works associated with the sacraments, especially
   with the eucharist and the feast of Corpus Christi) composed
   in honor of the saints. One should distinguish between the
   plays that are certainly authentic and some others that are
   less surely authentic. Juana's authentic pieces include those
   on St. Peter Nolasco, 1677; St. Peter the apostle, 1677, 1683;
   St. Joseph, 1690; St. Catherine, 1691; St. Hermenegild and
   Joseph of Egypt, both of uncertain date. A few pieces, re-
   ferred to as "attributable" in Alfonso Méndez Plancarte's
   edition of Juana's works, are probably authentic, but they
   are not attested by Juana herself or by her contemporaries:
   St. Peter, 1680, 1684, 1690, 1691, 1692.

4. religious pieces and plays written in honor of the Virgin
   Mary and on the occasion of her liturgical feasts, chiefly her
   conception (1676, 1689) and her assumption (1676, 1679,
   1685, 1690), plus, as attributable, the assumption (1677,
   1681, 1686)

5. the *Carta atenagórica,* a systematic critique, in the style of baroque Scholasticism, of the Christology of a sermon by Antonio de Vieira

6. religious pieces and dramatic works in honor of Christ: Christmas (1689), and, chiefly, the auto sacramental, *Divino Narciso* (1690); as attributable, Christmas, 1678, 1680

7. several lyric poems relating to devotional themes, which reflect Juana's personal piety and spiritual experience

8. several religious pieces in prose, some of which, of uncertain date, take the form of spiritual exercises for the Hieronymite sisters (for the novena before Christmas; in honor of the fifteen mysteries of the rosary), while others, of a highly personal nature, relate to Juana's entrance into silence.

Some writings by Sor Juana Inés have disappeared, notably one that was entitled *El caracol,* a study of musical theory, a topic in which she was highly interested. As a rule I shall generally avoid quoting the attributable poems, since there remains a doubt about their authenticity; in any case, the ideas they contain can already be found in the authenticated works. I will quote extensively only the poems and compositions that are certainly from Juana's pen.

Chapter 1 (First Dream) will analyze Juana's conception of the world and of the soul, which implies a definite theological view of creation and the Creator. Chapter 2 (The Baroque Edifice) will explore Juana's depiction of the saints, which is closely related to the shape of baroque piety. Chapter 3 (The Temple of God) will focus on her understanding of, and piety towards, the Virgin Mary. Chapter 4 (Narcissus) will study her Christology as it is formulated in her literary and theological masterpiece, the play *Divino Narciso,* in her villancicos for Christmas of 1689, in a few other poems, and in the *Respuesta.* Chapter 5 (The Finesses of God) will analyze Juana's systematic critique of Antonio de Vieira's Christology. Chapter 7 (The Silence) will try to arrive at a balanced understanding of her renunciation of further writing in 1692. Chapter 8 (The Theology of Beauty) will draw conclusions regarding the nature and shape of Juana's theological imagination.

1

First Dream

After she entered the convent, Juana Inés de la Cruz quickly became the quasi-official poet of New Spain. She has remained, in the judgment of later critics, the only great poet of the Spanish colonies in the Americas. Her religious convictions and theological conceptions are naturally related to what she learned about herself in her own experience of life. Her upbringing in the countryside and in the city of Mexico as well as her sojourn at the court of New Spain had given her a special sense of her motherland, of the Church, and of the world of nations. Her extensive reading and study provided her with a basic philosophy, even if they were not systematic in the modern academic sense. Her information and her ideas touched on both literature and the sciences such as they were then known in Mexico. She became familiar with classical Latin poetry, with the liturgical poetry of the Latin liturgy, and with Spanish poetic literature; in all three poetic spheres she found inspiration and models.

An investigation of the theological ideas to which Sor Juana Inés gave expression in poetry and prose should attend to the conclusions, provisional or definitive, that she may have reached about herself and about humanity. Juana often alludes to a scale of creaturely being: the physical world of nature; the world of animals (birds occupy a special place in her imagination); and the world of spiritual creatures, such as angels, including the fallen angels of the classical tradition. In Juana's works, humanity itself includes two levels: the men and women of the present world in their several categories; the saints in heaven. Regarding the former, Juana alludes to, and to some extent depicts, differences in class, caste, or culture. She is well aware of what separates Spaniards, recently arrived from the mother country, and Creoles, descendants of the early conquistadors and of later immigrants, from Indians, the proud but generally impoverished inheritors of the dethroned culture of the Aztecs and the other pre-Colombian tribes, from the less numerous blacks, the offspring of Africans who had originally been imported as slaves to the West Indies and who somehow had made their way to the land of New Spain, and from mulattoes, people of mixed blood, who were fairly numerous, since the Spaniards, following the example of Hernán Cortez, had not been reluctant to take native mistresses or wives. At the time of Juana Inés, many mulattoes and blacks still had the status of slaves.

Juana suffered from the official or customary differences between men and women in society and in the Church. For better or for worse, she herself never fit the stereotypes of her time on the assumed complementarity of men and women. She saw what inequalities society unjustly imposes on women. Not for nothing did she know that she was illegitimate. As her poetry abundantly shows, she could empathize with women of all kinds, qualities, and experiences. She sings of human love, of the waxing and waning of happiness, of the absence of the beloved, of the sorrows of widowhood, of the plight of despised and abused women, of the great heroines of the past, of the ideal woman who was raised by God to become the queen of heaven.

Juana's plays feature most of humankind as she knew or simply imagined it. Blacks and mulattoes speak a dialect of Castilian that she herself had heard as a child. The language and culture of the Aztecs she knew well. She liked to compose dancing songs modeled on those that were familiar to the natives of the Anáhuac, the central plateau of Mexico. The Spaniards called this kind of song a *tocotín*, from the triple meter of the music; in Nahuatl it was a *netotilichtli*. The rhythm was created by two different drums and several other instruments.[1] In fact, Juana's villancicos and the loas that introduce her religious plays are interspersed with tocotínes, most of them in Spanish, in the form of a romance made of hexasyllabic verses; a few are in Nahuatl.

Juana also acquired a profound knowledge of the Latin language and its literature as well as of the mythology of Greece and Rome, to which she constantly alludes. This latinizing tendency is derived from the taste of the Renaissance, which passed into the baroque and whose effects were still felt in the Spanish world, especially in poetry, thanks to the example of Juana's beloved poet Góngora. Juana's Latin poetry, chiefly in the form of quasi-liturgical hymns, is of good quality. She also acquired a smattering of Basque, her father's tongue, of Portuguese, and of Italian: she knew at least some words in these languages, and she placed them at strategic points in some of her poems.

From her experience of life, her reading, and her reflection, Juana Inés reached certain conceptions and convictions regarding human nature and destiny. These conceptions should serve as background and context for her theological views. Two documents are of special importance for what one may call Juana Inés's anthropology: the poem entitled *Primero sueño,* and the response to Sor Filotea de la Cruz's criticism, the *Respuesta.*

The *Primero sueño*

Of *Primero sueño* Juana declares in the *Respuesta* that it is the only poem that she composed entirely on her own initiative, just for herself:

> I naturally confess my baseness and vileness, but I do not think that anyone will have seen a stanza of mine that would be unbecoming. Moreover, I have never written anything of my own free will but because of requests and commands from others; so that I do not recall having written anything for myself, except a little paper called *El sueño.*[2]

Even if, as seems likely, Juana is understating, she gives a unique importance to the *Sueño,* a long, loosely structured poem of 975 lines without stanzas or paragraphs.

The exact date of its composition has not been ascertained. It was not included in *Inundación Castálida,* published in 1689 after the return to Spain of the marquis and marchioness de la Laguna. The *Sueño* was printed only in the second volume of Juana's works, which appeared in Seville in 1692 with a special dedication written by the author herself. One may therefore date the poem from the years between 1688 (Lysi's departure) and 1692.

The very title suggests that the poem deals with two related topics, for the word *sueño* has the twofold meaning of "sleep" and "dream." The poem is, in fact, a description both of sleep in general and of one special dream. That the meaning "dream" prevails without abolishing the meaning "sleep" tallies with Juana's confession concerning the activity of her mind during sleep:

Not even sleep is free from the continuous movement of my imagination: rather, it commonly travails in it with more liberty and neatness, comparing with more clarity and tranquillity the images it has kept from daytime, arguing, making verses, of which I could make you a very long list, as also of some reasons and ingenious points that I have found while asleep better than while awake.[3]

Why the poem is called "first" neither Juana nor her editors and critics make clear. Yet *First Dream* implies at least that there may eventually be a second one, even if, as is the case, Juana never wrote it.

There is no need at this point to study in detail the several hypotheses that have been made concerning the actual division of material in *Primero sueño*. That of Alfonso Méndez Plancarte, in twelve parts, is the most elaborate. Some students of Juana's works have slightly modified it (Sabat de Rivers). Others have preferred to read the poem in six parts (Chavez), five (Pfandl), four (Elías Rivers, followed by the American translator, Luis Harss), or even three (Carilla).[4] My own division modifies Méndez's hypothesis considerably. I suggest the following seven divisions:

lines 1–80 the coming of night
   81–233 night and the sleep of the universe
  234–291 the origin of dreams
  292–780 description of one special dream
  781–826 reflections on the dream
  827–886 the awakening
  887–975 the return of day

The description of the dream, the center of the poem, may be subdivided in this way:

lines 292–339 the soul, freed from the body, begins an intellectual flight above the mountains, close to the sky
  340–434 nearness to the sky evokes the "two pyramids" of Egypt and the tower of Babylon as symbols of the soul's ascent

435–559   the soul ascends by way of intuition; reaches
           the limits of it
560–780   the soul ascends by way of discursive reason
           and also reaches the limits of it

One could discuss at length whether the philosophical background of *Primero sueño* is Platonic or Aristotelian. Juana's philosophy was eclectic, and she was more poet than philosopher. Platonic and Neoplatonic themes run through the poem: the liberation of the soul from the body; the constraints that the body imposes on the soul's ascent; the intuitive glance with which, once on top of the first pyramid, the soul, as "supreme sovereign Queen of the sublunar," enjoys "the acute sight of its beautiful intelligent eyes."[5]

There are also Aristotelian themes: the ten categories of Aristotle are tools in the ascent of the second pyramid, as the soul climbs up the scale of being. Starting "from the lowest degree / of inanimate being," it passes through the "nobler hierarchy." This hierarchy begins with "the firstborn, though uncouth, / of Thetis" (p. 195). Thetis, a Nereid who is the mother of vegetation and lives at the bottom of the sea, represents, with her "motherly breasts," the sea, mother of life. Eventually, the soul reaches the "superior stars." It finally contemplates humanity, the fine point of creation,

> the supreme wondrous
> threefold composition,
> ordered in three harmonious lines,
> and of all inferior forms
> the mysterious compendium:
> the hinge tying together
> one that rises, enthroned,
> pure Nature,
> and one that, a creature
> less noble, sees itself lower:
> not only adorned with the five
> faculties of sense,
> but also by the inner ones,
> the three leading ones, ennobled. . . .

al supremo pasar maravilloso
compuesto triplicado,   ˋ
de tres acordes líneas ordenado
y de las formas todas inferiores
compendio misterioso:
bisagra engazadora
de la que más se eleva entronizada
Naturaleza pura,
y de la que, criatura
menos noble, se ve más abatida:
no de las cinco solas adornada
sensibles facultades,
mas de las interiores,
que tres rectrices son, ennoblecida. . . .

(P. 195–96.)

In touch both with the angels (the "pure Nature" of the poem) and with sheer matter, human nature is evoked by some biblical symbols. Its "mysterious image" appears in the "Evangelical Eagle's sacred vision" at Patmos, "which the stars / measured with equal feet as the ground" (p. 196). In the biblical text a woman is seen, whose feet stand on the moon and whose head is haloed by the stars: "A great sign appeared in heaven, a woman clothed with the sun, with the moon under her feet, and on her head a crown of twelve stars" (Revelation 12:1). Allusions to this text abound in the works of Juana Inés.

Not by inadvertence does Juana select the woman of the vision as the primary symbol of humanity: it fits what she will say elsewhere about womanhood. Did she also realize that a "woman clothed with the sun" is, according to the most natural understanding of the expression, a woman in the nude? Possibly the baroque imagination and its conventions prevented her from perceiving this point. In any case, Juana was acquainted with the interpretations of the biblical verse that identifies the woman with the Church; the text was also applied, in both exegesis and liturgy, to the Virgin Mary. In fact, Juana retains this second interpretation in a Latin poem of 1676 in honor of the assumption of Mary:

She ascends to heaven, and heaven
she covers with precious light. . . .

At the Son's right hand she sits
and, being Queen of heaven,
is crowned with full glory,
and glory she herself crowns. . . .

—Who is she? who is she?
ascending from the wild like a plant,
fairer than Stars, Sun, Moon?—Mary!

Ascendit Caelos, et Caelos
luce vestit peregrina. . . .

Ad dexteram Filii sedet
et, ut caelorum Regina
tota coronatur gloria,
et glóriam coronat ipsa. . . .

—¿Quae est ista? ¿quae est ista?
¿quae de deserto ascendit sicut virga,
Stellis, Sole, Lune pulchrior?—¡Maria!⁶

Humanity at its best is modeled on the apocalyptic image of
the woman in heaven, the Virgin Mary at the assumption; but hu-
manity is seldom at its best. Juana therefore proposes a secondary
biblical symbol in which humanity is much less exalted: the statue
seen in a dream by Nebuchadnezzar (Daniel 2:31–33). The upper
parts of the statue are of gold, silver, bronze, and iron, whereas the
feet, weaker than the rest, are made of iron and tile. When the feet
were struck, the whole construction fell down:

            or the tall statue
        that showed, in most precious metal,
        a rich, high forehead,
        and in most neglected
        material made a weak foundation
        which at the least movement collapsed—:
        Humankind, in sum, I declare a greater wonder
        than what human intellect invents:
        a compendium that absolutely

looks like Angel, plant, and beast;
whose high lowliness
shares the whole of nature.

---

o la estatua eminente
que del metal mostraba más preciado
la rica altiva frente
y en el más desechado
material, flaco fundamento hacía,
con que a leve vaivén se deshacía—:
el Hombre, digo, en fin, mayor protento
que discurre el humano entendimiento:
compendio que absoluto
parece a Ángel, a la planta, al bruto;
cuya altiva bajeza
toda participó naturaleza.[7]

The highest element in humanity is the soul. And in the soul the highest faculty is the intellect. The soul needs to be liberated from the body in order to experience the freedom of knowing: this is precisely how the dream evolves. Dreaming results from the soul's activity during the waking hours. When the body, asleep, has become "a corpse with soul, / dead to life and alive to death" (p. 187), the brain continues to produce "the four humors" of the human temperament. The "estimative" function still feeds "copies" of reality—the "species" of the scholastic theories of cognition—to the "imaginative" function, which in turn entrusts them to "memory" (p. 188). Out of these copies of reality the "fancy" is able to form "diverse images."

In the actual dream that is now described, the soul functions like the lighthouse of Alexandria's harbor. Located on the island of Pharos, in the estuary of the Nile, this was one of the seven wonders of the ancient world. Legends had grown around it: its mirror was said to reflect all the ships traveling in the Mediterranean, with their "light sails and heavy hulls." Likewise the soul: its faculty,

quiet, went copying
the images of all things,
and formed the invisible brush

of mental, lightless, ever-flaring
colors, the images
not only of all creatures
sublunar, but also of those
clear intelligent Stars
and, in the possible mode
in which to conceive the invisible,
in itself, skillful, depicted them
and to the soul showed them.

---

así ella, sosegada, iba copiando
las imágenes todas de las cosas,
y el pincel invisible iba formando
de mentales, sin luz, siempre vistosas
colores, las figuras
no sólo de todas las criaturas
sublunares, mas aun también de aquellas
que intellectuales claras son Estrellas,
y en el modo posible
que concerbirse puede lo invisible,
en sí, mañosa, las representaba
y al alma mostraba.

(P. 188.)

The high point of the soul is reached when the process of knowing has arrived at self-contemplation:

Which, meanwhile, totally turned
to its immaterial being and beautiful essence,
contemplated it,
partaking of high Being, a spark,
that similarly found joy in itself. . .

La cual, en tanto, toda convertida
a su inmaterial ser y esencia bella,
aquella contemplaba,
participada de alto Ser, centella
que con similitud en sí gozaba. . .

(P. 189.)

What is this "high Being" of which the human soul partakes when she has reached the supreme intuition of her own self? It can only be the Being of God. In biblical terms, the soul has been created in God's "image and likeness" (Genesis 1:26). In the Platonic perspective of the passage, it is also the divine Being, the source and model of the soul, the ultimate Being that is also Oneness, Goodness, and Beauty. In the context of the search for knowledge that runs through the *Sueño,* the idea of St. Augustine is also relevant: the certainty reached in cognition implies a participation in divine certitude under the impact of a spark—an illumination—from the divine light.

The scope of natural knowledge, boundless, includes "the immense dimension of the sphere . . . the course of the heavenly bodies." Yet, at the lower levels of knowledge, "in the first region of its height," the soul cannot obtain "the speedy, quick flight / of the eagle." In other words, the glance by which the soul reflects all things in herself through the phantasms that she stores up stands in need of a complement. This complement is obtained in two more ascents: along the intuitive way, which may be called Platonic; and along the discursive way, which would be more Aristotelian. Juana finds their models in the two great pyramids of Egypt.

The two ways are connected, since it is the final incapacity of the first, unable to reach the totality of its desired goal, that leads the cognitive process to the second way. Yet, in Juana Inés's vision, both ways ultimately fail. Although moved by an infinite desire to know, the soul can never know infinitely. This is precisely the heart of the human tragedy: "the defect / of not possibly in one intuition / knowing all the creation" (p. 194).

If the intuitive way does not reach infinity, the discursive way, which "from one concept / to another goes ascending step by step," is equally unable to obtain ultimate knowledge of all things. Before the immensity and complexity of the universe, Juana wonders

> How in such a frightful
> immense system can it travel?

> ¿Cómo en tan espantosa
> máquina inmensa discurrir pudiera?

(P. 198.)

She cites the mythological example, as at several other points in her writings, of young Phaëthon, son of Helios (the sun), who obtained permission from his father to drive the fiery chariot for one day. But he was unable to control the horses, and the chariot came dangerously near to the earth. To avoid a cosmic disaster, Phaëthon was slain by Zeus in a flash of lightning. This is Juana's way of giving voice to the Promethean wish of "the proud soul, / who, despising life, determines / to eternalize its name in its ruin" (p. 198). Many years later and in another cultural context, Dostoyevsky's *The Possessed,* this is the drama of Kirillov, who thinks that he will become God if he kills himself, for he will have stolen the creative power. It is the death-wish that Freud discovered in the depths of the human psyche.

Human nature's unrestricted desire to know is never satiated. And, since falling from heaven brings no solution, an inner wound is forever unhealed in the soul. The Creator himself placed such a desire in the soul when he made her the queen of creation:

> —that she might be the lady
> of the others, not in vain
> did the Wise Mighty Hand adorn her—
> the end of His works, the circle that links
> the Sphere with the earth,
> the ultimate perfection of creation
> and ultimate pleasure of its eternal Author,
> in whom with satisfied contentment
> His immense generosity rested. . . .

> —que para ser señora
> de los demás, no en vano
> la adornó Sabia Poderosa Mano—
> fin de Sus obras, círculo que cierra
> la Esfera con la tierra,
> última perfección de lo criado
> y último de Su eterno Autor agrado,
> en quien con satisfecha complacencia
> Su inmensa descansó magnificencia. . . .

(P. 196.)

Like a burning flame, the soul bends, as it were, all her faculties as they converge toward their acme. Thus the lines of the pyramid's edges converge toward the point at the top:

> so the human mind
> its shape copies,
> and to the First Cause always aspires
> —central point whence straight is drawn
> the line, if not circumference,
> containing, infinite, all essence—.

> así la humana mente
> su figura trasunta,
> y a la Causa Primera siempre aspira
> —céntrico punto donde recta tira
> la línea, si ya no circunferencia,
> que contiene, infinita, toda esencia—.

(P. 191.)

Juana Inés de la Cruz has encapsulated in these verses what she takes to be the heart of the mystery of knowing. But let us not be misled by her philosophical and mythological language: the First Cause of Aristotle and of philosophy is also the Creator of the biblical story of creation. Already at the natural level, the soul aspires to full knowledge of the First Cause, the Creator. It may well be that, as Méndez Plancarte suggests,[8] one should read "Su terno Autor" ("her trine Author"), rather than "Su eterno Autor" ("her eternal Author"); by thus inserting the doctrine of the Trinity into her description of the human soul, Juana would set this description in the light of the Christian revelation. Even if this is not so, the analogy of the point and the circumference indicates Juana's intent: God has placed limits to human conquests, even at that moment when the human soul is engaged in its highest natural achievement, the cognitive process.

The analogy of the point and the circumference was quite traditional. Juana Inés may have known it from her mentor, Athanasius Kircher. Luis Harss gives Kircher's version as follows: "All things issue from God, who is at once the center and circumference from which and in which all lines begin and end."[9] Juana's version is very different: the First Cause is the central and original point of the lines but is not the circumference.

The analogy appears again in the *Response to Sor Filotea de la Cruz,* still in the context of creation but in a different form. This time it is quite similar to what Kircher had written: "All things emerge from God, who is at the same time the center and the circumference from which all created lines emerge and where they end."[10] Juana's two formulations of the analogy differ substantially. In the *Sueño,* God, the First Cause, is also the Final Cause to which the straight line of creation goes as to its own center, but the First Cause is not also a circumference containing all essence in its infinity. In fact, this is faithful to the traditional form of the saying as formulated in the twelfth century by Alanus de Insulis (Alain de Lille), who himself had received it from the Neoplatonist Proclos: "God is an intelligible sphere, whose center is everywhere and whose circumference is nowhere."[11] For Alanus, the center that is everywhere coincides with all human souls. God, imagined as a spiritual sphere, has, as it were, reduced himself to a spaceless point at the very center of all souls; and he has no circumference because, being infinite, he cannot be bound by any limits. In the *Sueño,* therefore, God, at the center, attracts all the created lines, including the soul, but the creaturely world is not in God as in an infinite circumference that would contain it: it is not a part of God. God has no parts.

The perspective has been reversed in the *Respuesta.* God is both the center and the circumference. The created lines begin at the center and end at the circumference. They are like radii within the divine sphere. The poem comes closer to the classical use of the analogy without being quite identical with it. But the prose opens a bolder conception that is in fact quite opposite to that of the *Sueño:* all creation is located within God.

The doctrine of the *Sueño* does not profess to go beyond what a purely rational vision can see of human nature. The dream is confined within the data of sense experience and science. This may well be intended by the title, *First Dream.* A second dream could investigate the meaning and scope of human nature under the impact of the divine grace revealed in Christ. What Juana writes in the *Respuesta* of the dangers of theology for those who are insufficiently prepared suggests that she never intended to compose such a second dream. Yet this is not to say that she never dreamt it; her title left the possibility open.

Does Juana, going further, relate human nature to the incarnation? She does in fact raise the question of the purpose for which humanity was created:

> For what? Perhaps so that luckier
> than all, raised
> by the grace of loving
> union it be! Oh, though repeated,
> never well enough known
> grace, even ignored,
> little appreciated
> it seems, or in evil responded to!

> ¿Por qué? Quizá porque más venturosa
> que todas, encumbrada
> a merced de amorosa
> unión sería. ¡Oh, aunque repetida,
> nunca bastantemente bien sabida
> merced, pues ignorada
> en lo poco apreciada
> parece, o en lo mal correspondida![12]

In his paraphrase of the *Sueño*, Méndez Plancarte reads this passage as endorsing John Duns Scotus's conception of the purpose of creation.[13] The union in question would be the hypostatic union that in the classical Christology deriving from the Council of Chalcedon (451) unites the divine and the human natures of Jesus in the Person of the divine Word. This reading has the merit of paying due attention to the theological dimension of the poem. Other scholars have not been so discerning. Thus Raúl Levia, in keeping with his general approach to Sor Juana's poetry, reads *Primero sueño* as the poem of Eros. He suggests that "loving union" refers to "her mysterious drama of passion."[14] Juana would have experienced an unshared erotic passion for some man, whose name she never divulges. Unrequited love would be the key to her poetry.

Both interpretations are unacceptable. The second disregards a well-attested fact in religious literature: the language of Eros comes naturally to the pens of mystical authors, as the example of St. John of the Cross, known to Juana Inés, proves sufficiently.[15] As to the first interpretation, it is not theologically accurate, for the hypostatic union is unique. It cannot be "repeated," like what Juana Inés has in mind. Admittedly, it is, in the text, God's grace that is repeated and "never well enough known." But the divine grace in question is the "union," or the elevation of human nature through this union. In order for it to designate the incarnation, the word *repeated* would have to refer to the preaching or proclamation of the doctrine of the incarnation. But this would be farfetched, since the poem nowhere alludes to the teaching of doctrine; it would be out of tune with the general tone of the poem.

Another theological interpretation is proposed by Luis Harss in the commentary on his English translation of the poem. The union in question would be the eucharistic communion. Harss sees in this no more than "a conventional apostrophe . . . , a pious after-thought": "Sor Juana is merely paying her dues to the Eucharist (a routine 'constantly repeated' and as easily 'forgotten')."[16] This, how-ever, would trivialize the eucharist in a way that would jar with Juana's approach to it in her religious plays.

Another reading fits perfectly both the language and the se-quence of thoughts. The union that is envisaged here is the mystical union between the soul and God, the high point of prayer and of creaturely existence, the ultimate crowning of the contemplative life that Juana espoused when she made her religious profession.

That Juana alludes to the mystical ascent in a description of the higher levels of the cognitive process that has drawn considerably on Greek philosophy is in fact a delicate touch. As she well knew, much of Greek philosophy, especially in the currents influenced by Plato and above all in the Neoplatonism of Plotinus, aspired to union with the One, who is also the Good and the Beautiful. Furthermore, having attempted to become a Carmelite, Juana sill considered her-self in a key passage of the *Respuesta* to be a daughter of the great St. Teresa. She could not ignore that Teresa gave the name *union* to the highest mystical state that she experienced in her life and described in her writings.[17] This fits Juana's previous contention that the soul is "partaker of high Being," ever desiring the First Cause and long-ing for the Final Cause.

Elsewhere, Sor Juana will take sides concerning the motive for the incarnation, the discussion of which goes back largely, though not exclusively, to the Franciscan John Duns Scotus.[18] It is humanity as such that is destined to reach the acme of its ascent in the Word of God incarnate. The destiny of each human person is to reach the high point of existence in mystical union with the Divinity.

The *Respuesta*

Juana's *Response to the Most Illustrious Sister Filotea de la Cruz* explains at length, in the very personal perspective of a reflection about her life and works, her conception of human nature and destiny. The *Respuesta* is basically a defense of her life as a nun who happens to be the best-known poet of the land and, in a sense, the poet laureate of New Spain, to whom distinguished personages of both state and Church have recourse when they need suitable poetry to grace some civic or religious celebration. Why, asked the bishop of Puebla in introducing the *Carta atenagórica*, does so gifted a Hieronymite sister devote so much time to secular poetry? Ought not her great talent to be entirely at the service of religion and theology? This would fulfill her religious vocation as a nun and fit her natural and social status as a woman.

The reality was simple. Juana's insight and her capacity to empathize with others made it natural and easy for her to sing of human love and sorrow or to celebrate secular pursuits when she was invited to do so because some private or public occasion made such poetry appropriate. But this does not suffice to answer the query of "Filotea de la Cruz." The bishop of Puebla had a point: the life of a nun should be devoted to the service of God and the Church, not of the viceroy and the state. But the reproach assumed a distinction between the sacred and the profane that was clearly foreign to Juana Inés. She still lived in the classical world of the Spanish Reconquest, when Church and kingdom were one. Madrid was the center of faith, as she wrote in *Divino Narciso*;[19] the profane is the locus of the daily experience of the sacred; and true politics is the politics of faith.

Juana would have preferred not to answer at all. She was indeed prepared to admit the veracity of reproaches and criticisms; she knew herself to be sinful. Indeed, when she received the pirated publication of the *Carta atenagórica*, she "burst into tears of confusion," for she sensed that what the bishop of Puebla considered a favor to her was rather God's punishment for her sins. In regard to her sins, she did not consider herself subject to human judgment; as she said in this admirable prayer:

Be blessed, Lord, for not only have you not placed the task of judging me in the hands of another creature or even in my own hand, but you have reserved it to yours, and you have freed me from myself and from the sentence that I myself would pronounce—which, forced by my own knowledge, could not be less than of condemnation—and you have reserved it to your mercy, because you have loved me more than I can love myself![20]

Juana would have preferred silence, but silence "is a negative thing . . . , for its proper task is to say nothing." It belongs in the realm of mystical experience. St. Paul had recourse to it concerning "words which cannot be uttered, words which no one may speak" (2 Corinthians 12:4). If Juana reached such an experience, a point that is denied by most scholars, it is covered by her broad statement: "I do not say what I see, but I say that I cannot say it." Yet she chose to answer "Sor Filotea" lest her eventual silence be misunderstood: "Because it is a negative thing, although it explains much by its insistence on not explaining, it is necessary to put on it a certain brief label, so that one may understand what is claimed to be said by silence. If not, silence will say nothing, for this is its proper task: to say nothing" (p. 828).

Juana complains politely that her *Carta atenagórica* was published and given a title (by "Sor Filotea," whom everybody must have known to be the bishop of Puebla) without her own knowledge. She did not wait for Filotea's letter, however, to feel the accuracy of the bishop's main point: her occupation and writing are "repugnant to her sex, her age, and above all to customs" (p. 829). She was afraid of trespassing into areas from which she might be barred by public opinion. Many a time has "this fear taken the pen from her hand." But "a heresy against art" is not punishable by the Holy Office; it can only be laughed away in the public forum. Nevertheless, Juana may well ask: Is it true that she has (as a nun) "no obligation to know, and (as a woman) no capacity to succeed"? As she confesses,

I do not study in order to write and still less to teach (which in me would be excessive pride) but only to see if by studying I am less ignorant. Thus do I respond and thus do I feel. Writing has never been my own decision, but an alien power. (P. 829–30.)

In a very personal and moving autobiographical passage, Juana tells the story of the profound desire to know that she already felt at the tender age of three. She tells how this led her, through the court of the viceroy, to the community of the Hieronymites, where it is proper to follow the example of the learned founders, St. Jerome and St. Paula: "It would be degeneration for the daughter of such learned parents to be ignorant" (p. 831).

This passage illustrates Juana's conviction that the highest dignity of human nature resides in knowledge, and that the highest knowledge is the perception of beauty. This corresponds exactly to her experience of the desire to know. In the hierarchy of knowledge that she has inherited from the Scholastics, theology stands at the top; all other sciences are its servants. This conviction shaped Juana's studies: "Thus did I pursue, always, as I have said, directing my steps to the summit of sacred theology, for it seemed to me necessary, in order to reach it, to climb the stairs of the human sciences and arts." This is of course faithful to the classical notion of theology and Holy Scripture, to which all other sciences are subordinate and to which their investigation contributes. Simply, Juana has had to linger longer in the lower sciences than formally trained students. But this is not all, for theology is not only science; it is also wisdom:

> Being the Book that contains all books and the Science in which all sciences are included, the understanding of which they all serve, . . . it demands, more than what has been said, another condition: permanent prayer and purity of life, in order to ask God for the purgation of the soul and the illumination of the mind that are necessary to understand such high things; and if this is lacking, the others are useless. (P. 832.)

The rest of the *Respuesta* is mainly concerned with Juana's admission that she has not written more about the heights of theology because she has no trust in her own knowledge. She has not been sufficiently well versed in the preliminaries to handle difficult questions of theological interpretation. This is not due to her attention being dispersed in too many subjects but, as she confesses in a way that is not entirely convincing, "to my ineptitude and to the weakness of my intellect" (p. 833). Community life and obligations of justice and charity have interfered with her studies. To some persons this would not matter: "Knowing has not cost them anxiety!" With irony Juana exclaims, "Blessed are they!" And she adds that "it is not knowing (for I do not yet know), but only the desire to know, that has cost me so much . . . !" (p. 833–34).

Even though she states that she does not know enough theology to write about it, Juana hints at the direction that her theology would take:

> If we look at his [Christ's] presence, what jewel is more lovable than this divine beauty? If any human beauty has jurisdiction over the wills and knows how to subject them to itself with delicate and desirable violence, what would this one do with its great prerogatives and sovereign gifts? What would this incomprehensible beauty do, what would it move, what would it not do, what would it not move, through whose beautiful face as through smooth crystal the rays of the Divinity made themselves transparent? (P. 835.)

Attracted to a theology of beauty, Juana Inés de la Cruz has retained from "the holy Mother and my mother Teresa" a vision of "the beauty of Christ." But beauty has its price. Those who have access to divine wisdom cannot aspire higher than Christ; and Christ's head, the depository of wisdom, was crowned with thorns: "The triumph of the wise, reached through suffering and celebrated with tears, is wisdom's way of triumphing; and since it is Christ, as the King of wisdom, who wore the crown, for that reason it has been sanctified in his own, and therefore the others who are wise feel no fear any more, and understand that they should not aspire to any other honor" (p. 836).

Juana's main suffering came from the conventional opinion of society that women should not pursue knowledge. When her mother superior, unreasonably fearful of the Inquisition, forbade her to study, she stopped reading. But she could not help observing the book of nature, for "there is no creature, however low, in which one does not recognize the *me fecit Deus*" of St. Augustine in the *Confessions*.[21] On one occasion, a young girls' game, by the geometric figures that the players formed among themselves as they jumped and ran, brought to her mind "the shape which, it is said, was that of Solomon's mysterious ring, in which there were distant lights and representations of the most Holy Trinity" (p. 838). Another time, being forbidden to read by her physician because of a stomachache, Juana reflected interiorly: "And my thoughts were so powerful and vehement that in four hours they tired my spirits more than a study of those books in four days" (p. 839). Even sleep could not stop the movement of her imagination but on the contrary liberated it, in keeping with the theme of *Primero sueño.*

The last section of the *Respuesta* pleads eloquently for the right of women to study. Juana adduces the examples of many learned and holy women of the past. She shows that the statements of St. Paul that are used to keep women in a state of ignorance have no bearing on the question. Furthermore, hallowed by great saints of the Old and New Testaments and by great theologians like Gregory Nazianzen, poetry has also been written by women. Did not "the Queen of Wisdom, our Lady, intone with her sacred lips the canticle of the Magnificat?" (p. 845).

Having made this plea, Juana Inés returns to her own writing: the only piece she composed for its own sake was the "little paper called *El sueño.*" The only ones printed with her consent are "some *Exercises on the Incarnation,* and some *Offerings of the Sorrows,* for public devotion, but without my name. . . . I did them only for the devotion of my sisters, years ago, and afterwards they spread" (p. 847). She again complains that the *Carta atenagórica* was printed by "an alien decision which does not fall under my dominion."

The *Respuesta* is dated 1 March 1691. Along with *Primero sueño* it constitutes Juana's most elaborate statement concerning the condition of humanity in God's basic purpose. Another point, which is not underlined in these documents, is also extremely important in Juana's eye: the idea, derived from St. Augustine, that, if men and women are for whatever reasons unequal in society, they do not differ in any way in their soul. In the same year, 1691, Juana's villancicos in honor of St. Catherine were performed at the cathedral of Antequera (today, Oajaca). In the traditional legend, Catherine exemplifies a woman who is not only holy and beautiful, but also learned:

> Victor, victor Catherine!
> who with her divine science
> the sages has convinced,
> and victorious has escaped,
> —with her sovereign science—

the profane arrogance
that to convince her came!

By one Woman they were convinced,
all the sages of Egypt,
of the proof that sex
is no essence in the intellect.

––––––––––

Víctor, víctor Catarina,
que con su ciencia divina
los sabios ha convencido,
y victoriosa ha salido
—con su ciencia soberana—
de la arrogancia profana
que a convencerla ha venido!

De una Mujer se convencen
todos los sabios de Egipto,
para prueba de que el sexo
no es esencia en lo entendido.[22]

"Sex is no essence in the intellect." And God, who has so
created humanity, intends women to serve the Church through the
activity and creativity of their minds:

She studies, argues, and teaches
and this is the Church's service,
for He does not want her ignorant
who created her rational . . .

Never of a famous male
equal triumph have we seen;
for God has wanted in her
to honor the female sex.

––––––––––

Estudia, arguye y enseña
y es de la Iglesia servicio,

que no la quiere ignorante
El que racional la hizo . . .

Nunca de varón ilustre
triunfo igual habemos visto;
y es que quiso Dios en ella
honrar el sexo femíneo.

(P. 291.)

This was Juana's profound and constant conviction. As she had been made rational by the Creator, she owed it to him to become learned. For this purpose she entered the convent. And if she spent a great deal of time cultivating her innate talent for poetry, she did so largely in order to be free at other times to study and to learn.

At this point, however, Sor Juana's desire and what she conceived to be her vocation to learn ran counter to the customs and prejudices of her time and place concerning the female sex. This was part both of her early disagreement with the Jesuit Antonio Núñez and of her later problems with some sisters in her convent.[23] Accommodations with the viceregal court were acceptable. The prioress herself, Mother Juana de San Antonio, ordered Juana Inés to meet the marquis and marchioness de la Laguna when they paid their first visit to the monastery and Juana was reluctant to meet them.[24] Transgressions of the intellectual and social limits assigned to the female sex were more difficult to swallow.

Yet Manuel Fernández de Santa Cruz y Sahagún, bishop though he was, disguised himself as Sor Filotea de la Cruz when he published Juana's private writing, the *Carta atenagórica*, and urged her to devote her talents exclusively to religion and to theology. At least the bishop of Puebla was not shocked by her gender. He had no qualms passing himself off, on this occasion, as a woman. His problem was not with gender but with the religious vocation. Juana seems, in 1693, to have agreed with him. But nothing even remotely hints that she also agreed with the restraints imposed on her sex: like St. Catherine, she had to be and to behave as God had created her.

2
The Baroque Edifice

The motherland of Juana Inés de la Cruz, New Spain was, by virtue of its dominant classes, an image of Spain itself. The viceroy in Mexico represented the king in Madrid and acted in his name. Juana's religious universe was therefore that of the Spanish Counterreformation, not, as is assumed by some authors, a belated form of the Middle Ages.[1] In turn, the Spanish Counterreformation is part of the broader movement of the Counterreformation in general, whose effects in theology, piety, and church architecture and decoration were felt first in central and northern Italy and in the southernmost German-speaking areas of Austria, Bavaria, and Switzerland. This broader movement is commonly designated in art and literature as the *baroque,* a term that gains a wider meaning when applied to the period: the baroque age. Militant against the inroads of the Reformation, the baroque's triumphalism is more moderate in France than in Italy, Spain, and the Germanic territories. It is the most exuberant kind that Juana Inés knew.

One of the characteristics of this new trend in Catholic sensitivity was the growing importance of the saints and their representations in the arts. The cult of the saints that had been practiced at the end of the Middle Ages was criticized generally in chapter 21 of the *Confession of Augsburg* (1530). More specifically, the invocation of saints and its abuses were carefully examined in a critical yet constructive mood in the corresponding chapter of Melanchthon's *Apology for the Confession of Augsburg* (1530). This was in fact the most systematic tractate on the saints since the age of Charlemagne. But while Melanchthon and the Lutheran movement criticized devotional practices that had been traditionally honored and upheld for centuries, the theologians of the Counterreformation argued in favor of the old customs. They defended the legitimacy of invoking the saints in prayer, maintaining that this need not detract from the sole mediatorship of the Lord Jesus in the order of salvation. Occasional abuse is no reason to stop legitimate use.

In a different yet related order, the Catholic liturgy continued to evolve. As a rule, the two chief components of the liturgical calendar, the temporal and the sanctoral, are frequently in tension. After the Council of Trent (1545–1563), liturgy and piety tended to reemphasize the sanctoral cycle at the expense of the temporal. An increasing number of feasts of saints was gradually obscuring the way in which basic liturgy, focused on the celebration of Christ, illustrates both the doctrine of the Trinity and the pattern of redemption. Running parallel to the theological and the liturgical trajectories, the education of the Catholic people in the spiritual life often promoted devotion to the saints in personal piety.

The typical baroque church differs from the devotional buildings of the Renaissance by the predominance it gives to decoration. At the service of decorative motifs, structure brings attention to special, highly decorated segments. Such are the sanctuary and the main altar, enhanced by a reredos that often covers the entire wall behind the altar. The ceiling of the transept is often shaped in the form of a dome, as in St. Peter's at the Vatican; and the dome, with daylight coming in through clear windows, suggests in sculpture and painting the high tiers of heaven. Saints, in sculptured rather than painted form, abound; they are shown as forming one society with the angels, and at times with the seven archangels. The Christian virtues—such as religion, faith, charity, fortitude—are often featured, exemplified by allegorical personages. There is a striking correspondence, unknown in older churches, between the front porch of the church and the high altar. The faithful inside the building worship between an altarlike entrance and an entrancelike altar. The triumph of the eucharist is unmistakable. The liturgy of earth mirrors the liturgy of heaven. And the inhabitants of heaven are the angels and the saints.

In the seventeenth century the great development of Mexican baroque architecture was still to come (it flourished in the eighteenth), but the movement was on the way. The architecture and the decoration of the churches of New Spain were, like their Spanish models, to feature the emphases of the baroque age. The great church of the Jesuit college of Tepotzotlán, some forty kilometers north of the capital, was built in the twelve years between 25 May 1670 and 9 September 1682. The college was set apart for the education of

Indian boys, while the church was appropriately dedicated to St. Francis Xavier, the first of the great Jesuit missionaries. Like all baroque churches, the interior structure and decoration were intended to represent the victory of Christ in his Church. And this was shown, as in many other buildings of the seventeenth and eighteenth centuries, through his triumph in the saints. Juana, who followed the rule of enclosure in the convent of St. Jerome, never saw this new church. She must, however, have heard it described by some of her frequent parlor visitors. At least she had seen the unfinished cathedral on the Zócalo. The church of her own convent exuded the same baroque spirit.

Juana lived under the Hapsburg dynasty. After the examples of Charles V and Philip II, champions of Catholic Christianity against the Reformers, the Spanish kings were more deeply religious and more restrained in external show than the Bourbons were to be at the beginning of the next century. In all respects modeled on the court in Madrid, the viceroyalty of New Spain was expected to honor the acquired rights of its subjects. In particular it protected and, in some areas, deferred to, the Church and the archbishop of Mexico. At one time during Juana's life the archbishop also served the king as viceroy of New Spain. In 1673, following the unexpected death of the duke de Veragua five days after his inauguration as viceroy, the archbishop, Don Payo Enríquez de Ribera, was made viceroy, retaining both positions until his recall to Spain in 1680. In this unusual instance, the delicate balance that was achieved between the two powers in the hands of one person served to convey a higher notion of heaven, where all is ruled in harmony at the hands of the great king.

As the kingdom, at its best, imitated heaven, heaven was depicted on the model of the royal court. The court of the king of heaven is, in imagination, like the court of His Catholic Majesty. In the exuberance of the later period of the baroque, the interior decoration of the church will correspond to the organization of the great court of Louis XIV at Versailles, which will serve as a model for the court of the Spanish Bourbons in Madrid. (Philip d'Anjou, grandson of Louis XIV, became the first of the Bourbon kings of Spain under the name of Philip V [1700–1746]).

The church building was conceived as a miniature of heaven, and the place of the saints in the decoration of baroque churches is well defined. They constitute God's royal court; their place is not unlike that of the aristocracy in Madrid. As members of the court they are associated with the king but are first of all his subjects. They are not intermediaries or mediators: they are adornments. They enhance the glory of God and that of the queen of heaven, the Virgin Mary, who received the crown from God after her assumption, and whose glory was already bestowed on her through her immaculate conception.

Mexican piety was generally in line with these aspects of Catholic life and culture. Thus Juana's world was filled with saints. Several in particular held a prominent place in her writings, as she was occasionally commissioned to write pieces that would enhance the celebration of a saint's day. In addition, she naturally echoes the traditional devotions and practices of the Hieronymite order. A few saints or holy personages, historical or legendary, provide the topics of Juana's religious plays: St. Joseph, whose feasts were, in the Roman calendar, on 19 March and the third Sunday after Easter; St. Peter the apostle, celebrated along with St. Paul on 29 June; St. Peter Nolasco (c.1189–c.1256), the founder or cofounder of a religious order devoted to redeeming captives, whose feast fell on 31 January; St. Catherine of Alexandria (died c.305), a more or less legendary martyr and one of the fourteen Auxiliary Saints of late medieval piety, whose feast was held on 25 November; St. Hermenegild (died 586), a Visigothic prince condemned and executed by his father, the Arian King Leovigild (died 587), against whom he had rebelled, celebrated on 13 April; and, from the Old Testament, Joseph of Egypt, who, however, had no liturgical day.[2] Joseph and Peter also inspired several separate poems. The great saint of the Hieronymites, Jerome (c.345–419/20), received occasional pieces, though there are none for Paula (347–404) or her younger daughter Eustochium (c.368–418/19). St. Juan de Sahagún (1429–1479) was the object of one isolated piece; a Spaniard of the order of St. Augustine, he was credited with having had a vision of Christ in the host while celebrating mass. In honor of St. Bernard, Juana composed an important sequence of poems.

All this need not mean that saints were of major importance in Juana's personal piety. Her devotion to the saints may have been less exuberant and of a narrower range than her poetry. She gave a hint about this matter in 1694, when she vowed to defend the immaculate conception of Mary even unto death. She made this promise "before the Most Holy Trinity" and "the Virgin Mother of the Eternal Word

Incarnate, our Lord, and of all the citizens of the heavenly court."
In this vast cloud of witnesses, however, Juana selected the following
for special listing: "the most glorious patriarch, lord St. Joseph, my
holy guardian angel, my father St. Peter, St. Jerome, St. Paula, St.
Augustine, St. Ignatius, St. Rose, St. Philip de Jesus, St. Eusto-
chium."[3] She added in a general way "all the holy men and women
who are the patrons, advocates, and protectors of my nation and
fatherland, and all the creatures of heaven and earth." Jerome,
Augustine, Paula, and Eustochium were venerated among the Hie-
ronymites. Devotion to St. Joseph had been popularized by the *Au-
tobiography* of St. Teresa of Avila.[4] Ignatius, the founder of the Society
of Jesus, is presumably mentioned in deference to Juana's director
of conscience, Antonio Núñez de Miranda, a Jesuit. Rose de Lima
was the first canonized woman of Spanish America. Philip de Jesus
(1571–1597) was Felipe de las Casas, born of Spanish parents in
Mexico; a Franciscan, not yet ordained, he was among the martyrs
of Nagasaki in the great persecution of Toyotomi Hideyoshi. The
final generality leaves no one out of the account. But Juana, usually
reticent about herself, does not reveal how and to what extent she
honors the saints.

St. Peter the Apostle (1677, 1683)

Religious plays devoted to the mysteries of the Christian reli-
gion and to the saints had been composed by some notable Spanish
writers, not least of them the great Calderón de la Barca (1600–
1681). The texture of such theater belonged to the popular genre of
the villancico, which was considered minor and was often neglected
by recognized literary figures. Sor Juana's religious villancicos are
many. She liked their simple structure and their varied musicality
even after the first publication of her poems in 1689 had suddenly
propelled her into fame. Juana's autos (acts, meaning, however, a
whole play) generally fall into a pattern that may be illustrated from
her treatment of the theme of St. Peter in a play that was commis-
sioned for the cathedral of Mexico City in 1677.

Inspired by matins, the monastic prayer of the night or early
morning that was traditionally sung before daybreak, the composi-
tion is built around the three nocturns of the office of matins, a
nocturn consisting of a sequence of three psalms with antiphons and
the Our Father, a short prayer, and three lessons with benedictions.

The first two of Juana's nocturns in the auto on St. Peter, 1677, comprise three villancicos; the last nocturn has only two. The central theme is usually expressed at the beginning, either in a preliminary dedication, or in a loa or introduction, or else at the opening by the first villancico. Here the theme is that of Peter the Teacher.[5] The public is invited to go to school to learn from Peter, who, with the pen of his oar, writes the ABCs of faith on the pages of the sea. With puns and contrasts based on diverse types of lettering, Juana describes his writing. Her smile or laughter is never far from deep seriousness, for, as her dedicatory letter to one of the cathedral canons explains, *jocularis sermo* (joyful speech) for the celebration of St. Peter was recommended by St. Jerome as being allowed by Scripture.

Peter's writing is able to make the "bastard type" (a style of lettering) into a "daughter of the Church."[6] This undoubtedly alludes to Juana's origins: in Mexico an illegitimate child was registered for baptism as "son" or "daughter of the Church." Heresy cannot alter Peter's writing. But this writing cost him his life. Peter is also the best teller of tales and the keeper of the keys. He puts "the rule of three / in a creed" (an arithmetical allusion to the Trinity and to the legend that the Apostles' Creed was composed, under Peter's leadership, by the twelve apostles). "He could of the sky gather up the stars, / of the ground the flowers, / of the sea the sands." Yet Juana does not hide Peter's sin: "once, / by mistake, / he denied a charge / by miscalculation."[7] This was his betrayal of Jesus. Subsequently, however, "what he missed in gold / he made up in pearls" through the tears of repentance.

The second nocturn begins with a villancico in Latin. Peter, now in Rome, makes the city "the queen of all the cities of the earth" and a "disciple of the Truth" instead of "the Mistress of error."[8] He protects it with "Christian humility" rather than "military discipline"; in doing so, he takes the place of Romulus, the founder of the city. The fifth villancico celebrates Peter's rhetorical ability:

> Latin and Greek *quantity*
> his faith learned in Christ,
> though blind,
> for in Him *Alpha* it saw,
> *and Omega.*

Cuantidad latina y griega
en Cristo su fe aprendió,
aunque ciega,
pues en Él el *Alpha* vio,
et Omega.[9]

Then, in typical baroque style, Juana extols Peter's mastery of diphthongs, feet, measure, pause, heroic verse, pentameters, liquids, declension, short syllables, and sapphic hymns. This leads, in a jocular mode, to Peter's philosophical difficulty, when, in the high-priest's courtyard, he created a new kind of syllogism, unacceptable to Aristotle: holding to the premise of the divinity of Jesus, he denied the conclusion, namely, the humanity in hypostatic union. In his subsequent repentance, however, Peter practiced "the art of finding the *means* / of not staying with his *conclusion.*"[10]

The third nocturn brings the celebration to a more jocular level, with a *jácara* (ballad) and an *ensalada* (medley). The ballad describes Peter's use of the sword with the vocabulary of fencing.[11] In the medley, a person of mixed blood celebrates Peter in Spanish as the doorkeeper, and a Portuguese sailor hails the apostle in Portuguese as the great steersman of the good ship *Church;* finally, in a mixture of Spanish and Latin, "a cowardly sacristan," afraid of Peter's roost-er, borrows the rooster's song, "qui-qui-riqui," in a series of lively stanzas.[12] Sacristans (representing the all-male clergy) and scholars (the all-male university) are often the butt of Juana's not so inno-cent jokes!

The literary genre required the form and tone of a popular entertainment. Juana excelled at this. Yet the light tone of these pieces underlines her versatility as she treats of the saints' lives with fitting concreteness, and of holiness, with depth.

In 1683 Juana returned to the apostle Peter. She built her play, which was also destined for the cathedral in Mexico City, around the "examination" that Peter must have taken before he was raised to "prelacy."[13] This shows that Juana was not chary of inventing legends and building myths to illustrate her topics. Peter in fact failed the test, for Jesus found him wanting at the moment of the betrayal in the highpriest's courtyard. Since the apostle wept and repented, however, he learned "neither to despair as sinner / nor, as saint, to presume of self." These words express the comforting news of the *Felix culpa*—"O happy fault!"—sung by the deacon during the Easter vigil to designate Adam's sin: "past faults contribute to present merit."

Juana is aware, at this point, of treading on soft ground. Her theme is paradoxical. Peter "has great holiness." He is "the Head of the Church," "the Key-holder / of the whole divine Alcázar" evoked by the central fortresses of Spanish cities.[14] Yet while we know this, we do not know "what the Head comprehends." We hardly understand Peter's holiness. And "to know and not understand / amounts to not knowing." In fact,

> So numberless are Peter's
> high marvels
> that although all are known
> never are they all told.

> Tan sin número, de Pedro
> son la maravillas altas,
> que aunque todas son sabidas
> nunca son todas contadas.

Sor Juana Inés finds that Peter's sin is often passed over in silence. She herself is not afraid of mentioning it. Nevertheless, a claim of ignorance recurs in her writings. While "all will tell what they know," she "alone" will speak of "what she does not know."[15] With a depth of thought that may have escaped her audience, Juana also confesses the negative dimension of all human theology when it is contrasted with the positive knowledge that angels enjoy:

> The winged Seraphim
> joyful sing
> Peter's greatnesses,
> for they know
> with angelic voices
> how to praise him only;
> but here below, as to us,
> only what has not been
> can we praise.

Serafines alados
alegres canten
las grandesas de Pedro,
pues ellos saben
con Angélicas voces
sólo alabarle;
que acá, nosotros,
lo que no fue, alabarle
podemos sólo!

Juana's humility is no mere literary device. Even when, as is the case here, her lessons are addressed to those who have authority in the Church, they also apply to herself. The very short second nocturn highlights the heart of the matter: the nature and significance of Peter's sin. Peter is indeed the "beautiful divine Shepherd," the "angular Foundation," "such a lucky Fisherman," the "Pilot of the one Ship," the "sovereign Key-holder."[16] Yet one thing alone makes him a "loving Shepherd": he is a "Stone wounded by the blows / of penetrating pain." In a remarkable villancico Juana invites him, with emotion and familiarity, to repent: "Weep, weep, my Peter. . . ."[17] All the universe witnesses his weeping: "the earth, the sea, the air, the Sky / . . . / the rivers, the creeks, sources, seas / . . . / the lights, the sun, moon and stars." Peter's repentance reversed his failure:

Weep, weep, my Peter,
for this weeping
more than ten thousand treasures
is worth.

——————

Llora, llora, mi Pedro,
que aquese llanto
más que diez mil tesoros
es estimado.

Peter then becomes the "loving Fisherman," who takes his "little boat" on the "immense Sea."[18] There "the whole Universe" will be his catch. The refrain delicately carries him Juana's wish: "Boatman, boatman, / may the waters sustain your oars!"

The third nocturn formulates the same lesson in simpler terms. After a moralizing villancico to the effect that "divine Providence" allows the leader to err in order to teach him mercy toward others,[19] a medley closes the play on a burlesque tone, as is frequent in Juana's autos. She likes to exploit the double meaning of the Spanish word *ensalada* or its diminutive *ensaladilla,* a "salad" as well as a literary "medley." On the eve of St. Peter's feast, we are told that the collation should end with a salad that is not too spicy![20] Then Juana's attention turns to another point and the analogy shifts to another mixed image that joins together the dancing choir of the cathedral and card games. Entering the church, one meets "a Six that is not more than one, / and one that is worth a hundred." In a Spanish cathedral, a *six* is a member of a sextet of choirboys whose function is both to sing and to dance. In most card games a six is less than an ace. In a game with which I am not acquainted, however, an ace must be worth a hundred in the final tally. The six in question, who mixes in himself these various factors in a rather clownish way, is San Juan de Lima

Juan Massias (1585–1645), who in Juana's time should have been called "venerable," since he was beatified only in 1837, was a Dominican lay-brother. Born in the Spanish province of Estremadura, he had visions of the Virgin Mary and John the Evangelist that inspired him to travel to South America. He entered the Order of Preachers, the Dominicans, in Lima, where he died. Whether Juana had a devotion to him, we do not know, but, given the similarity of their names, it would not have been impossible. In the present context, Juan de Lima sings of Peter's attempt to walk on the sea, a not unlikely theme, since Juan had traveled to the Americas to find the Lord. There follows a "Carder who does not know a tune," for whom Peter becomes a "Wool-carder." This apparently farfetched idea begins to make sense when one realizes that the Spanish word *carda* has a double meaning: it is a kind of dinghy as well as the act of carding. Peter the carder remains boatman and fisherman.

Finally, another person asks serious questions in Latin about the fruitful results of Peter's weeping. He is answered by a chorus, whose refrain, built on a pun, sums up the whole play:

> Because he knew how to love
> he knew how to weep bitterly.

> ――――――――――――

> Quia sapit amare
> sapit amare flere.

The pun makes use of the two meanings of the word *amare,* the infinitive of the verb "to love" and an adverb of the adjective "bitter." The statement reflects deep psychology, spiritual realism, and a sound theology of grace.

The apostle Peter must have provided a favorite topic to Sor Juana Inés, if one takes account of the five other autos (1680, 1684, 1690, 1691, 1692) that her modern editor classifies as "attributable" to her. In any case, Peter is the only one of the saints—not counting, for reasons that will be given in the next chapter, the Virgin Mary— in whose honor Juana wrote more than one liturgical play. Three other saints—St. Peter Nolasco, St. Joseph, and St. Catherine— received one play each.

St. Peter Nolasco (1677)

For St. Peter Nolasco, in 1677, Juana proposes this theme, enunciated in a preliminary dedicatory poem: "It is always right for an image / to return to its original,"[21] a principle that she relates cleverly to the image of Caesar on the coin (Matthew 22:21). The "glorious Spirits" in heaven rejoice over the "happy triumph" of Peter, "who united the French fleur-de-lis / to the Stripes of Aragon."[22] Juana took Peter Nolasco to have been French (a point that is questioned by some historians, who think that he may have been Spanish); and the kingdom of Aragon bears stripes on its coat of arms. There is a deeper reason for joy: "in such a holy squadron / he showed more gallantry / for he was a son of Mary." The captives receive the good news that there is no more cause for weeping.[23] Likened to a needle—an allusion (through a needle's motion both in sewing and on a compass) to his travels back and forth between Spain and Morocco—Peter, the marcher, is told to hasten, for the hole (*carrera*) to be mended is big. *Carrera* is also the career, the life, the journey, of Peter Nolasco, who carries with him on his travels "the Pilgrim, / . . . / the hidden Viaticum,"[24] that is, the eucharist.

In the second nocturn Peter is both "the Swan," or poet, "of Mary"[25] and a wonderworker, whose "greatest miracle is / that I can tell" of his miracles.[26] A ballad about Peter's actions and qualities takes the form of a litany. Presented as "imitator of Christ, Preacher of his glories," "crusher of jails," "valiant Frenchman," Peter is also a *bandolero,* a "Robber who, in a village, / stealing all the souls, / to have dinner with Jesus Christ / dispatched many persons."[27] He challenged the nobility and the people. Peter is he who, among his many achievements, defended Mary's purity, and he finally died a beggar.

The third nocturn draws peculiar parallels between Nolasco and Christ: both are redeemers (of captives, of all humankind); the names of their native lands, Gaul and Galilee, have similar sounds.[28] The superficial parallels would be disappointing were they meant seriously. But there is a glint in Juana's eyes; she intends her analogies to be taken with a grain of salt. The last "little medley" is sung by a Negro in his dialect, by a "pretentious student" who speaks Latin and Spanish, and by an Indian who sings a tocotín in a mixture of Spanish and Nahuatl.[29]

St. Joseph (1690) and St. Catherine (1691)

In the years 1690 and 1691, shortly before Sor Juana Inés de la Cruz abruptly ended her writing career, she was engaged in producing a rich and abundant series of works. Among many pieces, she composed an auto in honor of St. Joseph (1690) and one in honor of St. Catherine (1691), the only woman besides the Mother of Christ whom Juana celebrated in this fashion.

The auto on Joseph was destined to be performed in the cathedral of Puebla, whose bishop, Don Manuel Fernández de Santa Cruz, Juana's occasional visitor in the convent parlor, would soon release to the public the *Carta atenagórica.* In a personal dedication, Juana begs Joseph, in paradoxical language, to receive her play. Although she is "unable to say what no one guesses," it

> at least deserves to be
> the token of a finesse
> that thinks of your glories
> all that it does not think.

> al menos merezca ser
> índice de una fineza
> que piensa de vuestras glorias
> todo aquello que no piensa.[30]

Alternate choruses, representing earth and heaven, introduce the theme. Each claims Joseph as its own: earth, because, born of it, he is, unlike Mary in her assumption, buried in it; heaven, because Joseph is so much like an angel.[31] His unique perfection as "Virgin and Pure" is a "greatness without measure, / for only the eternal Father / gives him his natural Son / to call his own."[32] Accordingly, "his perfection is so great / that to be his Son / Christ alone was sufficient." Therefore the refrain proclaims:

> Then all Angels his glories sing,
> which is not much, if Christ calls him Father!

> ---

> ¡Pues los Angeles todos sus glorias canten,
> que no es mucho, si Cristo le llama Padre!
>
> (P. 272.)

The third villancico discovers types of Joseph in various servants of God of the Old Testament: Moses, Joshua, King Achaz, Jacob, and Elijah. Yet Joseph is greater than they all.[33]

"Father of the Word," Joseph is contrasted to Zachary, "father of the Voice."[34] Zachary was silenced, for he doubted the archangel's message. Joseph, however, has always remained silent; not one word of his is recorded in Scripture. This is precisely the measure of his extraordinary virginity: "Virgin and silent, / he neither fondles nor fecundates / the bridal chamber with offspring, / or the air with his echo's softness." The reason for Joseph's basic self-effacement is both simple and profound:"the divine Word is his Speech!"

The theme of virginity, dear to Juana since her youth, when she felt a deep aversion to matrimony, is at the heart of her view of Joseph. This state in life is not negative. Her own virginity is the counterpart of her love of learning. That of Joseph is greater. It is all the more fruitful, as "any untouched Virgin / is Virgin only once; / but to be twice a Virgin / is Joseph's laurel alone."[35] Twice: for he kept both his virginity and that of his bride. He thus offered "two pure holocausts / in one faith." Juana's imagination attempts to discover God's greatest finesse (the concept of *fineza* will retain us at length in chapter 5 in relation to Juana's Christology). In the present context, finesse concerns the most delicate demonstration of love. As Juana wishes to be understood by ordinary people even when she discusses a point of some subtlety, she proposes an unsophisticated image. Joseph and the divine Word bet against each other on this precise point: Which of them shows the greater finesse?

Two voices alternate, in favor of the one and of the other, in a villancico that ends on a lively exchange between the protagonists. No one wins the argument and the bet, but Joseph, not God, draws the conclusion:

> 1. I gave you as your Mother
> my own Bride.
>
> 2. I as your Bride
> gave you my own Mother.
>
> 1. Then no one wins,
> since in the tally
> the payment is equal
> to the debt.

> 1. Yo te dí, para Madre,
> mi misma Esposa.
>
> 2. Yo, para Esposa tuya,
> mi Madre propria.
>
> 1. Luego ninguno alcanza,
> pues en la cuenta
> tanto vale la paga
> como la deuda.[36]

In the third nocturn Juana asks the classical question: Why was the Word born of a married Virgin rather than of a single Virgin? Of four reasons given by St. Jerome, Juana mentions only the last: "I say that it was to reward / Joseph's perfection, / for his only worthy reward was / that God called him Father." In the final medley Juana builds a ballad on the theme of the "good Carpenter." This is of course Joseph, who had "in his workshop" a "rich sacrarium, / with a Child who had no / equal, of good red color."[37] *Encarnado* (red color) also means "incarnate," leading Juana to give full rein to her partiality for multifaceted symbols: if it is the sacrarium that is red—the color of blood—then the child is also *de bien Encarnado* (honestly incarnate)![38]

As God entrusted Joseph with the "trusteeship / of a most wealthy estate," he became "the tutor of God / not knowing how or when." But "since no sweet fruit is without tartness, / Justice came, and it threw / on the goods an embargo." The holy carpenter had to give up the claim of being a hidalgo (p. 276), or nobleman (of the lineage of King David), and flee to Egypt with the boy. Later, "he lost the Child / among certain fools, / so that Wisdom / be not lost among the wise." At this point, Juana presumably remembered the episode of her own youth, when the viceroy of New Spain, Antonio Sebastián de Toledo, invited a number of scholars to interrogate her and test her wisdom. Juana admits that she has chiefly listed the carpenter's difficulties. But this should be a lesson for all trustees: if a good trustee has problems, "how shall it be with bad ones?"

The jácara leads to a *juguete*, or "comedy," whose chief point is that a *Señor Doctor* is made to look foolish by a group of children. To the scholar's question about Joseph's job, they answer that Joseph was the shepherd who protected the paschal lamb, the sower who sowed the one grain that gave the "sovereign Bread," and the carpenter who made "the Wood" that was to be the remedy of our evil. For the doctor, however, who is knowledgeable in the study of liturgy, Joseph is an officer with a liturgical "office of the first class," for he is "the beloved Patron, Protector, and Advocate of Spain" (p. 277). An Indian and a Negro add their special notes. The Indian points out that one need not be a Doctor at the university in order to know God ("*quimati* Dios");[39] furthermore, the best Joseph is at Xochimilco, a point to which all assent. Xochimilco is a small town by the shallow lake of Chalco, on the south side of Mexico City, in which there remain floating gardens—artificial islands—of Aztec making; presumably there was an impressive statue of St. Joseph at the church of Xochimilco. Juana must have passed through, or near, Xochimilco when, as a child, she traveled to Mexico City, for a portion of the trip was by boat along the waterways leading to the lake of Texcoco, the original setting of Tenochtitlan.

As for Juana's Negro, he affirms that "Señol San José" was black, since the queen of Sheba, who became, in legend if not in history, Solomon's wife, counted among his ancestors. This makes perfect sense, given Juana's concerns for the lower levels of society in New Spain.

The auto on St. Joseph is prolonged by four villancicos destined to accompany the mass. Illustrating the epistle, the offertory, the elevation, and the dismissal (*Ite missa est*), they add some subtle points to Juana's encomium on Joseph. At the epistle, Joseph, who was satisfied "to believe and not to see," is contrasted with the apostle Thomas, who wanted "to see and to believe."[40] Juana Inés, never afraid of frank language, remarks:

> But José, who only
> assents to Faith,
> sees Mary's Belly
> as though not seeing.
> *To believe, not to see.*

> Mas José, que sólo
> asiente a la Fe,
> ve el Vientre a María
> como que no ve.
> *Creer y no ver.*

The theme is pursued at the offertory, with the kind of convoluted construction that was favored by baroque taste. In this case, the style gives a singularly halting quality to the proposed sight:

> So as not to see the Pregnancy,
> José, that made him angry,
> of Mary, his two eyes
> has closed.

> Para no ver el Preñado,
> José, que le daba enojos,
> de María, los dos ojos
> ha cerrado.[41]

Because Joseph's eyes were closed—and here too Joseph was a man of silence, guarding his eyes as well as his tongue—God sent him a dream in which "a glorious Angel" spoke. This prodigious dream provides the topic for the elevation: God acts against the usual order of nature, "for he makes sight uncertain, / making a dream the truth," a unique, even miraculous, event. Yet Juana Inés wants to make a deeper point. Joseph's task exceeds that of any other saint, since his adoptive fatherhood relates him uniquely to God the Father:

> For he feels among the Saints
> only this torment:
> that he is Father of Christ, and must
> resemble the Eternal Father.

> Pues sienta el entre los Santos
> solamente este tormento:
> que es Padre de Cristo, y debe
> parecerse al Padre Eterno.[42]

Finally, at the dismissal, Juana returns to her baroque concern about *fineza*: "Listen to the finesse that God wants to do / in showing his great Power!"[43] The ultimate finesse is that God has the capacity "to make another God, as good as Himself." This he did with Joseph, to whom Jesus became obedient and who "gave him to eat" while he "sustains all." The lesson, however, is universal:

> All our greatness
> comes from littleness,
> and it is,
> our being, so low,
> in such high Being!

Que toda nuestra grandeza
venga de la pequeñez,
y que esté
nuestro ser, por bajo,
en tal alto Ser!

Well may Sor Juana confess: "I do not understand such a great Saint!"

Juana's villancicos for St. Catherine of Alexandria were composed for the cathedral of Antequera (today, Oaxaca) in 1691. The theme was bound to have pleased Juana Inés for two reasons. First, Egypt, was, in her imagination, the land of science and civilization. Second, the traditional legend presented Catherine as a gifted and learned young woman not unlike Juana herself.

In fact, Juana improves on the legend. Not only is her heroine "the beautiful Catherine, / whom Gypsy glory, / vain, vain, / raised to be Divine."[44] She also surpasses, in beauty, wisdom, and strength, all the great women of biblical history: Abigail, Esther, Rachel, Susanna, Deborah, Jael, Rebecca, Ruth, Bethsabe, Thamar, and Sarah. Catherine is the counterpoint to Cleopatra. These two glories of Egypt belong together in their differences. "The loving Cleopatra, . . . valiant Gypsy, . . . offered her breast to the poison" and killed herself when she was "faced with infamy or death."[45] But "heroic Catherine" was "the better Egyptian," when, "by greater love wounded," she offered "to the sharp knives / . . . her beautiful limbs." A hymn to divine providence celebrates Egypt as the privileged land where the Septuagint was translated and the Old Testament preserved in its purity: these are antecedents for Catherine's defense of the purity of the Gospel.[46] And there are other precedents. The hieroglyphs of Egypt used the symbol of the cross, which was even "adored on the breast of Serapis." Catherine thus inherited both "the Law and the Cross." She was crucified on the wheel, which is, "with two opposite diameters, / the sovereign image of the Cross / divided in four right angles." She did not die on the wheel,

> . . . for, being
> God's hieroglyphic infinite,
> instead of death, she found breath.

––––––––––––

> ... porque siendo
> de Dios el jeroglífico infinito
> en vez de topar muerte, halló el aliento.

The poem's conclusion invites Egypt to rejoice: "in one single Rose of Alexandria, / God has granted you an eternal spring." Developing her metaphor, Juana calls Catherine a "cut Rose" that yet lives.[47] Angels and gardeners are invited to admire her.

Catherine also won the victory over the scholars who tested her, a point that is dear to Juana Inés:

> By one Woman they were convinced
> all the wise men of Egypt
> of the proof that sex
> is no essence in the intellect.

> De una Mujer se convencen
> todos los Sabios de Egipto
> par prueba de que el sexo
> no es esencia en lo entendido.[48]

Juana's following remark is not without humor: the miracle is not that Catherine vanquished the wise, but that they conceded her the victory! "Indeed, God wanted in her / to honor the female sex." This is why she became the "sacred tutelar Patron" and the "refuge" of Letters.

Mountains are altered by time, stones can be broken—and have been, even those on which Moses wrote the Law—but on Catherine's body God wrote "the new Table / of the Law of the Gospel."[49] Unlike the corpses of the pharaohs that lie under the weight of the pyramids, her body lay lightly on top of Mount Sinai, near to heaven (this is part of the legend of St. Catherine). In conclusion, a comedy (*juguete*) compares the famous marvels of antiquity with Catherine's greater marvels: she is wall, colossus, "Jesus' sacred Mausoleum in the Sacrament," Temple, statue, "Tower that touched heaven."[50]

Three additional poems accompany the mass. At the epistle, Catherine, "ever beautiful / is the Rose of Alexandria," while she is also, "ever pretty, / the Star of Alexandria."[51] At the elevation, when "the Heavens open from side to side / for Christ comes down and his Bride enters," the rose of Alexandria is "fragrant Lily," "Morning Star," "ever-bright Moon."[52] At the *Ite missa est,* the devil discovers that Catherine, though still in her teens, is "a woman who knows / more than he knows."[53]

Theological Concerns

Juana Inés's liturgical theater is both serious and jocular. She was fond of the genre and took it seriously, but laughter is never far. She fills her scenes with puns and jokes, some of them of frankly popular taste. She obviously enjoyed writing villancicos, even though they may have been deemed unworthy of "the tenth Muse" by some of her admirers. But when, with her extraordinary talent with words, she illustrates the lives of the saints and makes their meaning interesting to the people of New Spain, Juana does more than promote devotion and piety. She literally decorates the spiritual edifice that is the Church in Mexico and, more generally, the Church in all Hispanic lands. If the first nocturn commonly describes the saints according to the accepted legends of their lives, the second relates them to some basic aspects of the Christian faith, and the third brings in the local people in all its variety to share in the poet's enthusiasm. Somewhere in the unfolding of the theme, the angels are invoked; Juana's world is seldom without angels. She likes to evoke, directly or through the medium of a chorus, the heavenly hosts, the "winged Seraphim," who seem eager to be invited to sing.

One may discern in this a pattern of theological concerns. In telling history as it is known to her, with a good deal of legend and possibly of fiction, Juana Inés teaches the core of faith. As she makes the humblest inhabitants of Mexico the heralds of true devotion, she shows up the learned as pretentious and confused. In so doing, Juana, who undoubtedly drew on her own experience, was enjoying herself; she had fun. She excelled at making subtle puns and remote allusions. Perhaps to compensate for her preciosity, the *gongorism* of Spanish literature, she sometimes explored the bizarre, the trivial, and even the vulgar. Such elements are likely to be generally grasped, in her times as in ours, by high and low alike.

St. Hermenegild and Joseph of Egypt

Two plays with a quasi-liturgical intent belong to a different genre. Rather than being humorous imitations of matins, they are plays in their own right. When such a work illustrates the sacraments, it is known as an *auto sacramental;* illustrative of the life of a famous person, it is *historical-alegórico.* At some undetermined date, Sor Juana Inés composed one such play in honor of St. Hermenegild and another for Joseph of Egypt.

Hermenegild (died 585) was honored among the Hieronymites, presumably because he was the son of an early king in Spain and the Hieronymites were a Spanish foundation. Whether Hermenegild should be considered a saint is admittedly questionable. In the story that is reported by Gregory the Great, he was killed at his father's order because he refused to receive holy communion from an Arian bishop. But the communion was to have been a test of reconciliation: Hermenegild had rebelled, in the name of Catholicism, against his Arian father, Leovigild (died 586, king from 569). Married in 579 to the Catholic Ingundis (567–585), a daughter of Sigisbert I (died 575, king of Austrasia in 561), Hermenegild had converted to Catholicism. Does religion, even true religion, justify military rebellion against legitimate political authority?

In a prologue of eight scenes followed by five *cuadros* (tableaux) in twenty-four scenes, Sor Juana treats this theologically delicate topic with profound dramatic imagination. *The Martyr of the Sacrament, St. Hermenegild,* is in fact her only attempt at composing a Christian tragedy on the ancient Greek model. It was not, however, her only attempt at tragedy. Despite the humorous title, which parodies Miguel de Cervantés's *El laberinto de amor* (1585), her *Amor es más laberinto* (1689) begins in the tragic mode, with an entirely Greek setting. After the first act, however, it switches to the comic, mixing genres in a way that is not unrelated to the eclecticism of baroque decorators.

The prologue to the play is less than promising: two students debate scholastically about Christ. As is in keeping with Juana's frequent critique of Mexican society, her students are usually meant to be ridiculous: they highlight the pedantry of vain scholars who do not know enough, just as her sacristans show up the absurdity and ignorance of many in the clergy who claim to be experts in theology. Arguing from St. Augustine, one of the students claims that the greatest act of the incarnate Word was his death, the other, arguing from St. Thomas, maintains that it was his gift of the eucharist. Again we encounter the question of the finesses of Christ, of the proofs of his love. This will detain us later, as Juana, who frequently alludes to it, discusses it at length in a more dramatic personal setting.

Meanwhile, a third student decides to approach the question differently: the eucharistic dilemma in the life of St. Hermenegild will be acted out in a play. The stage is now set on a cosmic plane. In order to show that Mexico enjoys continuity with Spain, the student presents Christopher Columbus as winning an argument with Hercules, whose columns in the Straits of Gibraltar were believed in ancient times to mark the limits of the world. Is there a *Plus ultra* beyond Spain? No, says Hercules. Yes, affirms Columbus: Spain has been "fertile," and he has himself shown by reaching them "that there are more worlds, that there is *Plus ultra*."[54] In context, the cosmic stage serves two purposes. First, showing is a more effective method than arguing. Second, since New Spain is self-evidently part of the *Plus ultra* of Spain, the example of St. Hermenegild is proper in this new setting: he is indeed, for the inhabitants of the Hispanic New World, "Hermenegild, our King."[55]

The play itself, faithful to the tragic genre, vividly delineates the inexorable dilemma on whose horns both son and father are caught. Hermenegild is torn between fidelity to his father and fidelity to his faith, which cannot accommodate the heresy of an Arian kingdom. Leovigild is torn between love for his son and fidelity to his royal duty; the king must demand obedience. The dilemma is emphasized by conversations between allegorical personages. Truth, Faith, Mercy, and Peace side with the unfortunate son, while Fancy and Apostasy support the king. The plot is thickened by the son's expectation of military assistance from the emperor Tiberius (578–582), which makes him twice a traitor to the Visigothic kingdom, and by the mediating but ineffective intervention of the king's other son, Recared (died 601). (At the time, Recared was still an Arian; he was in fact to become Catholic after succeeding his father in 587, and he would officially convert the Visigothic nation at the Third Council of Toledo in 589.) In addition, the archbishop of Seville, St. Leander (c. 555–600/1), who acts as Hermenegild's adviser, passes on the emperor's demand that Hermenegild hand over his wife, Ingundis, and his son, Theodoric, as hostages and pledges of alliance. In fact, Ingundis fell sick and died on the way to Constantinople; but the play does not allude to this.

The cosmic point of view of the prologue is maintained: Leovigild's emissary, General Genseric, traces back the origins of the present monarchy to the days of Noah. Leovigild sees in a vision all the glory of the Spanish crown. In a second vision the king and his predecessors appear in succession, from "Toma, the first king of Spain," to Leovigild's father, Athanagild. This vision deepens the king's tragic position: the monarchy that he has inherited is, by religion, Arian.

Undoubtedly the stage is set for tragedy in masterly fashion. But setting the stage takes so long that there is little time for action. Neither of the main protagonists evolves or even hesitates. From start to finish, Hermenegild is the uncompromising Catholic set against the uncompromising Arian, Leovigild. The battle in which Hermenegild is taken prisoner is not acted out on the stage; even the clash of Faith with Apostasy is narrated rather than depicted. The spectators heard more than they saw.

It would be anachronistic to dwell on the theme's ecumenical possibilities, to which Juana Inés could not have been sensitive. To her audience, as presumably to the author herself, the Arians were the Protestants and Hermenegild was the hero of an embattled Counterreformation.

The title, *The Martyr of the Sacrament, St. Hermenegild,* emphasizes the sacred, rather than the political, aspects of the play. The sacrament comes in accidentally. It appears at the beginning, in the debate of the three students; next, in the king's condition for reconciliation—suggested to him by Apostasy, "the chief Prelate" of Arianism;[56] in Hermenegild's refusal;[57] and finally, in the assurance, given by the final chorus, that "this is the Martyr only / of the Sacrament."[58] The theme is not brought out well by the structure. Juana Inés has not been able fully to integrate her theological emphasis on the eucharist as Christ's finesse into the political and national plot of Hermenegild's history.

Although not presented as a tragedy, *The Scepter of Joseph* is no less ambitious than the play on St. Hermenegild. In five tableaux of twenty-five scenes, *Joseph* tries to build a biblical epic in which the theme of Egypt dovetails with that of salvation history. In the preliminary loa, scene 1, the law of monogamous marriage is explained in an allegorical dialogue among Music, Natural Law, Nature, Law of Grace, and Faith. In scene 2, the differences between Faith and Idolatry are indicated.

The play itself opens with Judah and Reuben's decision to sell their brother Joseph rather than kill him. [59] Then, as Lucifer (*Lucero*, the "morning star"), his bride ("beautiful Intelligence"), and his companions Conjecture, Envy, and Science are engaged in conversation, Music, the voice of God, is heard uttering the curses on Adam and Eve and on the serpent. As Lucero tries to understand the mystery of the woman's foot on his neck, he looks at several visions engineered by Intelligence: Abraham receiving God's blessing and the promise of a son in whom "all Nations / will receive benediction";[60] then Jacob; and finally, Joseph the dreamer, whose name, meaning "God's Increase," signals a further mystery.

Lucero and his companions take part in Joseph's temptation by Potiphar's wife. Several scenes show Jacob and his sons, then the pharoah and the wine steward, Prophecy and Joseph, Joseph and his brothers, later joined by Jacob, while Intelligence, Science, and Conjecture, talking with Lucifer, provide a running commentary on the events. In another commentary, Prophecy reveals the key to Juana's play:

> This Table is for another Table,
> and these Twelve for other Twelve . . .
> and there will be the Bread of Life
> when it will no more be Bread . . .
> and another Benjamin, there,
> will be preferred to all . . .

> Esta Mesa es de otra Mesa,
> y estos Doce de otros Doce . . .
> y allá será el Pan de Vida
> cuando deje de ser Pan . . .
> y otro Benjamín, allá
> será a todos preferido . . . [61]

The last words are spoken by Prophecy:

> If José preserves
> seven years the Wheat,
> here the Bread lasts
> infinite centuries.

Si José conserva
siete años el Trigo,
aquí dura el Pan
infinitos siglos.[62]

A chorus responds:

For it is the Mystery of Mysteries
it is the Prodigy of Prodigies!

¡porque es el Misterio de los Misterios
y es el Prodigio de los Prodigios!

Like the *auto* on Hermenegild, *The Scepter of Joseph* fails as a literary piece. In spite of splendid passages, Sor Juana cannot sustain the high pitch that would be needed. Her forte lies in lyrics, in the lively exchanges of contrasting voices, in dancing songs, and in descriptions of the naturally and the spiritually beautiful, rather than in the nobler genres of tragedy and epic.

Angels

Angels are often featured in Juana's liturgical plays and religious poems. Her *Sacred Poems at the Solemn Profession of a Nun,* which comprise four villancicos, have the nun proclaim: "An Angel of the Lord / assists me courageously."[63] The fourth villancico urges the "winged Seraphim" and "heavenly Courtesans" to sing to the king.[64] In Juana's loas and plays, angels celebrate the conception and the assumption of Mary, who is "Regina Angelorum,"[65] the "Queen of Heaven and Earth"[66] and of all the creaturely universe. They form "the celestial Choirs."[67]

In the more prosaic *Exercises for the Incarnation* Juana Inés outlines her angelology in some detail. We will return to this text in the next chapter, for it speaks of the Virgin Mary at considerable length. But we should at this time outline its teaching on angels. That the angelic world is divided in nine choirs or hierarchies had been generally accepted in western theology since *The Celestial Hierarchy* of Denys (Pseudo-Dionysius the Areopogite) had appeared in the ninth century in Latin translation. Several translations were in fact available. Clearly, Juana Inés is well acquainted with Denys's general view: the angelic choirs belong, three by three, to three ascending levels, the lowest (Angels, Archangels, Virtues) being the nearest to us, the highest (Thrones, Cherubim, Seraphim) the nearest to God. The middle ones—Powers, Principalities, Dominations—act as channels of communication between the upper and the lower levels; for there are, in the Dionysian scheme, descending and ascending activities between the nine choirs, the higher ones illuminating the lower ones, and the latter in turn contemplating the former. Each level is an image of the Holy Trinity.

According to Juana's description, the three levels of the Heavenly Spirits embody the divine gifts of power (first level), wisdom (second level), and love (third level) "that have been communicated to them by the three divine Persons."[68] Within each gift, which obviously reflects one of the divine attributes, each Person is also represented: "In the first [Angels], God is honored as Spirit, in the second [Archangels] God is revealed as Light, in the third [Virtues] God works as Virtue," that is, as strength or power. This threefold action is experienced in the life of the faithful: "to Angels there pertain the protection and care of humans, to Archangels the annunciation of great mysteries and happenings, to Virtues the working of miracles." In the classical theology derived from St. Augustine, on which Juana Inés depends here, light and virtue are attributes of the divine essence. They are "appropriated" respectively to the second and the first Persons, whose proper characteristics they evoke in the believer's mind. Through them and through the angelic activities of protection, revelation, and wonderworking, the divine Persons are adumbrated and indicated. And thus the lowest angelic hierarchy mirrors, however remotely, the holy Trinity.

Juana applies the same principles to the other hierarchies. The Powers, Principalities, and Dominations of the second level represent the three Persons in their wise government of the world, for "Powers control and dominate demons; Principalities rule the governance of kingdoms; Dominations rule the offices of angels."[69] At the highest level, the Heavenly Spirits are absorbed in the contemplation of God. A fruit of love, contemplation is an inner experience of God's being and action: "Thrones see the Equity of God, Cherubim the Virtue, Seraphim the Goodness. In the first, God rests as Equity; in the second, God knows as Truth; in the third, God loves as Charity."[70] The celestial choirs are the object of Juana's loving admiration, for, as she says, the angels are "elevated spirits, most beautiful creatures, admirable examples, and powerful revelations of the Divine Omnipotence."

St. Bernard (1690)

The *St. Bernard Poems* (1690) provide a suitable transition to the Marian themes of Juana Inés's writings, the topic of the next chapter. Composed at the request of the Bernardine sisters of Mexico City for the inauguration of their new church, the poems were apparently not used on that occasion, presumably because something in them did not please the Bernardines. Thirty-two villancicos are built around the theme of the Church-temple, chiefly focusing on the identification of the Virgin Mary as the spiritual temple of God. Bernard appears in the poems as their inspirer and the singer of Mary's glories. As is characteristic of Juana's religious works, she gives a prominent place to the altar, the mass, the sacrament, and finally the faith in which alone they make sense. The temple is of course a baroque edifice, centered on "the Sun of the Monstrance,"[71] that is, the eucharistic host presented to the adoration of the faithful. In the last poem of the set, Juana's pen, like a painter's brush, depicts "this famous Edifice," and thus "the minimum"—her pen and her talent—becomes "the means of the maximum,"[72] the temple of God. It is typical of her art that the author enters the movement of her subject. Juana is totally involved in what she does, she says, and she sings. Likewise her saints: they always illustrate some aspect of the faith; they refer to some dimension of Christ and some attribute or action of God. Bernard vanishes behind Mary, and Mary herself vanishes behind the sacrament. They are part of a building, which is no less a temple for being conceived in the baroque style.

The saints and angels of Juana Inés's theological vision point beyond themselves. The poet in turn tries to vanish behind them, to be no more than a stone in the edifice. But she does not quite succeed. And this is not surprising, since she is also the architect of what she builds.

3

The Temple of God

Temple, Trinity, Eucharist

Not all the thirty-two poems of the *Letras de San Bernardo* mention Mary, but she is present in nine of them (1, 3, 12, 20, 25, 26, 27, 28, 30), quite enough to designate her as a major focus of the series. The Virgin is seen primarily as the temple of God, as was suggested quite naturally by the dedication to Mary of the new church of the Bernardine sisters in 1690, the occasion for which the poems were written. The material temple evokes the spiritual temple. The church's dedication also underlines a basic principle formulated in the first poem:

> If Mary is God's best Temple,
> when one dedicates
> a Temple to God, it can be
> only in the name of Mary.

> Si es Mariá el mejor Templo
> de Dios, cuando se dedica
> Templo a Dios, no puede ser
> sino en nombre de María.[1]

Indeed, Mary's name acts, Juana dares to say, as a "sweet bait," attracting God to the church. And since a church needs a chaplain, who should it be if not St. Bernard, who was devoted to God and to Mary as to "his two Lords"? God, Mary, Bernard: in her imagination, so tied to the baroque taste, Juana finds a symbol of the Trinity in their association. These three, "making a holy league, / imitate the Trinity / in noble cipher."

Poem 3 also associates Bernard and Mary, "for She is life and sweetness / for every creature."[2] Her sweetness is explained: "to who invokes her, / the sound of her Name is / suavity in the ear / and sweets in the mouth." Juana must have remembered the traditional title of Bernard, *doctor mellifluus* (the honey-flowing doctor):

> The cadence of her name
> is clear harmony,
> occasioning melody
> with sweet correspondence;
> the suavity in it
> differentiates it from all:
> and to me it is honey.

> De su Nombre la cadencia
> es una clara armonía,
> que ocasiona melodía
> con dulce correspondencia;
> de todos la diferencia
> la suavidad qua hay en él:
> que para mí, él es miel.

The association of Bernard and Mary recurs in poem 12. He has given her his temple; she is his "Lady and Mother."[3] She is also "the divine Dawn," for dawn comes before full daylight, the mother before her son. Again, in poem 20, Bernard and Mary are linked in the triptych, "Temple, Bernard, and Mary," which soon becomes Christ, Mary, and Bernard: Bernard can never be "without them both, / since his soul he has given to Christ / and to Mary his heart."[4] Further, Bernard has brought "his family to his mansion, / for his Mother is Mary, / and Christ his elder Brother." The three are always one: "for in the goods of the Three / one cannot admit division." These ties and harmonies would offer a preacher a wonderful occasion to exhibit his talents; "but," Juana exclaims with modesty that is not entirely convincing, "no, no, no, no, / I am not the tailor / of such beauty."

Beauty—here the word is *primor*—is never far from Juana's concerns. The beauty of "the divine Dawn," universal, encompasses the whole created world. In a bold image, Juana Inés likens Mary's womb (the Spanish word *vientre*, like the Latin *venter*, means "womb," "belly," and "pregnancy") to the harvested wheat of the universal sacrament of the eucharist and to the monstrance of eucharistic festivities:

> Compare with the wheat's
> beautiful stack
> the Divine Bride's
> delicate Womb
> that conceives the Sacramented God.
>
> Then her beautiful Womb
> is the sacred Monstrance
> that keeps it sheltered. . . .

> De trigo comparado
> es a la parva hermosa,
> de la Divina Esposa
> el Vientre delicado
> que representa a Dios Sacramentado.
>
> Luego su Vientre hermoso
> es el Viril sagrado
> que lo tiene guardado. . . . [5]

The perception of beauty rests on a discernment of harmonies and correlations. In the churches where Juana attended expositions of the blessed sacrament, the glorious monstrance was commonly set in the midst of flowers, notably lilies. (One may recall here that expositions of the blessed sacrament, which remained popular until the liturgical reforms of Vatican II, were a typical devotion of the baroque age.) Juana wonders:

> But why is it adorned
> with a fragrant fence,
> if not because he wanted
> to show, mysteriously,
> that Lily and Nard are only one thing . . . ?

¿Mas, por qué de olorosa
valla está guarnecido,
sino porque ha querido
figurar, misteriosa,
que el Lilio y Nardo es una misma cosa . . . ?

The lily and the nard—a perfume—are Mary's symbols or attributes, at least if the Song of Songs, where they recur, is interpreted in a marian perspective. Juana Inés draws on the biblical poem as she weaves a text in which beauty, lily, and nard are intertwined with the image of the bride of God. The poet places these words in Mary's mouth:

To the cellar
of his fragrant wines
my Bridegroom leads me,
to give my senses all delight . . .

and from then on my suave
fragrant Nard
exhales in suavities
all the scent of its native virtue.

———————————

En la botillería
de sus fragrantes vinos
me introduce mi Esposo
por dar todo deleite a mis sentidos . . .

y entonces el süave
fragrante Nardo mío
exhala en suavidades
toto el olor de su virtud nativo.[6]

Mary, however, cannot be the lily. "Christ is the Lily, and Mary / is like the Lily." This refrain of poem 27 illustrates a twofold basic principle of Juana's Mariology: "Mary is not God, but she is / the one who looks most like God."[7] The Lily that Juana identifies with Christ contains all the "divine Perfections"; it is the sum total of the attributes of God. But the Holy Spirit has proclaimed in the

Scriptures that Mary "is like a Lily among thorns." The Lily's sweet fragrance belongs to God. If, by divine choice and gift, Mary exudes the same scent, this occurs only "by participation." Here again the abbot of Clairvaux appears, where hardly anyone would expect him: "in his mortification / Bernard has been her image." A graded scale thus leads the thought up to God, in that "Mary seems like God, / and like Mary the great Bernard."

Music provides analogies for the next poem, but Juana Inés mixes her metaphors: "It is St. Bernard and the Virgin / who control the violin's neck: / She, sweeter than sugar, / and he, whiter than geese."[8] Whether the Bernardine sisters would have appreciated the comparison of Bernard to a goose must have carried little weight in Juana's mind, if it occurred to her at all. The poet made full use of the richness of rhyme (*azucáre, ánsare*) and her pervading sense of humor. (Perhaps this was one of the points that displeased the sisters: Juana's poems were in fact not used at the dedication of their church.)

Toward the end of the series, Juana brings in again her cherished theme of the eucharist, as would of course be appropriate in the context of the dedication of a church. More unusual is the image of Mary as the immaculate temple of God. Juana's sacramental symbolism exploits a traditional connection between the church, as the eucharistic banquet hall, and the Virgin Mary:

> Wishing to hold a banquet,
> the eternal Wisdom,
> to prepare the Table
> first builds the house:
> and for such food
> she who serves it
> must be a new House.
>
> Virginal House, Untouched House,
> only Mary can be,
> by God alone indwelt
> and for God erected,
> who without blemish,
> to become his Temple,
> was conceived.

Queriendo hacer un convite
la eterna Sabiduría,
para preparar la Mesa
antes la Casa edifica:
que a tal Comida
ha de ser Casa nueva,
la que la sirva.

Casa Virgen, Casa Intacta,
sólo puede ser María,
de sólo Dios habitada
y para Dios erigida:
que sin mancilla,
para ser Templo suyo,
fue concebida.[9]

In spite of her devotion to the immaculate conception, Juana's
Letras de San Bernardo do not end on this theme. Like all aspects,
virtues, or privileges of the Virgin, the immaculate conception does
not have its ultimate purpose in itself. In poem 31, this purpose is
identified as the Church's wedding with Christ:

In the Sun of the Monstrance
God has placed his throne,
and as a gallant Bridegroom
from his bedchamber has come;

and when of a new Temple
Dedication is made,
there goes to Church one like a Bride
at the arm of her Love:

thus on the day when the Bride
reaches her happy union,
Christ celebrates his wedding
in the bedchamber of the Sun.

En el Sol de la Custodia
colocó su trono Dios,
y como Esposo galán
de su tálamo salió;

y cuando de un nuevo Templo
se hace la Dedicación,
va a la Iglesia como Esposa
a los brazos de su Amor:

con que el día que la Esposa
llega a su feliz unión,
celebro Cristo sus bodas
en el tálamo del Sol.[10]

The Immaculate Conception

Among the marian dogmas, the immaculate conception holds a special place in Sor Juana's doctrine and devotion. Not only did she compose in its honor at least two liturgical plays, one of which dates back to the early years of her writing, but also, when entering into silence, she consecrated herself to this mystery in a unique way. We shall return to this point later; for the moment, we shall sketch her doctrinal approach.

Although the basic argument in favor of Mary's immaculate conception had been proposed in the late thirteenth century by the Franciscan John Duns Scotus (1266–1308), it did not yet count in the seventeenth century among the officially defined doctrines of the Catholic Church.[11] There had indeed been a doctrinal definition at the Council of Basel on 17 September 1438, but this council had not been received as ecumenical by the popes and by the Church in general. According to Duns Scotus, the redemption wrought by Christ may have been applied by anticipation to Mary so that his mother would be exempt not only from the guilt that follows original sin but also from original sin itself. The definition of Basel had spoken more vaguely of a "prevenient and operative grace" that redeemed Mary "by a more sublime kind of sanctification." This was connected by the council with God's sovereign act of creation. But how could grace flow backward from the historical events in which Jesus Christ wrought the redemption of humanity? This ques-

tion was not answered by the formulation adopted at Basel. Some
theologians did argue from the statement of Basel in favor of Mary's
immaculate conception; nevertheless, by and large the force of this
definition was not admitted.

As was inevitable in the Hispanic possessions in the New
World, however, Juana Inés lived within the doctrinal and devotional
framework of the Church in Spain, where the doctrine of the im-
maculate conception had received the most enthusiastic welcome.
Since Alphonsus V (1416-1458), the crown of Aragon had assumed
the task of bringing political pressure to bear on the cardinals and
on the bishop of Rome in favor of a formal definition of Mary's
immaculate conception. Spanish influence had been strong at the
Council of Basel.

In fact, Juana's theology of the conception underwent a devel-
opment. In the villancicos of 1676, composed for the cathedral of
Mexico City, the ties between the redemption by Christ and the
immaculate conception of Mary are not explored. They are clearly
stated, however, in those of 1689, written for the cathedral of Puebla.

In 1676, the scene opens on an invitation to attend "the fiesta
of heaven," that is being celebrated in honor of "a Queen, Pure and
faultless."[12] The manner of the queen's conception is

> so new that she has no sin.

> There in the divine Mind
> her pure, intact splendor
> not needing absolution
> has been a reserved case.

> tan nueva, que no ha pecado.

> Allá en la Mente divina
> su puro esplendor intacto
> sin necesidad de absuelto
> fue éste un caso reservado.

(P. 213.)

Juana does not long maintain this sober language of canon law. She
soon perceives a "miracle": although it runs through the whole

world, sin has not been able to touch Mary's "Immaculate Being."
The fiesta is described further, as "Today with festive joy, / filled
with virtue and grace, / in her Conception there begins / a Temple
of God, Mary."[13] The next five stanzas highlight popular titles and
names of Mary: she is *Concepción*, St. Mary of Grace, *Porta-Coeli*
(Gate of Heaven), *Mercedes* (Mercies), Queen.

The theme of the lily follows in the third villancico, where Mary
herself is the lily *(Azucena)*, which in its purity outshines all other
flowers. To the question of the envoy, "Who is this Queen of earth
and heaven?"[14] this answer is given:

> She is the Bird of grace, by eternal God
> conceived without blemish,
> that is for glories, that is for graces,
> and in one Instant
> God freed her from guilt to be his Mother.

> Es el Ave de gracia, por Dios eterno
> concebida sin mancha,
> que está para glorias, que está para gracias,
> y en un Instante
> la libró Dios de culpa, para ser su Madre.

In light of the developed doctrine of the immaculate conception ar-
ticulated in 1854 the formulation of this last verse remains insuffi-
cient. As it stands, it can still express the opinion of opponents of
the immaculate conception, such as Bernard himself and Thomas
Aquinas, who thought that Mary had been freed from guilt imme-
diately after incurring original sin.

Whether Juana Inés was aware of the ambiguity of her formula,
she continued as though there were no problem. She imagined a sort
of parable, in which "a foreign Herbalist, / who is all Wisdom, / in
order to cure diseases / displays a blessed Herb."[15] This wonderful
herb is identified with a number of medicinal plants, known to the
herbalists of the time: the *Sánalo-todo* (cure-all), and also *Hierba-Buena*
(good herb), *Santa-María*, *Hierba-Santa* (holy herb), *Celidonia* (celan-
dine), Salvia, *Siempre-Viva* (ever-living), *Mejor-Ana*, *Yerba de la Puebla*
(seed-grass). It is, in sum, "the sweet Antidote / that dries up all the
venom / and heals all evils." The foreign herbalist is called Manuel,

a standard Spanish rendering of the word, *Emmanuel,* one of the messianic titles of Jesus. In the next villancico, God is "the Divine Gardener."[16] The enemy has sown darnel "in the garden of the world." But the gardener "has planted the most noble Rose," which is so different from all other flowers "that Nature even / in It does not recognize itself." All gardeners and laborers should go and see it:

> Without the thorns of sin
> you will see it preside over the meadow,
> without blemish,
> so beautiful,
> that being Heaven's Rose,
> it is the meadow's Marvel.

———————

> Sin espinas de pecado
> vereis que preside al prado,
> sin mancilla,
> tan hermosa,
> que siendo del Cielo Rosa,
> es del prado Maravilla.

After the parable, the explanation. Villancico 6 tells the story again in terms of the young girl Mary. "Before all things / there was a dainty Child, / by the Creator's eyes / graciously foreseen."[17] She was to become the mother of "a Humanized God" and "the defense of mortals." She was to fight with the devil and win. God gave her such grace "that, being a pure creature, / she seems to be a Divine Woman." A daughter of Adam yet conceived without guilt, she does not look like him. "From the universal debt / the Sacred Power freed her, / foreseeing that she had to be / our Queen without fall." The last nocturn of the composition offers pure praise, piling up marian symbols borrowed from nature. Mary is, through her conception, "of pure lights / the well-ordered Squadron";[18] "white Dawn, beautiful Sun, / and Moon full of grace"; "the shining divine Dawn." She is also "like a Moon ever filled / with pure, undamaged candor," for she has been conceived "from the clean, clear splendor / of indefectible Light." Finally, in villancico 8, a Negro sings the queen's praises in his colorful dialect.

At this point in her career, Sor Juana understands the immaculate conception as a special effect of God's creative power. Its purpose or final cause coincides with the incarnation of the Son of God and the divine motherhood. Its efficient cause lies in the power and authority of the divine Creator. The doctrine is more theocentric than christocentric. God can do it and, since it is fitting, does it. We are not far from the idea of God that was entertained by the nominalists at the end of the Middle Ages. God being essentially will and power (rather than being or goodness), divine actions are accountable only to his will. In Juana Inés's theology, however, the accent on the divine will has become an aspect of a broader emphasis on God as essential beauty. The divine will is a will for beauty.

The production of 1689 is much more theological than that of 1676, and the theology is somewhat different. At the start of the first villancico, Juana Inés lets us know that we are dealing with a mystery; that this mystery, though "not of faith, is believed";[19] and that it is self-evident, granted that, as she rightly admits, "self-evidence is not Faith." In so posing and delimiting the problem, Juana Inés challenges herself to a new task: in order to avoid dismissal as warmhearted but light-headed, she needs to show why she holds the doctrine of the immaculate conception to be self-evident. This is precisely the central theme of these villancicos.

Under the refrain, "That [or, If] self-evidence is not Faith," villancico 1 formulates three arguments. First, since Mary was preserved in order to be "the beloved Mother, / then before being created / she was already foreseen." Second, "Mother of God and sin" being mutually repugnant, they cannot coexist in one person. Third, since God has ordered all to honor their parents, and she is his mother, "why would he not do / with You what he decreed / for the others?"

The second villancico highlights the cosmic context of the immaculate conception. According to Genesis, at least as Juana reads it, "the creation of Humankind was / the perfection of the Heavens / and the complement of the Earth."[20] Because of sin, however, "all the universal order, / although perfect in its parts, / became, as a whole, formless." God restored perfection to the universe by preserving Mary from sin. Her pure conception includes the perfection "of Man, of Angel, of Heaven, and of Earth."

In the third villancico, two alternating voices relate dialectically Mary's motherhood and her conception, so that each throws light on the other and justifies it:

> 1.—The sacred Motherhood
> is in Mary
> the proof that without blemish
> she was conceived.
>
> 2.—Of this Conception is
> the clear premise,
> since it is for that alone
> that she was Preserved.

> 1.—La Maternidad sacra
> es en María
> prueba de que sin mancha
> fue concebida.
>
> 2.—La Concepción es, de eso,
> premisa clara,
> pues para tanto sólo
> fue Preservada.[21]

Those who see that Mary is the mother of God cannot doubt her immaculate conception; and those who see her as immaculately conceived know that she is the mother of God. Each vision implies the other; they are interchangeable. Juana Inés sums it up neatly: "Sinless? Therefore Mother! / Mother? Therefore sinless!"

So far, the argument is entirely compatible with the position of the ancient theologians on the matter of Mary's sinlessness: she was made sinless after incurring original sin. There was no agreement on the exact moment: Was it shortly before the age when one is able to fall into personal sin? Or perhaps before, at the annunciation, when she became the Theotokos? Or even in the womb before she was born? Or, finally, just after she was conceived?

The three villancicos of the second nocturn do not remove this ambiguity, but they introduce two new ideas. According to the first, Mary's conception, in all its purity, was not, strictly speaking, "a privilege of grace"[22] that would have been entirely gratuitous. Rather, it was a point of justice that God owed to himself; or, as Juana puts it, "grace made itself justice."

> It was in God's own interest
> her Conception without blemish:
> for, to whom is it more important
> to be born of a clean Mother?

> His mercy was in choosing her;
> for once she had been elected,
> it was God's point of honor
> to ennoble his Family.

> Proprio interés fue de Dios
> ser sin mancha Concebida:
> porque, ¿a quién le importó mas
> el nacer de Madre limpia?

> La merced fue el escogerla;
> pero una vez ya elegida,
> era pundonor de Dios
> ennoblecer su Familia.

The second idea focuses on the notion of *instant*. A singer asks for one instant of patience to hear his song, which is only about one instant. The immaculate conception took place in one instant, "outside of time,"[23] in God's eternity. Juana takes the occasion of this to denounce as illogical the older theology of Mary's preservation from sin after she was conceived:

> God, who with a pure act
> sees all that is created,
> from the infinite past
> to the infinite future,

> determined in his Power
> that considers all,

to forestall what was not
for the sake of what had to be.

To be his loving Mother
Mary he destined,
and *ab aeterno* saw her
ever Clear and ever Beautiful.

Then in such great dignity,
how come that it is said
that she was, an instant, Enemy
and Mother, an eternity?

———————

Dios, que con un acto puro
mira todo lo crïado,
del infinito pasado
al infinito futuro,

determinó de su Poder
que todo lo considera,
prevenir lo que no era
para lo que había de ser.

Para su Madre amorosa
a María destinó,
y *ab aeterno* la miró
siempre Limpia y siempre Hermosa.

Pues en tanta dignidad,
¿cómo cabe que se diga
que fue un instante Enemiga
y Madre una eternidad?

In villancico 6, Mary's beauty is admired by "Heaven, Sun,
Moon, and Stars"[24] and by the pagan goddesses "Venus, Cynthia,
Pallas, Flora," while the women of the Old Testament ("Judith,
Esther, Rachel, Sarah") paint her "only in glimpses," and the four
elements—"Water, Earth, Wind, and Fire"—surrender at her feet.

The third nocturn is the most far-reaching in regard to theology. Juana composes a striking commentary on the verse of Song of Songs 1:5: "I am black, but lovely." Quite correctly if one reads the Hebrew text carefully, the blackness in question is not that of skin pigmentation; it comes from suntan. This is the point of the envoy, which also serves as refrain:

> Dark is the Bride
> for the Sun is in her face.

> _____

> Morenica la Esposa está
> porque el Sol en el rostro le da.[25]

The sun is God. Given the sun's brightness, darkness easily symbolizes evil. Sor Juana joins the two symbols together:

> If the pure light is compared
> of each other, between them,
> before God's clear Sun
> the Creature is dark;
> but it acquires beauty
> as it comes nearer thereto.

> _____

> Comparada la luz pura
> de uno y otro, entre los dos,
> ante el claro Sol de Dios
> es morena la Criatura;
> pero se añade hermosura
> mientras más se acerca allá.

The same point is repeated in the next two stanzas. In the last one the bride declares herself to be the slave of God, who is her lord; she is free from the other lord, the devil. For her, slavery is freedom.

In the concluding *ensalada* of the very last villancico the theology of the immaculate conception is fully formulated. The previous points, comparisons, explanations, commentaries, images, and symbols were steps toward this theological conclusion. Appropriately, it is formulated by three angels, for Mary is "de Angeles la Puebla," "the Seed of Angels / in title and in all."[26] (These villancicos, composed for the cathedral of la Puebla de los Angeles, carried Juana's delicate compliment to the spectators.)

The first angel sings and dances a *jácara,* as he wishes to "alleviate with lightness / the gravity of the tone." It opens on a light note, with the appearance of "that divine Portent," the vision of the one who was "foreseen at the beginning / preserved *ab aeterno,*" whom in Revelation 12:1 "the Sun serves as her tailor / and the Moon as her shoemaker." Four stanzas begin with "the one who" (La que . . .), thus building up a haunting crescendo that enriches the vision of the woman in Heaven: the one who overcame the dragon; the one who in one instant won the victory; the one who,

> . . . in the Golden Age
> was conceived, for it is certain
> that at the time of her conception
> there was no instant of *iron.*

> . . . en el Siglo de Oro
> se concibió, pues es cierto
> que, al tiempo de concerbirse,
> no hubo un instante de *hierro.*

This play of words, "Golden Age" / "instant of iron," hints at Mary's virginity both *ante partum* (before being pregnant) and *in partu* (in giving birth), when she would give birth without the iron instruments of midwives. Mary is finally the one whose name means "Deus ex genere meo," "God from my genus." That this is a fanciful etymology need not affect the symbolic nature of the argument.

The name of Mary leads directly to Sor Juana's theological statement on the immaculate conception:

> Redeemed like all
> as to infinite cost;
> but as to the mode, no,
> for this was much higher:
>
> since the Passion of Christ,
> that redeemed the Universe,

for Her was preservative,
for others, remedial.

Then the sovereign Physician,
as a singular privilege,
before the disease arrived
applied to her the medicine:

for when the Soul was infused
in her most pure Body,
sanctifying Grace
had prepared the means;

thus, with no priority
or real instant of time,
no shadow in her could be
of sin, oh, no indeed.

This has ever been my doctrine
and shall be, and I protest
I shall never say otherwise,
I vow to God I believe it!

Redimida como todos
cuanto al infinito precio;
pero cuanto al modo, no,
porque fué con más supremo:

pues fue la Pasión de Cristo
que redimió al Universo,
para Ella, preservativo,
para los demás, remedio.

Que al Médico soberano,
por singular privilegio,
antes que llegara el daño
le aplicó el medicamento:

pues al infundir el Alma
a su purísimo Cuerpo,

la Gracia santificante
tuvo prevenido el medio;

con que, en prioridad ninguna
ni instante real de tiempo,
pudo en ella haber vestigio
de pecado, ni por pienso.

Este siempre mi sentir
ha sido y será, y protesto
que nunca diré otra cosa,
¡y voto a Dios, que lo creo!

In 1689, Juana was five years away from her private vow to
defend the immaculate conception; she may well have already been
thinking of such a vow when she wrote this poem. Nevertheless, as
a court poet she would not burden her audience with excessive grav-
ity. The serious tone is soon alleviated by the song of a second angel,
who compares Mary's purity to the Sierra Nevada and the dawn.
The Sierra Nevada is the mountain range of Juana's early childhood
at Nepantla and Amecameca, when she could see the snows of the
Popocatepetl, near to which she was born, and of the Ixtlaltepetl.
Finally, as a game, the other members of the angelic choir sing a
kind of litany of Mary in stanzas of eleven lines:

Like among thorns the Rose,
like in the clouds the Moon,
unique and like no one else
shines the divine Bride:
all pure and all beautiful,
purple and colorful,
protected City of God,
Ark of his Covenant,
Throne of the Trinity,
beautiful Iris of peace,
and three hundred things more!

> Como entre espinas la Rosa,
> como entre nubes la Luna,
> única y como ninguna
> luce la divina Esposa:
> toda pura y toda hermosa,
> púrpura y biso vestida;
> Ciudad de Dios defendida,
> Arca de su Testamento,
> de la Trinidad Asiento,
> Iris hermoso de paz:
> ¡y trescientas cosas más![27]

Three other stanzas with the same light tone and fast pace end with the refrain, "and three hundred things more!" Juana could have written many more lines in honor of the Immaculate Conception.

The Presentation

Three short pieces for the feast of the presentation of Mary provide a transition to the other doctrine to which Sor Juana Inés de la Cruz devoted considerable attention, Mary's assumption. The two feasts are similar in that both Mary's presentation in the temple at the age of three and her assumption into heaven were first formulated in the early centuries of Christianity, in apocryphal writings that were excluded from the New Testament. The presentation, however, is entirely based on a nonhistorical legend. Of eastern origin, the feast is attested in England around 1060, though it disappeared after the Norman conquest. It spread again in the West during the fourteenth century, being celebrated at the papal court of Avignon for the first time in 1372. The feast became universal in the Latin rite toward the end of the sixteenth century; its liturgical celebration falls on 21 November although it has at times in some places been celebrated on 26 November or 30 September. The assumption, liturgically much older, was formally defined as a dogma by Pius XII in 1950.

In the seventeenth century, the presentation was no more than a pious belief. The assumption, however, while equally based on a legend, was universally celebrated on 15 August, was generally taught by the Church's ordinary magisterium, and was believed by the faithful, so that it could be held, according to Catholic principles, as pertaining to the deposit of faith. Whether Juana took the presentation as fact or as legend she does not tell; but she was by no means naive in matters of history.

Juana's *Letras a la presentación de Nuestra Señora,* of uncertain date, have a theological content that is, given the frequent accent of Juana's Mariology, hardly surprising: Mary is the true temple of God. As understood by Juana, the feast does not commemorate Mary's entrance into the temple at the age of three, but, rather, dedicates Mary as the temple of God.[28] In addition, the poems celebrate Mary's beauty:

> If the beauty of Mary
> is the best throne of God,
> to which Temple of God goes
> She who is his best Temple?

> Si es la beldad de María
> de Dios el mejor asiento,
> ¿a qué Templo de Dios va,
> siendo Ella su mejor Templo?

She is "of God himself the high, beautiful Concept." As the "beautiful Child" ascends the steps of the temple, her walk is "dainty":

> Yea, yea, yea, beautiful Child,
> how daintily you go!
> Yea, yea, yea, how dainty
> are your steps!

> ¡Ay, ay, ay, Niña bella,
> qué linda vas!
> ¡Ay, ay, ay, y qué lindos
> pasos das![29]

Although the little girl can hardly walk, she is spiritually flying! Today she seeks God in the temple; God, "some day, will come to seek" her. The last poem develops the theme of Mary's spiritual flight. As she brings her purity to the temple, she measures the stairs with her feet and with her soul, the spheres. Her walk is light, but lighter still is the flight of her soul. Her body and her soul struggle, for her body wants to detain her and her soul wants to raise her up. Her soul would win if she did not bow to a higher reason:

> She concedes; but her impulse
> yielding to so high a purpose,
> she manages in a Sacred Place
> to deposit her Beauty.

> Cede; mas ya que el impulso
> a fin tan alto suspenda,
> procura en Lugar Sagrado
> depositar su Belleza.[30]

The Assumption

Juana Inés's treatment of the theme of Mary's assumption must have pleased the canons of Mexico City who were responsible for the cathedral, and presumably the successive archbishops as well, for the Hieronymite nun was invited four times to compose villancicos for the feast—in 1676, 1679, 1685, and 1690. Her manner is always brilliant and, in spite of the identity of the topic, always varied. She takes a new approach each time: a special aspect of the feast may be underlined; new ideas may be tried; new symbols proposed and deciphered; new rhythms attempted; even other languages than the customary Spanish employed. As she says,

> Since in the Church it is in style
> to sing new things,
> and if in the *Jacarandina*
> there is nothing new,
> in vain does one scream,
> for no one has to listen.

> Porque en la Iglesia se estila
> que se canten cosas nuevas,
> y si en su Jacarandina
> no hay algo de novedad,

en vano se desgañita,
porque nadie ha de escucharle.[31]

Juana Inés makes full use of her amazing versatility to bring variety to her compositions on the assumption. Besides Spanish, she introduces the Negro dialect that she likes to feature in the "salad" of her third nocturn:[32] the Indian language, Nahuatl, that she had most likely spoken in her childhood;[33] Basque, called "the same dense language of my ancestors,"[34] of which she knew at least a few expressions; and, finally, Latin.[35] She even performed an extraordinary feat with a hymn of praise that, depending on how it is pronounced, is in Latin or in Spanish.[36]

In the four works on the assumption, Juana's treatment of the opening scene and her proliferation of symbols attest to her versatility. The work from 1676 opens with an invitatory in which heaven and earth argue about which is better: that God descends to the earth, or that Mary ascends to heaven. In 1679, all creatures salute the dawn. In 1686, Mary's body and her soul struggle at the moment of the assumption. And, in 1690, a question is debated: Is the assumption an ascent or a descent? New Marian symbols are created: Mary is not only the divine dawn and the queen, the city and the temple of God,[37] she is also the sovereign physician,[38] the choirmaster,[39] the teacher,[40] the "Great Astronomer,"[41] the beautiful empress,[42] the slave who becomes queen.[43] Each symbol is explored and developed in suitable ways, as when the choirmaster takes us through the notes and intervals of the musical scale.

Juana draws on the Song of Songs and the Revelation of John to explore what she takes to be the scriptural basis for the doctrine of the assumption.[44] Mary is "this Shepherdess,"[45] who, "wounded with her eye, / caught with her hair," the chief shepherd of the mountain (Song of Songs 4:9; 7:6). "Daughter of the eternal Prince,"[46] she is a "Sweet Bride," called from "highest Lebanon" to receive the three crowns "of Amana, Hermon, and Sanir" (Song of Songs 4:8).

Of Amana for the Mother
(for this is the Hebrew sound),
of Sanir for the Bride,
and of Hermon for the Temple.

La de Amaná, como a Madre
(pues eso suena en Hebreo);
la de Sanir, como a Esposa
y la de Hermón, como a Templo.

Meanwhile, God, the chief shepherd, calls to her:

Come, my Friend,
get up fast;
come, my Turtledove,
fly the sweet flight!

Come, my beautiful One,
and in three calls
enjoy the three Crowns
that I prepare for you!

¡Ven, Amiga mía,
levántate presto;
ven, Paloma mía,
alza el dulce vuelo!

¡Ven, Hermosa mía,
y en tres llamamientos
les tres Coronas goza
que te prevengo!

(P. 284.)

Mary is also the rising dawn (Song of Songs 6:9), identical with the dawn that brought an end to Jacob's struggle with God.[47]

Juana refers to the apocryphal legend of the dormition: the twelve apostles were in attendance when Mary passed away. Through the voice of a sacristan she relates that "all the Apostles rushed to the Virgin's transitus."[48] She adds, through another voice: "This does not matter!"

The earth's round shape provides a striking parable in support of a biblical argument, prompted by the query: Is the assumption an ascent or a descent? This question of the first villancico of 1690 receives a twofold answer. It is an ascent, for, among other reasons,

Mary went "from earth to Heaven,"[49] and she "ascended with joy /
to the arms of her Son." Yet it is also a descent: "Heaven ascended
to Mary, / and Mary descended to Heaven; / in that She gave more
joy / than Heaven could give." Moreover, the vision of the City of
God in Revelation 21:2 refers to Mary:

> John saw a City
> descending from Heaven,
> like a Bride adorned
> for her Bridegroom, with royal pomp,
>
> and a voice told him:
> —"This is the supreme
> Tabernacle, where
> with humankind dwells eternal God";
>
> and then he adds that
> he saw no Temple in it,
> for God alone
> was his Temple, and the Lamb.
>
> In this way it stands out,
> according to the text,
> that it is the Temple of God
> and God is his own Temple at the same time.
>
> But who can understand
> so great a mystery,
> except when Mary enters
> in Glory, and Jesus in the Castle?
>
> God entered the Castle
> when the Word became Man,
> and today Mary enters God
> to enjoy her Kingdom's crown.
>
> Therefore, today, in her Assumption,
> the Gospel tells us
> that when Mary enters,
> it is God who enters a higher Throne.

———————

Vio Juan una Ciudad
que descendió del Cielo,
como Esposa adornada
para su Esposo, de aparato regio,

y que una voz le dijo:
—"Aquéste es el supremo
Tabernáculo, donde
con los hombres habita Dios eterno";

y luego añade que
no vido en ella Templo
alguno, porque Dios
solo era Templo suyo, y el Cordero.

De manera que sale,
según consta del texto,
que ella es Templo de Dios
y Dios es Templo suyo, a un mismo tiempo.

¿Pues a quién figurar
podrá tanto misterio,
sino al entrar María
en la Gloria, y Jesús en el *Castelo*?

Dios entró en el Castillo
cuando se hizo Hombre el Verbo,
y hoy María entra en Dios
a gozar la corona de su Reino.

Con que hoy, en su Asunción,
nos dice el Evangelio
que, cuando entra María
es Dios quien entra en Trono más excelso.[50]

Descent can be ascent, as is demonstrated by the very shape of the earth. Juana's interest in the sciences comes to the assistance of her theology. One recognizes, "in good Philosophy,"[51] that "the center of the Earth / is only a point, distant / equally from the whole Sphere." Those who go down to the central point and pass through finally go up to the circumference on the other side. So is it with the Virgin:

> This happens today in Mary:
> reaching the extreme line
> of Humility, descending,
> she goes through the center and ascends. . . .

> Her Assumption was not an ascent
> through desire of greatness,
> but she passed into Heaven
> by penetrating the Earth.

> Esto pasa hoy en María,
> que al tocar la línea extrema
> de la Humildad, por bajarse,
> pasa al centro y se eleva. . . .

> No fue, su Asunción, subir
> por apetecer grandeza
> sino que se pasó al Cielo
> por entrañarse en la tierra.

Theologically, the pieces of 1685 and 1690 are richer than the earlier ones. In the first nocturn of 1685, Juana develops the theme of Mary's death. She imagines that Mary's body and her soul struggle together because neither is willing to abandon her. And why should they abandon her? Mary's death was not required, for she had no sin; her death was freely offered: "Since Death had no / reason to accomplish its work, / She did not pay it as a debt / and accepted it as a test."[52] Further, Mary wished to be like her Son: "She died by imitation, / so that no one could find / some item in the Son / that the Mother shared not." Then, after a traditional litany to Mary, villancico 3 returns to the question of Mary's death. As a herald proclaims God's decree, Juana Inés shows the coherence of her Mariology:

> The Supreme King orders
> that because Mary

lived without guilt,
she will die without pain.

She lived Immaculate;
and thus, there was reason
for Mary to die
as she had lived.

Her death was merit,
not obligation;
for she paid the debt
that she never owed.

———————

Manda el Rey supremo
que, porque vivió
María sin culpa,
pára sin dolor.

Vivió Immaculada;
y así, fue razón
que muera María
conforme vivió.

Mérito es su muerte,
y no obligación;
pues pagó el tributo
que nunca debió.[53]

Well may one say that Mary died "for other reason than others," namely, "not as Adam's daughter, / but as God's Mother."

What is Mary's Assumption? Behind the luxuriant metaphors, Juana expounds with enthusiasm what Martin Luther would have called a theology of glory, that was to her a theology of beauty. "Who is this Beauty," she asks in an envoy that paraphrases Song of Songs 6:9,

who hastens her exit,
nimble like the Dawn,
beautiful like the Moon,

select like the Sun,
armed like a Squadron
with every powerful weaponry?

———————

que su salida apresura
cual la Aurora presurosa
y como la Luna hermosa
y como el Sol escogida,
como escuadrón guarnecida
de toda fuerte armadura?[54]

This question is answered in the stanzas. Mary is like the dawn

because she is the primordial light
gilding the fields with light:
and the forerunner of the Sun,
whose divine red sky
is begotten by the Sun,
and also the Mother of the Sun.

———————

Porque Ella es la luz primera
que de luz los campos dora:
es del Sol la precursora,
cuyo divino arrebol
es engendrado del Sol,
y es Madre del Sol también.

(Stanza 1.)

Her beauty is like the moon: whereas the sun both illumines and burns, "she illumines and does not burn" (stanza 2). Stanzas 3 and 4 explain that the Sun—Christ—keeps "the rays of Justice" (stanza 3), but Mary "is only Advocate; / only protection becomes her / and attending to our good." For this reason, she, "the pure Bride, / from her celestial lips, / only distills honeycombs / with milk and honey of sweetness" (stanza 4). By contrast, Christ, the bride-groom, also distills "sourness." She is "elect" like Apollo (whose symbol, in Greco-Roman myth, is the sun), even if Juana's etymology is less accurate than her mythology:

because Sol is from *solo,*
and she is alone in perfection:
alone in glory,
alone in purity,
alone in beauty,
and also in dignity.

Porque Sol se dijo *a solo,*
y es sola en la perfección:
una sola en el blasón,
una sola en la pureza,
una sola en la belleza,
y en la dignidad también.

(Stanza 5, p. 282.)

Finally, Mary is like a squadron because she has vanquished the dragon (stanza 6, p. 282).

What, then, is the assumption? Since Mary is, first and last, the temple of God, something is missing in heaven as long as she is not there. The Apocalypse shows that in heaven there is no temple but God; this applies, however, only until Mary's assumption. Juana exclaims: "Go up, up, up, with light flight, / for till you go up God misses his Temple!"[55] God has built a throne in all his creatures, but a dwelling only in Mary. He has not found a suitable one "in all the greatness of the Heavens." He has confined himself "to the generous cloister / of the virginal Womb that shelters him."

Therefore, as long as Mary is on earth,
God has no dwelling in the heights;
for only his Mother's womb is one,
a Throne, a Resting place, a Temple, an Urn.

Luego mientras María esta en la tierra,
no tiene Dios morada en las alturas;
pues sólo lo es el pecho de su Madre,
Trono, Reclinatorio, Templo y Urna.

This is the ultimate reason for Mary's assumption:

She ascends, then, to make Heaven, Heaven,
for till it is adorned with her beauty,
Heaven misses its ornament, God his dwelling,
and creatures their accidental glory.

Suba, pues a hacer Cielo al mismo Cielo,
pues hasta que le adorne su hermosura,
al Cielo falta ornato, a Dios morada,
y gloria accidental a las criaturas.

The Sorrowful Mysteries

Juana Inés did not regard singing the praises of Mary as merely a literary exercise but as a concrete and important action. Profoundly devoted to Mary, Sor Juana holds convictions deeply impressed by the mariological tradition, especially regarding the immaculate conception. In her religious life in the Hieronymite community, she was also devoted to her sisters and to many others, whether outsiders, like the clergy and lay people who assisted the nuns, or insiders, such as the oblates, servants, or slaves who shared the convent's life. It is therefore not surprising that when she composed spiritual exercises to be used in her community, they were focused on the Virgin Mary. Mentioned by herself in the *Response to Sor Filotea de la Cruz,* they had been printed "years before," at a date that is uncertain. The publication, which did not carry her name, had been made with her knowledge and consent. As Sor Juana testifies, she composed two works—*Exercises for the Incarnation* and *Offerings of the Sorrows*—"for my sisters' devotion."[56] The topics of the works, out of proportion to her own "lukewarmness and ignorance," dealt at considerable length with "things of our great Queen." And, as Juana remarks, "I know not what happens: treating of the Most Holy Mary, the coldest heart is inflamed."

The feast that Juana Inés de la Cruz calls the "Sorrows of Our Lady the Virgin Mary" dates back to the synod of Cologne of 1423. Celebrated on the Friday following Passion Sunday, it did not become universal in the Latin Church before Pope Benedict XIII, in 1727. Another feast on the same theme, created in 1668 by the Order of the Servites of Mary, was celebrated on the third Sunday in September. Whichever feast Juana has in mind, she brings undeniable originality to her *Offerings,* fifteen meditative prayers to the Virgin that were destined to introduce the fifteen decades of the rosary. Her decades were not, as today, made of one Lord's Prayer, ten Hail Mary's, and one doxology; they consisted, rather, of ten Hail Mary's and one Lord's Prayer, so that the Virgin leads, in ten steps, to the Father.

Juana knew the practice of dividing the marian mysteries into three groups, Joyful, Sorrowful, and Glorious, for she mentions the first group at the end of the *Exercises for the Incarnation;* in the *Offerings,* however, she adopts another pattern. The fifteen mysteries, all of them sorrowful, refer to the pains felt by the Virgin: (1) at the denudation of her son, (2) at the crucifixion, (3) at the raising of the cross, (4) at the words from the cross, especially the words to John and to herself, (5) at the offering of gall and vinegar, (6) at the dying of Jesus, (7) in her solitude at the foot of the cross, (8) at the piercing of the side, (9) at the descent from the cross, (10) at the burial, (11) at her return to the cenacle, (12) at the pains she feels when people die without baptism, (13) at the pains she receives from heresies, (14) at her pains from bad Christians, (15) at her pains from the venial sins of the just.

The details of the prayers need not detain us, but a few points are worth mentioning. Mary walked back to the cenacle along "Bitterness Street," where the "meek Lamb" had previously walked in the other direction (mystery 11). The sorrows caused to Mary by heresies are felt in her "indelible memory," her "infused wisdom," and her "most ardent love." Heresy implies leaving "the way of Light," insulting "Baptism with heretical dogmas," "smashing like ungrateful vipers the entrails of Holy Mother Church," "not only tearing the seamless robe of your Son, but disconnecting the harmony of the members of his mystical body, which is the Holy Church, interpreting and falsifying the Holy Scriptures" (mystery 13).

The Annunciation

The *Exercises for the Incarnation,* intended as a novena before the feast of the annunciation (25 March), are a more ambitious composition. They are dedicated to the "Supreme Empress of the Angels, Sovereign Queen of the Heavens, absolute Lady of all that is created."[57] Juana explains her purpose and plan. She has found inspiration in some suggestions made by "Mother María de Jesús," that is, Maria Coronel (1602–1665), who was born and spent all her life at Agreda in the province of Burgos in Spain. Having entered the monastery of the Immaculate Conception in her home town, she was elected abbess when she was only twenty-five years old. Her *Mística Ciudad de Dios,* written between 1655 and 1660, was published in 1670 in Madrid. The "City of God" in question is the Virgin Mary. Among the many fantastic ideas of Maria d'Agreda, Juana mentions only that the Virgin was shown the whole universe, was taken to heaven three times (the last time being her final Assumption in body and soul), and received extraordinary honors from God, the highest of these being that she would become the mother of God. Mary did not know this—though it was no secret in the heavenly court—until the annunciation.

Whatever she learned from Maria d'Agreda, Juana Inés presents, for each of the nine days of the novena, a meditation, followed by an offering or prayer to the Virgin and a list of exercises to be performed, some by those who are familiar with Latin, others by the less learned. The plan is original in that Juana follows the seven days of creation; each day as it is recorded in Genesis implies some point concerning the mother of God. The seventh day, which is taken to refer to the angelic choirs, is easily divided into three parts, in keeping with the organization of the angelic hierarchies three by three. The nine days of the novena being filled, final exercises were to be made on the day of the annunciation.

The meditations follow a pattern of contrast or opposition as the days of creation separate (1) light and dark, (2) the two firmaments, (3) earth and sea, (4) night and day, (5) fish and birds, (6) animals and Adam. For the last three days of the novena the pattern is threefold: (7) angels, Archangels, Virtues; (8) Powers, Principalities, Dominations; (9) Thrones, Cherubim, Seraphim.

The style varies considerably of course from that of Juana's poetry, but the thought is similar. Even in this prose destined for the edification of pious people, most of them neither learned nor theologically educated, Juana proposes images of considerable boldness for the participation of the Virgin in the process of salvation and sanctification. Comparing Mary to the firmament of the second day of creation, Juana Inés affirms: "Thus our great Queen not only was pure and holy, but she is the means of our cleanness and sanctification" (p. 850). On the third day, Mary is the *"mare magnum,"* the great sea, "of all greatnesses" (p. 852). Juana prays to her: "My

Lady, loving mother, sea of all perfections, mother of the living, for alone you make us, through your intercession, live the life of grace" (p. 853). Mary is "the means of our Redemption" (p. 857, sixth day). In the meditation on the creation of light on the first day, Mary, the "Queen of Light, . . . illumines all souls" with her gifts, for she is "nearest to the unfailing and inaccessible Light of the divine Essence." Not unusual in the heyday of the Counterreformation, such language was in harmony with baroque taste.

The archangel's visit on the day of the annunciation allows Juana to dwell on one of her favorite plays on words: the angel's *ave* (hail) is addressed to the Queen of *Aves* (birds) (p. 855). The pun enables the poet to imagine what kind of bird "this most pure Bird of Mary full of grace," "this heavenly Bird," can be. She, the "divine *Ave*," can, "like the eagle who teaches her young ones to fly, inspire the flights of our contemplation so that we may drink the rays of the Sun of Justice." Mary is indeed a "royal eagle, who has soared up as far as the sun of the Most Holy Trinity." She is not only eagle: she is also "the white and silvery Turtledove, . . . the hard working Bee. . . . " She is a "Heron so high, who gave chase to the Eternal Word and brought him down to the Earth so that we may feed on his Flesh and Blood." She is "the most true Phoenix," risen from Adam's ashes.

Of all the laudatory formulas with which Juana Inés extols the Mother of God, the most far reaching is undoubtedly the following:

God did not weary of favoring his chosen and most dear Mother, adding favors upon favors and greatnesses upon greatnesses; rather . . . not only did Mary's privileges equal the model of Adam in Paradise, the king of all inferior creatures, but the immense sea of her merits broke all the bounds of Nature, and its waves swelled not only to the point of flooding heaven, but even to that where the pure Angelic Substances drowned in it. (P. 859.)

Has Sor Juana so exalted Mary that Christ has been replaced by his mother, that Mary has become a substitute for the redeemer, that she has even been made divine? Juana's language is not so much a matter of theology as of style, a triumphalistic style in the baroque manner that was favored for reasons of taste and of theology in the Counterreformation, especially in Hispanic lands. Given the bent of her vivid imagination, Juana Inés carried this style to its farthest limits. But in all that she wrote on the Virgin Mary, she intended to describe the glorious works of God. Mary is what she is, because

> to welcome her there came out
> the Three Divine Persons,
> with whose approval she is
> Daughter, Mother, and Bride.

> A recibirla salieron
> las Tres Divinas Personas,
> con los aplausos de quien
> es Hija, Madre y Esposa.[58]

Beyond the problem of Catholic Mariology and its limits, Juana Inés's marian formulae underline a point that is important for a theology of beauty: How is the divine glory perceived, if it is not in an ecstatic experience of beauty? In describing this glory Juana echoes both older and more recent emphases in piety and theology. In addition, she creates new images, comparisons, and symbols.

Our Lady of Guadalupe

Juana Inés, though Mexican, alludes only once in all her writings to Our Lady of Guadalupe. This occurs in a sonnet that is not even directly focused on Guadalupe but on a Jesuit priest, Francisco de Castro, a Spaniard, the author of an unpublished "heroic poem in which he describes the miraculous apparition of Our Lady of Guadalupe of Mexico." Juana celebrates this poem as a second miracle, equal to that of Tepeyac:

> The Marvel made of flowers,
> divine American Protectress,
> who becomes a Mexican Rose
> appearing as a Rose of Castile;
>
> instead of the dragon—whose rebel neck
> she crushes in Patmos—who masterly walks,

hereto sovereign Intelligence,
the pure throne of its pure greatness;

but Heaven, copying her mysteriously,
a second time her heavenly signs
in figures of flowers clearly adds:

no less is she given a beautiful transcript
by the flowers of your peerless verses,
by the marvel of your elegant pen.

―――――――――――

La compuesta de flores Maravilla,
divina Protectora Americana,
que a ser se pasa Rosa Mejicana,
apareciendo Rosa de Castilla;

la que en vez del dragón—de quien humilla
cerviz rebelde en Patmos—huella ufana,
hasta aquí Inteligencia soberana,
de su pura grandeza pura silla;

ya el Cielo, que la copia misterioso,
segunda vez sus señas celestiales
en guarismos de flores claro suma:

pues no menos le dan traslado hermoso
las flores de tus versos sin iguales,
la maravilla de tu culta pluma.[59]

The apparitions of the Virgin to a Nahuatl-speaking Indian adult, Juan Diego, are dated, in the late story that was printed in 1648, from 9 and 12 December 1531. They took place on the hill of Tepeyac, a short distance north-northeast of Mexico City (in its original dimensions), at a spot where there already existed a small chapel built in the 1530s. This was replaced by a church, begun in 1556, and later by a much larger church, started in 1695 and terminated in 1709.

In the first period of the devotion, the early chapel was already dedicated to Our Lady of Guadalupe. This was an old miraculous statue, whose original was preserved in Spain at the monastery of Guadalupe, near Cáceres in Estremadura, the province of Hernán Cortéz, the conqueror of Mexico, who had a personal devotion to it. In the legend, the statue was of oriental origin, a gift of Gregory the Great to Leander of Seville.

Juana lived in the second period of the devotion, at the time of the first church, when the cult of Our Lady of Guadalupe was progressively indigenized. The Spanish statue, still venerated in 1582, had been replaced by the Aztec painting that is featured in the legend of Juan Diego and is still venerated today. Along with the painting, the legend was the chief vehicle of the cult's indigenization but was very distant in time—more than a century—from the date assigned to the apparitions. This alone makes the legend less than trustworthy, and it reveals its inauthenticity when it states that the Virgin, appearing to Juan's uncle, Bernardino, identified herself as *Santa Maria de Guadalupe:* had she appeared to two Christian Aztecs at that time, the Virgin must have spoken Nahuatl, not Spanish! At any rate, one cannot know for certain whether, during the years that Juana spent as a girl in the city, she ever made the pilgrimage to Tepeyac (today, Guadalupe-Hidalgo). This is probable, since the viceroys occasionally visited the church of Guadalupe.

The sonnet faithfully reflects several aspects of both the legend and the painting of Our Lady of Guadalupe: the flowers, roses, that Juan Diego is said to have picked up on Mary's instructions and carried in his *tilma,* or "cloak," on 12 December 1531; the identification of these roses as "roses of Castile," which did not grow in New Spain; the picture left on the cloth after Juan brought the flowers to the bishop; the fact that there previously existed a Spanish devotion to Our Lady of Guadalupe.

Juana adds her own interpretations. The vision seen by Juan Diego corresponds to that of Revelation 12:1–5 ("at Patmos"). The poet even suggests that Guadalupe has improved on this biblical vision. In her understanding of the Apocalypse, Mary crushes the head of the dragon. This is in fact not correct: the dragon of Revelation 12:3–4, sets himself in front of the woman, whom he threatens, not under her feet. Juana conflated the text of Revelation, chapter 12 and the verse of Genesis 3:15 (in the Latin Vulgate): "she will crush your head." At Tepeyac, however, it is not the devil that is under Mary's feet, supporting her: the "sovereign Intelligence" that acts as her throne is an angel. "Hereto"—that is, both chronologically, until this moment, and geographically, as far as the center of New Spain—the angel was sovereign intelligence, a pure spirit. Now, however, at the vision of Guadalupe, the angel becomes Mary's footstool. In a sense, then, this picture is the highest representation of the greatness of Mary. Whether Francisco de Castro's poem really deserves to be declared the equal of the picture is of course another matter!

Juana Inés does not mention or clearly allude to Guadalupe anywhere else. One should not infer from this, however, that this Mexican devotion has left no other traces in her writings. Her occasional and, in theological literature, somewhat unusual title for Mary, "Empress," may well reflect an early use of the appellation, "Empress of the Americas," that became official much later and was endorsed by Pius XII in 1945. More to the point, Juana's frequent encomia of the Virgin's pregnancy, like her repeated mention of Mary's beautiful belly, tally perfectly with the picture of Guadalupe, in which Mary is visibly pregnant. The title of "Pilgrim" (*el Peregrino*) that Juana uses both for St. Peter Nolasco and for Christ may have been inspired by the legend of Guadalupe, where it is a nickname given to Juan Diego because of his propensity for walking alone in the hills.

The *Exercises for the Incarnation* contain a striking example of the hidden presence of Guadalupe in Juana's thought and devotion. The meditation for the fourth day depicts Mary in the vision of the Apocalypse. On that day the sun and the moon, called "presidents of all the Orbs, and kings of all the republic of the other lights," are not only created; they also "recognize on that mysterious day their divine Queen, whom previously, in colors and shapes, the Sun clothed, the Moon fitted with shoes, and the Stars crowned."[60] The sun wanted to clothe her because she was already illuminated by the "Sun of Justice." The Moon wished to "serve as her cothurne," because even "all the angelic Choirs" were under her feet; "the stars wanted to crown her, but already the rays of the Divinity of all the Holy Trinity crowned her." Juana's description corresponds precisely to the Guadalupe picture, where the Virgin stands on the moon crescent and an angel holds the hemline of her garment.

Furthermore, it would be odd if not in Mexico, where the Aztecs had been great astronomers, that Juana Inés would then expound on the "highest wisdom"of the Virgin Mary, who "knew by most perfect intuition all the natures and qualities of all those lights:

their influences, revolutions, movements, retrogressions, eclipses, conjunctions, waning, waxing, and all the effects that they can produce in sublunar bodies." Moreover, the Virgin Mary also knew "the generation of rains, hails, ice, and the frightful monstrosity of lightning." Juana remarks that precisely these questions have "for so many centuries left hanging and tired the intelligences of men in their scruples, while they did not arrive at a perfect knowledge of them." Juana Inés then exclaims: "With what greater obedience will the Sun stop its luminous chariot at the order of the sovereign Empress of the Angels than at that of Joshua!" (p. 854).

The key to this amazing passage lies in the meaning of Guadalupe as the Virgin's apparition to the Indians, direct descendants of the Aztecs and other pre-Columbian tribes, among whom both astronomy and agriculture were far advanced. The Indians carefully studied the course of the planets, especially that of Venus. In their theology, the sun was the chief symbol of God. Huitzilopoxtli, identified with the sun, was the god of war and the chief protector of the Aztecs. Tláloc was the god of rain. It must be Huitzilopoxtli that Juana has in mind when she speaks of "the Great God of the seeds." One of the many rites in his honor included a meal: a cake representing Huitzilopoxtli was distributed and eaten.

Guadalupe therefore means that the Virgin Mary has been placed by God above all natural religions and above all worship of the forces at work in nature. She is higher than the highest things worshiped by the Toltecs, the Aztecs, the Mayas, and the lesser tribes of Mexico and Mesoamerica. The Virgin of Guadalupe is prominent in Juana's thought, even when she is not called by her folkloric name.

Juana in fact avoids giving Mary the names of apparitions or of local cults and shrines. It is part of her baroque conceptism that she prefers to call the Virgin with terms that have a theological content related to the mysteries of Christ, even though this content was more evident to the baroque imagination than it has commonly become to minds nurtured in the twentieth century.

Undoubtedly, much in Juana's marian writing is, by today's standards, couched in extravagant language. Is it also extravagant in doctrine? Juana knows enough theology to guard herself. The problem is not with the Inquisition, which, though active in New Spain, was unlikely to regard devotional exaltations of the mother of God as departing from the centrality of Christ. Juana well knows that this Christocentrism is the heart of the Christian faith. In her meditation for the day of the annunciation, she distinguishes among the privileges of Mary: the basic ones were unmerited gifts; others were consequences of these, merited in a secondary sense of the word, by virtue of the basic gifts. Her formula is this:

> But look, Gentlemen: although it is true that God gave his sacred Mother very many favors that were gratuitous, and, as theologians say, before looking at her merits—such as his preserving her from original sin and thereby from all the movements of a nature inclined to evil by the fault, so that all her operations were planned by reason with no resistance of the inferior part, and his lending her intelligence beyond the natural limits in which God had decided to infuse it in the other living beings—the other privileges were as though due in justice to her high merits, total fidelity, burning love, and the extreme finesse with which she responded to all divine benefactions, making herself worthy of conceiving the Eternal Word in her womb because she had already conceived him in her soul. (P. 864-865.)

In terms of traditional orthodoxy, this formulation, I believe, effectively clears Sor Juana Inés de la Cruz from the charge of Pelagianism that has been leveled at Catholic mariological speculation by many Protestant authors. It leaves her open, however, to another theological stricture. Her emphasis on Mary's privileges, whether merely given or also, in some sense, merited, conveys the impression of taking away the uniqueness and exclusiveness of Christ as the one "Mediator of the new covenant" (Hebrews 8:6). But formulas are one thing, meaning is another. Juana Inés's writing and theology are of one piece with the exuberant architecture and church decoration of New Spain. As there was a baroque art there was a baroque theology. It clearly raises the christological question: How does Juana Inés de la Cruz speak of Christ?

4
Narcissus

The Christology of Juana Inés de la Cruz pervades much of her writing; the saints, for example, are never isolated from Christ, since he and the gift of divine grace through the Holy Spirit make them saints. Three main sources in particular, however, provide especially rich documentation about her theological vision of Christ. First, just as Juana was led to devote a great deal of attention to some saints at the request of her patrons, she was also invited to compose joyful pieces to celebrate Christmas; the "attributable" pieces of 1678 and 1680 left aside, the villancicos of 1689, certainly authentic, deal almost exclusively with the conception and birth of Jesus (as do two other poems and a romance on the feast of the Nativity). Second, her liturgical play or auto sacramental *Divino Narciso* (1689) constitutes a largely original approach to the mystery of the incarnation. Because of its extensive and crucial evidence for Juana's theology of beauty, *Narcissus* provides the main focus of the chapter. The third locus for Juana's Christology consists of several passages in her autobiographical work, the *Respuesta a Sor Filotea de la Cruz* (1691), the "sister" being, as we have seen, the bishop of Puebla de los Angeles, Manuel Fernández de Santa Cruz y Sahagún. These three main sources for Juana's Christology belong to the same period of her life, when she was at the height of her poetic power and literary output. We should therefore expect consistency in the doctrine of these works, even though their different genres may favor different emphases. In addition, several individual poems also touch on the topics of Christ and the incarnation.

The Birth of the Divine Child:
The Villancicos of 1689 and Other Works for the Nativity

In keeping with a type of popular piety that originated in the Mediterranean lands of Catholic Europe, the entire motif of the eight pieces of Juana's villancicos for Christmas of 1689 is focused on the divine child, the wonderful *niño* to whom Mary gave birth. Although the marian accent remains prominent, as is not unusual in popular approaches to the nativity of Jesus, Juana never forgets that Jesus, not Mary, should be at the center of Christmas. The tone of the work is especially festive, popular, and familiar. The paraliturgical genre of the villancicos allows Juana Inés to explore the grotesque, a stylistic trait that she shares with many authors of the baroque.

Sor Juana brings a cosmic dimension to her perspective. The first nocturn focuses on the contribution made to the incarnation by the four elements. Water, earth, fire, and air, "clean, pure, fragile, and fresh,"[1] are internal constituents of the "Eyes, Breast, Flesh, and Breath" of the divine child. They also shape his human experience from the outside: fire warms him; air assuages his fatigue; water calms his weeping; and earth lets him rest his head. The theme of redemption is soon introduced as crying and joy are joined together. Like his birth, the life of the child is a paradox. Jesus is a "magnetic stone," attracted by the iron of ordinary human beings, since, in Juana's words, "God's coming to earth / is my rising up."[2] A more jocular vein is struck in the third villancico: the mayor of Bethlehem distributes Christmas lights to the people, a practice followed, presumably, by the mayors of some of the towns of New Spain.

The second nocturn is more solemn. In villancico 4, the great king holds court. Since Joseph and Mary are present, his grace is guaranteed to the guilty. Adam, Moses, Solomon, the patriarchs, and Joseph (Mary's husband) each ask for a favor. Villancico 5 asks, Should the child be awake or asleep? Being divine, he should watch; being human, he should sleep, and sleeping is the apprenticeship of dying. The contemplation of his wax statue in villancico 6 introduces a symbolic description of his skin, his eyes, his mouth. As in so much popular Christmas art, the baby is a cupid:

> Such a little Cupid
> to be the Soul's Jewel
> has been born.

> Tal Cupidillo
> para Joya del Alma
> viene nacido.[3]

In the third nocturn, the souls rush to see the baby. They turn
to him like a swarm, a loving butterfly, a fast stream; like an arrow,
a sunflower, and a magnetic needle:

> Thus go to the Child
> in a hurry the Souls,
> to the Center where they draw life:
> away from Him they are not even in themselves.

> Así se van al Niño
> presurosas las almas
> que es Centro do se animan:
> y fuera de El, ni aun en sí mismas se hallan.[4]

Read superficially, the ending of the third nocturn is the most
unsatisfactory of Juana Inés's paraliturgical villancicos: two sac-
ristans argue whether the child is *verbum caro* or *tantum ergo*. Both
logically and grammatically this question is absurd. Logically, the
expressions *verbum caro* (Word-flesh, from John 1:14) and *tantum ergo*
(So-great-therefore, from the famous eucharistic hymn "Pange lin-
gua" attributed to Thomas Aquinas) belong to unrelated categories.
Grammatically, *tantum ergo* cannot designate a person. Yet the ques-
tion raises a theological point that is dear to Juana: the dialectic of
redemption, within which the child is to live, is determined by the
two poles of the incarnation (*verbum caro*) and the sacrament of the
eucharist (*tantum ergo*).[5]

The birth of Christ is also the topic of "Two Poems for Sing-
ing" of unknown date that are highly theological. The first raises the
problem of faith:

> How is it, my God,
> that I believe in You,
> yet, though I believe what I see,
> I do not see all I believe?

¿Cómo será esto, mi Dios,
que yo creo in Vos,
y aunque creo lo que veo
no veo todo lo que creo?[6]

The birth of Christ is the case in point, where what is seen is believed, but what is believed is not seen:

If Faith and sight are
so contrary, why
is sight here to be faith
and not Faith to be sight?

―――――――――

¿Si la Fe y la vista son
tan encontradas, por qué
aquí ha de hacer fe la vista
y no hacer vista la Fe?

The faithful believe that the child they see is divine, but that he is divine is not seen. The eucharist follows a different logic: both the body and the divinity are believed, though neither is seen. This is, Juana remarks, easier, "for I know that the contrary / of sight I must believe." At the birth of Jesus, however, I should believe "what I see and what I see not, / what is and what is not" (p. 317). The Lord is seen as man but not as God; he is nevertheless also believed to be God. In sum, "there is / an Infinite more in what is / than in what comes to be seen."

Equally profound is the second poem, which better sounds the lighter tone of Christmas. The scene is related to some of the paintings of the nativity in which the cave of Bethlehem has been replaced by the solemn porch of a large house.

One day at sunrise,
filled with the lights of dawn,
the Shepherds saw God,
not knowing how, or how not.

―――――――――

> Un día que amaneció,
> lleno de luces y albores,
> vieron a Dios los Pastores
> sin saber cómo ni cómo no.[7]

The last line includes a pun, since *cómo no*, literally "how not," commonly means "why not?" The pun suggests the paradox of the birth of Christ, hinting at what is called apophatic theology. Juana's "not knowing" may well be reminiscent of St. John of the Cross, in whose commentaries the expression *sin saber* recurs at key points.[8] There is in the experience of Christ something that cannot be known. The poem, in four stanzas of thirteen lines each, provides pointers towards what this "something" is. The shepherd who speaks was called but does not know who called him. He saw a beautiful woman, and was told that she was "Married and Maiden": another puzzle! He also saw her husband, who is not the baby's father: "the recently born Child / is the One who gave him life." Finally, the very sun is nothing compared to this child, who is more beautiful than the lily and the rose. His mother is more beautiful than the dawn and the light, fresher than the morning; red like scarlet, she is also white like the lily and straighter than the verbena. All this the shepherd saw "in the Portal, / not knowing how or how not."

In addition to these villancicos for Christmas, Sor Juana composed a romance on the "Nativity of Christ" that she centered on the symbolism of the honeybee. She drew on the legendary assumption that bees are born of roses. Christ is the honeybee, and Mary, the "fragrant Rose."[9] *This* rose gives birth only to *this* honeybee "in the cloister / of her virginal purity." So interdependent are "Son and Daughter" that while neither owes anything, each is obligated to the other. They stand in a relationship of mutual correspondence. The note of suffering and redemption is not absent, for Jesus is crying: but "what he gives up as dew / he will later collect as nectar."

The Incarnation as Union of Humanity and the Word: *Divine Narcissus*

Christianity as Fulfillment of Paganism. The writing of Juana Inés de la Cruz that is, from a theological point of view, both the most ambitious and the most successful is undoubtedly *Divine Narcissus*. This liturgical-sacramental play (auto sacramental) was composed to be presented in 1689 in Madrid, presumably for the feast of Corpus Christi. The marchioness de la Laguna had asked for the work, as is stated in the title of the first printed edition, which was issued in Mexico in 1690 by a doctor who was also a poet, Ambrosio de Lima. Evidently, Marchioness Maria Luisa carried it in her luggage when she returned to Spain in 1688. As Juana declares at the end of the prologue, Madrid

> . . . is of faith
> the Center, the Royal Seat
> of its Catholic Kings,
> to whom the Indies will owe
> the lights of the Gospel
> that shine in the West.

> . . . que es de la Fe
> el Centro, y la Regia Silla
> de sus Catolicos Reyes,
> a quien debieron las Indias
> las luces del Evangelio
> que en el Occidente brillan.[10]

Whether the play was ever produced in Madrid is doubtful, but this does not affect its meaning or value. This auto provides the longest and the most complete poetic exposition of Juana's Christology.

The characters of the play's prologue are, in order of entry, Music (who sings in two choruses); then an Indian couple, West (who is a man of royal bearing) and America (a woman); and finally a Spanish team of two persons—Religion (who appears in the guise of a Spanish lady) and Zeal (a captain-general of the Spanish army, who is evidently modeled on the conquistadors). West and America represent the pre-Columbian religions of Mexico, devoted to "the Great God of the Seeds,"[11] who is, in the Aztec religion, Huitzilo-pochtli. The two Indians sing and dance a tocotín, the popular dance that is often featured in Juana Inés's plays. Religion represents Christianity in the dimension of faith and worship. Zeal is Christendom in its political and military arm, offering (but the offer is refused) to ensure the triumph of faith by putting all pagans to the sword.

The purpose of *Divino Narciso* is made clear in the loa, or pro-
logue, that introduces the play. As West and America dance, Reli-
gion forms the project of persuading them that what they now believe
will be found in Jesus Christ much more fully than in their gods.
When they inquire about the life and death of her God, Religion
describes her project and the reason for it:

> Let us go. In the idea
> of a metaphor, dressed
> in the colors of rhetoric,
> visible to your eyes,
> I will show you; for well
> do I know that you lean
> to the visible more
> than to what faith teaches
> by hearing; and so
> it is important that you use
> your eyes in order to
> receive faith through them.

> Pues vamos. Que en un idea
> metafórica, vestida
> de retóricos colores,
> representable a tu vista,
> te la mostraré; que ya
> conozco que tú inclinas
> a objetos visibles, más
> que a lo que la Fe te avisa
> por el oído; y así
> es preciso que te sirvas
> de los ojos, para que
> por ellos la Fe recibas.[12]

Religion justifies the project with "the doctrine of Paul," who,
speaking to the Athenians, did not attempt to teach them about a
"new deity" but about the "unknown God" to which they had al-
ready dedicated an altar (p. 387). Likewise, the Aztecs worship the
author of the miracles and prodigies of nature. Rather than being

the work of "lying Deities," however, such wonders are due to "the true God and his Wisdom" (p. 388). For

> . . . if the meadow
> in bloom is fertilized,
> if fields are fecundated,
> if seed beds grow,
> if rains are distilled,
> all is the work of His hand.

> . . . si el prado
> florido se fertiliza,
> si los campos se fecundan,
> si las sementeras crecen,
> si las lluvias se destilan,
> todo es obra de Su diestra.

The true God is already adored, though unknown, in natural religion. There is more among the Aztecs, however, than natural religion. America wants to be able to touch her God with her own hands, "like the Idol which, here, / my own hands make / with seeds and innocent blood": such a confection of corn and blood was eaten by the Aztecs in a sort of communion with Huizilopochtli. Juana finds in this practice a hint of the Christian eucharist.

Religion, whom one may regard as speaking for Juana Inés, briefly outlines the true faith. The "Divine Essence / is invisible and immense" but "already united / to our Nature" in such a way that it is touched by "the unworthy / hands of the Priests." As West asks if this God is made of precious material, like "blood that has been / offered in sacrifice, / and seed that is food," Religion sums up the doctrine of the eucharist, a theme that is dear to Juana's heart. And she normally presents it, as she does here, in the typical theology of sacrifice that was current in the Counterreformation:

> I have said that His infinite
> Majesty is immaterial;
> but His blessed Humanity,
> placed bloodlessly in the Holy
> Sacrifice of the Mass,

under white accidents,
avails itself of the seeds
of wheat, which is converted
into His Body and Blood;
and His Blood, which is in the Chalice,
is the Blood that, offered
on the Altar of the Cross,
innocent, pure, and clear,
was the Redemption of the World.

Ya he dicho que es Su infinita
Majestad immaterial;
mas Su Humanidad bendita,
puesta incrüenta en el Santo
Sacrificio de la Misa,
en cándidos accidentes,
se vale de las semillas
del trigo, el cual se convierte
en Su Carne y Sangre misma;
y Su Sangre, que en el Cáliz
está, es Sangre que ofrecida
en el Ara de la Cruz,
innocente, pura y limpia,
fue la Redención del Mundo.

Returning to her project, Religion repeats that she wants to set up "the allegory of an Auto" with educational value. Why, then, focus on Narcissus? Because it is not only among the Aztecs that there have been "symbols / of such a high Marvel" but also "among other Gentiles" (p. 389). That pagan religions pave the way for the Christian gospel is thus clearly implied. As Juana maintains, it is not unbecoming to discuss this question and to propose her answer to an audience in Madrid, where there are, presumably, no pagans. She simply wishes

to celebrate the Mystery,
and the personages introduced
are no more than
abstractions that paint

what is intended to be said. . . .

---

a celebrar el Misterio,
y aquestas introducidas
personas no son más que
unos abstractos, que pintan
lo que se intenta decir. . . .

(P. 390.)

This can be understood in Madrid as elsewhere in Christendom, "since for intellective species / distances are not in the way / and seas are no obstacles." Clearly, Sor Juana's deft allegories broach a topic regarding the knowledge of God and the incarnation that is of interest to the whole Church. The incarnation of the Word of God opens one way in which some, if not all, of the pagan religions can find their fulfillment in the Christian faith.

Juana's Narcissus and Its Models. In the ancient myth, Narcissus, son of Cephissus and Liriope, is unable to return love, so that Echo, a nymph who loves him, withers away from grief to the degree that she survives only in her voice, repeating the last words that she hears. As a punishment, Nemesis dooms Narcissus to be enamored of his own image in a pool and to die, like Echo, from the grief of unreturned love. Juana's play departs from the myth considerably: Narcissus is, in what he is and does, the model of love. Echo, who loves him in her own strange way, has become the devil. The characters are, in order of entry, two sisters—Synagogue and Gentiledom—with their mother, Human Nature; the bad nymph, Echo, with her two friends Pride (a shepherdess) and Self-love (a shepherd); then Abel, Enoch, Abraham, an angel, and Moses, all of whom make a brief appearance in a historical-prophetic sequence that refers to the Old Testament; the hero, Narcissus, a shepherd armed with a sling, who will be Christ; and Grace, a beautiful shepherdess. The Virgin Mary also appears, though not as a speaking personage: she will be the well in whose water Narcissus will see his image mirrored.

Since the eclogues of Garcilaso de la Vega (1503/4–1536), shepherds had become quite popular pastoral images in Spanish poetry. And there was nothing unusual about depicting Christ with the features of a shepherd in an idyllic garden; this image had had a long history in Christian iconography, going back to the art of the cata-combs. It also corresponded to an accepted reading of the Song of Songs that had been popularized in the Spanish-speaking world by the Augustinian friar Luis de León (1528–1591) in his vernacular translation and commentary of the biblical poem (composed in 1561–1562). Luis de León had also used the word *shepherd* as the fourth christological title in the first part of his famous book, *Los Nombres de Cristo* (begun in 1574),[13] in which the author justified the christolog-ical meaning of the word on the basis of the New Testament's allu-sions to Christ as shepherd (John 10: 11; Hebrews 13: 20; 1 Peter 5:4) and also on the basis of the Song of Songs. Luis considered that "finesse of feeling belongs to the countryside and to solitude," in which, precisely, shepherds live. Now, "Christ lives in the fields, and enjoys the free sky, and loves solitude and quiet."

Furthermore, Juana Inés, who had begun her religious life as a discalced Carmelite, was aquainted with the poems of St. John of the Cross (1542–1591). The reformer of Carmel had used the sym-bolism of the shepherd to describe Christ's longing for the soul, his beloved shepherdess, in the *Spiritual Canticle* and in the shorter poem that is called, from its first two words, "Un pastorcico."[14]

Juana's chief model for her play, however, was the auto of Cal-derón de la Barca, *Eco y Narciso*. She borrowed from Calderón the recurring words of her scenes i and ii, "Fuentes y flores." But Calde-rón's piece was a comedy while Juana oriented her work toward the tragic. This kind of transposition of genre had already been attempt-ed by two Spanish authors, though Juana is unlikely to have been acquainted with their works, which were both entitled *Auto sacramental alegórico Eco y Narciso*.[15]

Juana's play is composed of five tableaux in sixteen scenes. Each tableau features a moment in the Narcissus myth, with a rec-ognizable theological parallel:

1. Human Nature talks with her two daughters, Synagogue and Gentiledom: the world before the coming of Christ.
2. Echo tries to woo Narcissus: the temptation of Christ in the desert.
3. Human Nature narrates her search for Narcissus and the ideal human beauty, and Narcissus searches for his perfect image: the mutual search of humanity and the divine Word.

4. Narcissus sees his image in the fountain and dies of love: Christ finds his perfect image in humanity and dies of love.

5. Human Nature embraces Grace and through Grace is united with Narcissus: the union of humanity and God through the redemption.

Human Nature Talks with Her Two Daughters, Synagogue and Gentiledom: The World before the Coming of Christ. The plot is outlined at the beginning of the play, in scene i. The two daughters of Human Nature do not share the same religion. Synagogue worships "the Lord," while Gentiledom adores Narcissus, or ideal human beauty. In their opposite religions, the sisters really have the same desire: both are searching for divine beauty. Synagogue proclaims:

> Intone a new song
> to his divine Beauty,
> and as soon as the light shines
> may eternal praise ring
> of the glory of His name.

> ───────────

> Un nuevo canto entona
> a Su divina Beldad,
> y en cuanto la luz alanza,
> suene la eterna alabanza
> de la glorie de Su nombre.[16]

In parallel fashion but in opposite direction, Gentiledom proclaims:

> Applaud Narcissus, Fountains, and Flowers!
> Indeed his divine beauty
> of unequaled preciousness
> is above all the beauty
> seen in other creatures
> and inspires love in all.

> ───────────

> Aplaudid a Narciso, Fuentes y Flores!
> Y pues su beldad divina
> sin igualdad peregrina,

es sobre toda hermosura,
que se vio en otra criatura,
y en todas inspira amores.

In *Divine Narcissus* as often in Shakespeare, monologues hold
the key to the play. Two long monologues in scenes i and ii give
Human Nature's interpretation of the differences between her two
daughters. She has read the Scriptures and knows that Gentiledom
is wrong and Synagogue is right. Gentiledom is "blind, / mistaken,
ignorant, and stupid," attached to "perishable beauty" (p. 392);
Synagogue stands in the truth, certain as she is of what she has heard
from the prophets. But this will not always be so. As Human Nature
already knows from her study of the prophecies, a time will come
when Gentiledom will be right, and Synagogue, in error.

Already there is a mystery in what Gentiledom believes. Hu-
man Nature claims that Narcissus's beauty acts as "the magnet of
the hearts," that it is followed "not only by Nymphs and Shepherds"
but also by "the birds and beasts, / the hills and mountains, / the
brooks and fountains, / the plants, grasses, and flowers." This power
of attraction does not belong, however, to the Narcissus of Gentile-
dom's dreams. It belongs only to God, whose beauty is reflected by
the very orbs of the universe. Human Nature herself is intimately
connected with this truth: it is, as she confesses, what "I desire as
my Center / and I follow as my North Star" (p. 393). Indeed, Juana
Inés finds a broad humanism in the divine revelation:

As they many times concur,
the Divine and Human Letters
show that God places
even in Gentile Pens
views in which there appear
His high Mysteries.

Pues muchas veces conformes
Divinas y Humanas Letras
dan a entender que Dios pone
aun en las Plumas Gentiles
unos visos en que asomen
los altos Misterios Suyos.

In order to help her two daughters perceive the full truth, Human Nature will borrow ideas and images from both Synagogue and Gentiledom as she constructs converging metaphors. Synagogue will give "a body to the idea"; and Gentiledom will provide "the garment."

In the two monologues Human Nature also reflects on herself. Her faults, as she has learned from the Psalms, surround her like deep and dirty water; Narcissus's beauty cannot be reflected. She is thus led to desire other, pure, water, in a fountain that will mirror beauty:

> . . . Oh! may Heaven will
> that my hopes may find
> some Fountain that, free
> of these briny waters,
> reflects of Narcissus
> all the perfections!

> . . . ¡Oh, quiera el Cielo
> que mis esperanzas topen
> alguna Fuente que, libre
> de aquellas aguas salobres,
> represente de Narciso
> enteras las perfecciones![17]

She then resolves to start on a quest:

> . . . Let us go and seek
> the Fountain where my stains
> have to be washed away. . . .

> . . . vamos a buscar
> la Fuente en que mis borrones
> se han de lavar. . . .

The theme of the quest or pilgrimage is of course classical in religious and spiritual literature, and Juana Inés was undoubtedly acquainted with many examples of it, not the least with the biblical

Song of Songs and John of the Cross's *Spiritual Canticle*. She also knew of the pilgrimage to Our Lady of Guadalupe. Even when she makes use of conventions, imitates a style, or borrows rhetorical devices, however, she does not really copy anyone, for she shapes the material of shared language and literary convention in her own style.

She now describes a quest for the perception of absolute beauty. Modeled on the beauty of Narcissus, absolute beauty will be divine and human at the same time. Before it, Gentiledom and Synagogue may be reconciled; Gentiledom will find the supreme human beauty that she desires, and Synagogue should—but will she?—acknowledge the beauty of her Lord.

Echo Tries to Woo Narcissus: The Temptation of Christ in the Desert. Along with Narcissus and Human Nature, Echo is one of the play's three most important characters. Her self-appointed task is to thwart the efforts of Human Nature and Narcissus in the hope that they will never meet. She plans to muddy all the waters where Human Nature can possibly be reflected, so that Narcissus may never find the perfect image that he seeks. More profoundly, Echo enriches the plot and provides the spectators with an alternative hero. While the reflections and interpretations formulated by Human Nature and Narcissus are correlated in their mutual search, those of Echo stand in sharp contrast, offering other possibilities and another choice.

Echo does not see the beauty of this world in the same light as Narcissus and Human Nature. After Echo has been struck dumb, while her body and her mind are waning and only her echoing voice remains, she echoes the consoling words of Pride and Selflove, who try to assuage her agony. Next she echoes the words of Narcissus in Juana's rendering of the agony in the garden. Readers and spectators may then choose to identify and empathize with either agony, that of self-centered false beauty and false love, or that of true beauty that cannot yet be united with the perfect image that it has finally perceived. After the death and resurrection of Narcissus, Echo (who has somehow recovered her voice) proposes an alternative view of humanity's future: the struggles of the Old Testament will continue, for she, the devil, is still the prince of this world. This contrasts with the ending of the play, where the future resides in the union of Human Nature and Narcissus in the eucharistic mystery.

The play as such starts, in Christian terms, after the birth of Jesus. In her first major appearance, Echo reviews her own history.

Over against Human Nature, the "beautiful Shepherdess," Echo identifies herself as "she who, unfortunately beautiful, / for wanting to be still more, / shrunk to ugliness."[18] In fact, the devil in person has chosen Echo as a suitable metaphor of himself, for Echo is angelic being, though not the whole of it: she is "only that / reprobate part, which daringly / dragged down of the Stars / one third to the Abyss." The demonology is classical. Knowing herself to be "of my illustrious Angelic Nature the most perfect creature," the devil aspired to become "the bride of Narcissus" and thus to mount his throne, making herself "equal to his Grandeur." But Narcissus rejected her, leaving no hope that she still might, in a remote future, "be able to enjoy the rays / of his Divine Beauty."

Thus Echo became jealous of anyone whom Narcissus might choose as his bride. Ever since he started looking for his perfect image, she has been muddying the waters, and as long as she keeps doing it, he cannot find a suitable mirror to reflect his image. Echo tells of her success with "the careless Nymph," unnamed, in whom we may recognize Eve. Surviving as Human Nature, this nymph is still so much like Narcissus that if he ever looks into her eyes he may find in them the reflection of himself that he has been searching for. "So I fear that if he sees her, / His image that he sees in her / will oblige his Deity / to yield and love her." Because Echo's interference pushed Human Nature to sin, God destroyed the world through the flood. Later, the builders of the "high Tower" of Babylon were punished by "the confusion of tongues," for it is a just punishment that "he who maliciously thinks / that he understands all / should understand nothing" (p. 397). Next, Echo induced humans to worship the sun, to venerate beasts, to offer their belief to rocks, fountains, creeks, woods, forests. Having reached the point where they adore "their own inclinations," they have now forgotten "the true worship of God" (p. 398).

Echo has not, however, entirely succeeded. At all periods there have been true worshipers of God. The main ones—Abel, Enoch, Abraham, Moses—appear briefly in scene iv. Abraham, whom Echo calls "this monster of faith and obedience," is the only one who says nothing, while an angel tells what happened. Two choirs representing the prophets sing their hope in a savior to come. And now Echo, by "infused knowledge,"[19] knows "through certain signs" that Narcissus "is Son of God and that / he was born of a real / Woman."[20]

He might well be the expected savior. In order to find out, Echo
joins Narcissus on a mountain where he has retired.

The temptation in the desert is interpreted as a reversed reen-
actment of the temptation of Eve in paradise. Narcissus, in the
mountains, alone with animals, has not eaten for forty days. Echo
believes that he has forgotten to eat, being so absorbed in the search
for his perfect image. In reality, he wants to reverse—in traditional
theological terms, to *recapitulate*—the ancient pattern, when in para-
dise someone ate. The temptation itself is a long, flattering address
to "most beautiful Narcissus." Echo praises his beauty and points to
the beauty of the valleys below, in the human world. She is, so she
says, the richest shepherdess of these valleys. She praises the beauty
of the meadows, of dawn, of the winds, of the mines and their jewels,
of gardens and their fruits, of pine-covered mountains, of the har-
mony of birds singing in many choirs, of kingdoms and their ships
at sea, of animals in their variety. She concludes:

> All, beautiful Narcissus,
> subject to my orders,
> is my possession,
> the goods of my dowry.
>
> And all will be Yours
> if You with kind heart
> abandon your aloofness
> and consent to adore me.

> Todo, bello Narciso,
> sujeto a mi dictamen,
> son posesiones mías,
> son mis bienes dotales.
>
> Y todo será Tuyo,
> si Tú con pecho afable
> depones lo severo
> y llegas a adorarme.

(P. 401.)

Narcissus rejects the offer of this "Abhorred Nymph," declar-
ing: "My Beauty alone / is worthy of adoration." Echo vows to seek

his death. Later, in scene x, Echo finds Narcissus by the side of a clean fountain that she has not yet muddied. This is the beginning of her end. As she discovers that Narcissus is looking at his own image in the waters, Echo is struck dumb. She can only repeat the last words of what Self-love and Pride tell her (scene xi):

> I Suffer, the Fury
> of Seeing that Narcissus
> Loves a Frail Being
> Sickens Me.

> Tengo Pena, Rabia,
> De ver que Narciso
> A un Sér Quebradizo
> Quiere, A mí Me agravia.[21]

As Narcissus speaks, Echo also repeats his last words, which in turn are reconstructed as three stanzas. The first two are sung as a duet by Music and Narcissus. They suggest that the devil's actions unwittingly serve the glory of divine beauty:

> I Suffer Unbearable Torment;
> Since My Faultless Beauty
> Love Has Made Mortal,
> Inferior, Human, Suffering.

> Love, That can Wound,
> In Me has Shown Its power;
> And loving My image
> From Heaven I Came To Die.

> Tormento Paso Insufrible;
> Pues Mi Hermosura Cabal
> El Amor Hizo Mortal,
> Sujeta, Humana, Pasible.[22]

> El Amor, Que puede Herir
> En Mí Mostró Su pujanza;

Y amando A Mi semejanza,
Del Cielo Vine A Morir.

(P. 415.)

The third stanza is sung by Echo and Music:

Echo In Sorrow Answers,
Seeing That Your love wants
To Love an Inferior;
And so She hides From your eyes.

_____

Eco Quejosa Responde,
Viendo Que quiera To amor
Amar un ser Inferior;
Y así, A tus ojos Se esconde.

(P. 416.)

This, however, is not the end of the devil's story. After the resurrection, Echo will persist in her evil purpose. In scene xvi she will vow to continue her opposition to the mutual love of Narcissus and Human Nature.

The role of Echo throws considerable light on Juana's Christology. It distinctly shows the two main deeds of God, creation and incarnation, as focused on, and manifestations of, divine beauty. Echo is so enamored of her own God-given creaturely endowments that she claims equality with God at the level of beauty. By the same token, the purpose of the incarnation takes on a new coloration. Juana does not side exactly with either of the two medieval answers to the question of the purpose of the incarnation. She does not, with Anselm, Bonaventure, and Thomas Aquinas, understand the incarnation as primarily remedial, chosen by God to undo the effects of sin by way of redemption.[23] Juana comes closer to John Duns Scotus's idea: the purpose of the incarnation is that humankind should give God the highest possible glory. Yet her view cannot be simply identified with this. Rather, the purpose of the incarnation—identical to that of creation—is the ultimate union of two kinds of divine beauty: the beauty of the eternal Word and the beauty that has been given to creatures.

Where did Juana get this idea from? The Hieronymite nun gives her source away when she puts this ultimate union in terms of marriage, for St. John of the Cross had opened a similar perspective. In his *Romance on the Incarnation,* God the Father had declared to the Son: "A bride who loves you, / my Son, I would wish to give you."[24] And, further: "You see, Son, that your bride / in your image I have made." The nature of the incarnation follows from this nuptial view of creation. The bride's love for the divine son will greatly increase "if she sees you similar / to the flesh that she has."

The incarnation weaves the divine Word's nuptial garment for his wedding with humanity. This is precisely Juana Inés's conception: Human Nature is born with a deep desire for nuptial union with divine beauty, and the Word of God in turn desires a nuptial unity with his creaturely image. This appears clearly in the description of Human Nature. In Juana's vision, the nuptial character of the incarnation is what finally unites the rival sisters, Gentiledom and Synagogue, both of whom have been seeking divine beauty. They share one and the same beauty. At this point, however, the bad angels and humanity cannot be reconciled. Echo's passion for Narcissus is too selfish for sharing.

Human Nature Narrates Her Search for Narcissus and the Ideal Human Beauty, and Narcissus Seeks for His Perfect Image: The Mutual Search of Humanity and the Divine Word. The picture of Human Nature, a "beautiful shepherdess," is less flashy than that of Echo. In scene vi, Human Nature tells the story of her love and search for Narcissus and then engages in a dialogue with another beautiful shepherdess, Grace (scene vii). Later, in scene xiv, Human Nature weeps over the death of Narcissus until Grace reveals that he is still living. Like Mary Magdalen, she sees him without recognizing him (scene xv). At the end of the play, however, she and Grace embrace (scene xvi).

The most striking moment of Human Nature's part and what constitutes one of the high points of the entire play is her description of her search for Narcissus. This long monologue of twenty-three stanzas throws further light on the relations between God and humanity and complements what Echo has previously said of the Old Testament. The first part of the poem—eleven stanzas—surveys Human Nature's search for divine beauty outside the Old Testament, in the natural religions. In metaphors that are chiefly borrowed from the Song of Songs, Human Nature tells of the many days and ages when she has sought the beloved in the beauty of flowers and plants; she speaks of her weeping, of her sorrows, of "travails, pains, prisons,"[25] of her wounds when she was roughly handled by the city's guards. She has found numerous signs of her beloved's passage, and by comparing them, she knows that so many and so great beauties in the meadow can only derive from "having already kissed His feet": the beloved has been here. On the model of the Song of Songs, Human Nature begs the nymphs of "this flowering and pleasant meadow" to tell the beloved upon his return of her love for him. She describes him as in the biblical Song. She concludes the first part of this remarkable poem with an appeal to the nymphs:

> Tell me where the One is whom my soul adores,
> or in what place He feeds his lambs,
> or whereabout—at the hour
> of noon—he rests his eyes,
> lest I start wandering
> in the sheepfolds, for I go seeking him.

> Decidme dónde está El que mi alma adora,
> o en qué parte apacienta Sus corderos,
> o hacia dónde—a la hora
> meridiana—descansan sus luceros,
> para que yo no empiece a andar vagando
> por los rediles, que Lo voy buscando.

(P. 403.)

The second part of the poem also contains eleven stanzas (the twelfth does not belong to the sequence; it is a transition to the next scene). Human Nature discovers that the prophecies of the Old Testament are coming to their fulfillment. The weeks of Daniel have passed. She expects the prophecies of Isaiah to come true. "Then he is already born, the beautiful and handsome Child . . . " who is "Admirable, Powerful God, Counselor, / King, and Father of the world to come." The root of Jesse has blossomed, "the beautiful Flower in which there rests / in its beautiful cup / the Divine Spirit, the warrant / of Wisdom, Counsel, Intelligence, / Strength, Piety, Fear, and Knowledge." Already "the Fruit of David has the Throne / of His father." The sign granted to King Achaz is there, "the new, stupendous marvel, / so exceeding Nature, / that a Virgin conceives and remains Virgin." The promise to Abraham and to Isaac is fulfilled: "blessed are the people born / in all nations / to share in their blessings." The prophecy of Jacob has come true: "the Scepter of Juda has fallen" (p. 404). These are signs that "the Hope and Joy of the World" has arrived, "the Lord's Salvation, that it expected, / and in prophetic spirit saw." Only one thing is still missing: "the greater Sacrifice" has not been consummated.

At this point Juana Inés returns to the Song of Songs:

> Oh, my Divine Beloved, who will have the joy
> of approaching Your generous breath,
> of rarer fragrance
> than the most precious wine and scent!
> Your name is like oil poured out,
> and for this the Nymphs have loved You.

> ¡Oh, mi Divino Amado, quién gozara
> acercarse a Tu aliento generoso,
> de fragrancia más rara
> que el vino y el ungüento más precioso!
> Tu nombre es como el óleo derramado,
> y por eso las Ninfas Te han amado.

Human Nature can go no further. She has expressed her desire for divine Beauty. She knows that divine beauty is already here, but she cannot find it. At this crucial point, with great delicacy and remarkable theological acuity, Juana Inés places the encounter between Nature and Grace. Scene vii brings them face to face. In the guise of a "beautiful Shepherdess," Grace enters, proclaiming the good news like the angels at Bethlehem. In the ensuing dialogue, Grace reveals that she is able to lead Human Nature to a fountain whose pure waters have remained unsullied.

It is one of the notable features of *Divine Narcissus* that although the Virgin Mary is not represented by an actress she is is nonetheless present at the climax of the play: she is the well with clear water. Bent over it, looking into it, Narcissus will see his perfect image. This, precisely, is the message of Grace in her meeting with Human Nature. Grace identifies herself as the "Lady" who, "in that beau-

tiful Garden," was Human Nature's companion before sin. They
can embrace again if they go together to the pure fountain, to

> . . . that Fountain,
> whose crystalline waters
> free of impure liquid,
> ever clean, ever intact
> since their first instant,
> have always run without stain.

> . . . a aquella Fuente,
> cuyas cristalinas aguas
> libres de licor impuro,
> siempre limpias, siempre intactas
> desde su instante primero,
> siempre han corrido sin mancha.[26]

Juana's emphasis on Mary's immaculate conception is thus
maintained: the fountain is the immaculate Virgin.

> She is of the Songs
> the Sealed Fountain
> that flows from Paradise,
> abounding in life-giving waters.

> Aquésta es de los Cantares
> aquella Fuente Sellada,
> que sale del Paraíso,
> y aguas vivíficas mana.

Following this clue, Human Nature recognizes her as "She who is
Full of Grace," prefigured by Esther. She prays:

> O divine Fountain, O Well
> of life-giving waters,
> for from the first instant
> you were preserved
> from the original venom,

from the transcendental stain,
that infests all other Streams . . .

———————————

Oh, Fuente divina, oh Pozo
de las vivíficas aguas,
pues desde el primer instante
estuviste preservada
de la original ponzoña,
de la trascendental mancha,
que infesta los demás Ríos . . .

(P. 405-6.)

At the edge of the well—"sacred Fountain / of crystalline streams"—Human Nature becomes "Fortunate Nature" (p. 406). Grace has been "the Guard" of the fountain "since yesterday began / its stream, Immaculate / by singular privilege." Grace wants Human Nature to bend over the fountain so that Narcissus, when he comes, may see her reflection in the pure water. Both pray to the "ever crystalline, / clear and beautiful Fountain," to the "Fountain of perfections," where there is no "stain, peril, shadow, or sin," which runs "clean, preserved, exempt," whose crystals give "with their sweetness / strength and salvation, pleasure and wealth."

One may wonder if, like John of the Cross, Juana Inés took the word *crystal* to be etymologically connected with Christ; in the *Spiritual Canticle,* the fountain was said to be crystalline because "it is of Christ."[27] The fountain of the *Canticle*'s stanza 11, however, was faith itself, while in Juana Inés's work, the fountain is the Virgin Mary, the highest example of faith. Juana espouses a much higher Mariology than John of the Cross: the divine Word will recognize himself in Human Nature to the extent that Human Nature is reflected in the well—symbolically, the womb—of the Virgin Mary.

Narcissus Sees His Image in the Fountain and Dies of Love: Christ Finds His Perfect Image in Humanity and Dies of Love. We are now brought to the central symbol of the play, Narcissus, who is of course Jesus Christ as the embodiment of divine beauty, the incarnate Word of God. That Christ is the divine beauty has been suggested, said outright, and emphasized many times since the beginning of the play; indeed, it is already implied in Juana's use of the Narcissus myth. One point now becomes clearer: divine beauty is divine love. In scene viii, Narcissus, following the lost sheep, comes to the fountain over which Human Nature and Grace are bending. In this very fine scene Narcissus talks to himself in a monologue that is inspired in part by the *improperia* of the traditional Good Friday liturgy before the reforms of Pius XII and Vatican II.[28] Narcissus addresses the lost sheep, wishing for her recovery and health while regretting her insensitivity and sin. He is both lover and lord:

> See that My beauty
> by all is loved,
> by all is sought,
> with no creaturely exception,
>
> and you alone your fortune has chosen . . .
>
> See that I am sovereign,
> and no one has more power:
> that I give life and death,
> that I wound and I heal,
>
> and that no one escapes My hand.

———————

> Mira que Mi hermosura
> de todas es amada,
> de todas es buscada,
> sin reservar criatura,
>
> y sólo a ti te elige tu ventura . . . [29]
>
> Mira que soberano
> soy, y que no hay más fuerte:
> que Yo doy vida y muerte,
> que Yo hiero y Yo sano,
>
> y que nadie se escapa de Mi mano.

(P. 408.)

As Narcissus looks at the pure water, in scene ix, his tone changes, along with the poetic form and cadence. There is an exclamation of joy and surprise:

> I come; but what do I see?
> What sovereign Beauty
> faces with its pure light
> all the Heavenly Sapphire?

> Llego; mas ¿qué es lo que miro?
> ¿Qué soberana Hermosura
> afrenta con su luz pura
> todo el Celestial Zafiro?[30]

Narcissus continues with a description of the image in the water. In six stanzas of ten lines each he tells what he sees. Juana draws on her interest in astronomy:

> The Sun's shining trip,
> that shines in all its course
> from Setting to Rising,
> does not radiate in Signs and Stars
> so much light, so many sparks,
> as this Fountain alone gives.

> Del Sol el luciente giro,
> en todo el curso luciente
> que da desde Ocaso a Oriente,
> no esparce en Signos y Estrellas
> tanta luz, tantas centellas
> como da sola esta Fuente.

The whole sphere of the heavens seems to be concentrated in the beauty reflected in the fountain. Narcissus sees Nature and Grace together, or, better, he sees Nature through Grace, as their reflected images now form only one beauty in the Virgin Mary. The description is again inspired largely from the Song of Songs. Narcissus sees "a barely opened pomegranate, ... two lips" like a rose, and also "pearls, . . . eyes" with rays of sunshine in them, the "meekness of the dove," the "curl of a hair" (p. 409). "Heaven and Earth," the sun and the moon, contribute to Mary's beauty. The poem ends on an invitation:

> Come, Bride, to your Beloved;
> tear away this light veil:
> show me your beautiful flesh;
> let your voice sound in my ear!
> Come from elect Lebanon,
> I have just arrived,
> and I will crown the Ophir
> of your precious wood
> with the fragrant crown
> of Amana, Hermon, and Sanir!

> ¡Ven, Esposa, a tu Querido;
> rompe esa cortina clara:
> muéstrame tu hermosa cara,
> suene tu voz a mi oído!
> ¡Ven del Líbano escogido,
> acaba ya de venir,
> y coronaré el Ofir
> de tu madera preciosa
> con la Corona olorosa
> de Amaná, Hermón y Sanir!

Juana Inés had a special problem, as she needed a careful transition to the death of Christ. I suspect that she found a cue in the little poem of John of the Cross, "Un Pastorcico," where the shepherd climbs a tree, opens his arms, and dies.[31] His death is caused by the knowledge that his "beautiful shepherdess" has forgotten him. Juana Inés ends at the same point, in scene xii, when Narcissus gives Death permission to kill him. In order to arrive at this point, Juana has brought back Echo, the devil; in scene x, Echo finds Narcissus looking into the well whose waters have remained unsoiled. Out of anger and frustration she turns mute again, not "formally," yet "causally and efficiently."[32] In scene xi Self-love and Pride try to comfort Echo but can only make her suffer more from her own fury. In scene xii, Narcissus passes slowly from joy to agony, for his total love cannot be fully returned: "Who loves as I have loved? / . . . Seeing what I desire, / I am powerless to enjoy it."[33]

> . . . it is My own image
> that causes My sorrow.
>
> Of her I am enamored;
> and though love has to kill me,
> it is easier to renounce
> life than what I care for.

> . . . Mi propria semejanza
> es quien Mi pena causó.
>
> De ella estoy enamorado;
> y aunque amor Me ha de matar,
> Me es más fácil el dejar
> la vida, que no el cuidado.

Hiding in a tree, Echo repeats some of the words that come from Narcissus's increasing sorrow. A cumulative effect results as these words are in turn strung together into three stanzas that are then picked up by Music. At the end of the passage, Narcissus dies of love, having granted Death permission to separate his soul from his body but knowing that he has power to reunite them. He is willing to die "because the matter of a life is little / for the form of so great a fire" (p. 416). Narcissus then exclaims, in keeping with the gospels:

> Father! Why in such extreme peril
> do you abandon me? It is consummated.
> Into Your hands I commend My spirit!

> ¡Padre! ¿Por que en un trance tan tremendo
> Me desamparas? Ya está consumado.
> ¡En Tus manos Mi Espiritu encomiendo!

How Narcissus dies is not very clear. The instructions for scene xiii, just after his last words, specify that "an earthquake is heard; Narcissus falls behind the side curtains."[34] Some authors assume that Narcissus collapses into the well and drowns at the point where he fuses with his own image in the water. Despite the logic of this assumption, Juana Inés neither describes nor shows a drowning; rather, she simply makes Narcissus vanish from sight. His death is left to the spectator's imagination. I suspect that Sor Juana Inés was aware of a dilemma, literary at least in part: How could the symbol of the well—the Virgin Mary—coincide with the image of the cross? The cross had been discreetly suggested in scene x, when Narcissus was "as though suspended over the well"; but he walked away from it in scene xii.

The difficulty is also theological, however. If the entire purpose of creation and the incarnation is to establish a nuptial relationship between the divine Word and the creature, the crucifixion and death of Christ appear as surds in the system. Scandalous happenings in a process that could indeed make room for the death of Christ but hardly for that kind of death, the crucifixion and death are events hardly in keeping with the logic of the divine purpose.

Human Nature Embraces Grace and through Grace is United with Narcissus: The Union of Humanity and God through the Redemption. Juana Inés, always alert to theological issues, attempts to meet the objection. In scene xiii, Echo and her cohorts, impressed by the earthquake, are led to confess, "This Man truly was most Just!" and "This was the Son of God . . . !" (p. 417). In scene xiv, Human Nature, with Music and a number of nymphs and shepherds, laments the death of "my beautiful Narcissus."[35] She is affected by the earthquake, by the sun's hiding, by the tearing of the veil in the Temple. The whole universe seems to be crying with her. Nevertheless, she also understands that she must seek her own life in "this image of death," "for to give me life / is the purpose for which he dies" (p. 419). In the person of Mary Magdalen, who cannot find the corpse, Human Nature believes that it has been hidden. Then Grace appears and reveals the truth:

> Your Narcissus is living;
> do not weep, do not lament,

or seek among the dead
Him who is ever Alive!

Vivo está tu Narciso
no llores, no lamentes,
ni entre los muertos busques
Al que está Vivo siempre!

(P. 420.)

Returning in scene xv risen from the dead, Narcissus meets Human Nature who, still like Mary Magdalen, does not recognize him. He makes himself known: "But how, My Bride, / can you not know me, / if my Divine Beauty / nothing can equal?"[36] He warns her:

To touch me do not come near,
for I go to My Father
at His heavenly Throne.

A tocarme no llegues,
porque voy con Mi Padre
a Su Trono celeste.

The institution of the Church comes next, set in a discussion among Echo, who still claims power over Nature, Grace, who promises Nature her protection, and Narcissus. Echo argues on the basis of St. Anselm's theology of redemption: since human sin was infinite, Narcissus's death was necessary, for only a divine Person can erase the result of an infinite sin. But, she continues, "clearly it is not proper / that all the times that she / returns to sin, you also / should again die for her."[37]

Echo's logic would be correct if, in Anselmian theology, the death of Christ, effective for the past and the present, had not affected the future. Such, however, is not the case, for redemption by Christ is universal in time as well as in space. One may nonetheless wonder if it is not on purpose that Juana Inés has placed this theology in the mouth of the devil's symbol. For Anselm's theology of redemption conflicts with what Juana has identified as the reason for the incarnation. If God's ultimate purpose is indeed a nuptial union between the divine Word and humanity, then the redemptive effect of the incarnation follows. Once humanity has sinned, redemption still makes this union possible; but sin does not belong to God's basic design.

On the contrary, to focus God's entire incarnational purpose on humanity's need for redemption—as in Anselm's theology— makes sin a fundamental occasion and condition for the incarnation. In the play, and presumably in Juana's theology, this conception is diabolical. Echo may well like it; it gives her a key role that otherwise neither she nor temptation or sin could ever have played. But this is not Juana's own insight into the mystery. Rather than enhance the part played by Echo in the history of salvation, the Incarnation and its redemptive consequence highlight God's generosity, as is clear in Narcissus's response to Echo: the sacraments, and especially penance, have been given "as medicines for the Soul." Moreover, another sacrament that Narcissus instituted before his death—the eucharist—is, as he declared, "a Memorial of My Love," the "manifestation of my unequaled finesse."

The introduction of the eucharist in "the very metaphor" of the play leads to a remarkable ending. In a long series of quatrains, Grace surveys the whole process of salvation history and reviews Narcissus's reign over creation and nature. Totally happy in the glory of the divinity, "Sovereign Narcissus" was

> King of all beauty,
> Archive of perfection,
> Sphere of miracles,
> and Center of prodigies.

> Re de toda la hermosura,
> de la perfección Archivo,
> Esfera de los milagros,
> y Centro de los prodigios.

Fire, sea, earth, and air acclaim him. The sun is a "spark of His Beauty" (p. 422), the planets a "sketch of his light." Fields cover themselves with flowers "to imitate his beauty." Animals, birds, and fish adore him. The "infinite *mare magnum* of perfection," this "beau-

tiful Wonder" not only enjoyed the roses and lilies of nature but also
loved himself in his human image, where he saw "the beautiful
reflection / of His rare splendor." God alone is worthy of God's love,
and he loved himself in his human image until man hid behind "the
sea of his sins." Then Narcissus decided to die, in order "to show
that danger / is the measure of truth." Drawing from the Epistle to
the Ephesians, Grace declares:

> He humbled himself, Paul wrote,
> and (if it is licit to say so)
> consumed Himself, in the sweet fire
> tenderly enamored.
>
> He lowered himself like a Lover . . .
>
> He gave his life in testimony
> of his love . . .

> ———————————

> Apocóse, según Pablo,
> y (si es lícito decirlo)
> consumióse, al dulce fuego
> tiernamente derretido.
>
> Abatióse como Amante . . .
>
> Dio la vida en testimonio
> de su Amor . . .

(P. 422.)

Juana Inés seems to have harmonized now the views of re-
demption that were previously opposed. She has incorporated a mod-
ified Anselmian theology of justice in a Scotist focus on the glory of
God and a sanjuanist vision of the nuptial relationship between God
and creation. The perspectives of Anselm, John Duns Scotus, and
John of the Cross are reconciled in a theology of the divine love at
work in creation. Once creation has been damaged by sin, this love
becomes redemptive. The death of the Lord for the sins of human-
kind opens the way to the loving union that is the purpose of God
in creation and in the incarnation. In Juana's theology the concerns

for justice, glory, and oneness are joined together in the eucharist, instituted before Narcissus's death as the future memorial of his sacrificial love and as the instrument of his nuptial union.

This is clear in Juana's brief treatment of the eucharist at the end of her play. Narcissus left "a souvenir and a warning / as memorial of His Death / and as pledge of his Care." He who was called in the Scriptures "Flower of the Fields, / and of the Hills Lily" (p. 423) made himself a "white Flower." Lover and bridegroom of the soul, he hid himself, watching her "through the windows, / spying on her through the cracks." (The images come from the Song of Songs.) Then there appears, next to the fountain, a "beautiful White Flower," shaped like a chalice surmounted by a host—a frequent design in the decorative art of the Counterreformation. At this moment Narcissus pronounces the words of Scripture:

> This is My Body and My Blood
> that I surrendered to so many martyrdoms
> for you. In memory
> of My Death, do it again.

> Este es Mi Cuerpo y My Sangre
> que entregué a tantos martirios
> por vosotros. En memoria
> de Mi Muerte, repetidlo.

After a few suitable words—of gratitude from Human Nature; of anger and pain from Echo, Self-love, and Pride—Grace and Human Nature fall into each other's arms. The play ends as they sing Juana's rendering of the liturgical hymn attributed to Thomas Aquinas, the "Pange lingua":

> Sing, my tongue, the glorious Body's
> high Mystery, given to us
> as worthy price of the World, Fruit
> Royal, generous, of the most limpid Womb!

¡Canta, lengua, del Cuerpo glorioso
el alto Misterio, que por precio digno
del Mundo Se nos dio, siendo Fruto
Real, generoso, del Vientre más limpio!

(P. 424.)

In these words Sor Juana Inés de la Cruz links the eucharist with
the conception and birth of Christ from the Virgin and with the
glorious body of Christ after the resurrection.

The Imitation of Christ: The *Response to Sor Filotea de la Cruz*

The reflections on her life and experience that were occasioned
by the publication of Juana's *Carta atenagórica* inspired some remarks
on the life of Christ that are worth considering in this chapter. Al-
though they do not constitute the central topic of the *Respuesta,* they
show that Sor Juana Inés was aware, in bearing what she calls her
persecutions, of practicing the imitation of Christ. She has told her
correspondent and critic, Sor Filotea de la Cruz (the bishop of Pueb-
la), how persecuted she has been. Most painful have been the stric-
tures coming from good but narrow-minded persons who found
Juana Inés too learned, or too intelligent, or too versatile in her
writings, or too much aware of her accomplishments. Learning, they
felt, was unbecoming in nuns: "This scholarship does not fit the holy
ignorance that is their duty."[38]

Juana remarks first that ancient Athens had a "politically bar-
barous law": the citizens who were too seductive and brillant had to
go into exile, for fear they would use their talents to dominate the
city. Machiavelli made it a principle of government "to abhor the
one who stands out, because he discredits the others." Mediocrity
would seem to be necessary to share the common life of a society.
Juana concludes this section with the pessimistic reflection: "Thus
it has been and it will always be" (p. 835).

This law of human society was the reason for "the Pharisees'
rabid hatred of Christ." Christ was too beautiful for them. His beau-
ty threatened them because it could so easily inspire the crowds to
follow him: "What could this incomprehensible beauty do and move,
and not do and not move, since through his beautiful face the rays
of Divinity made themselves transparent as through pure crystal?"

The great Teresa, whom Juana Inés calls at this point "the Holy Mother and my mother," testified that "after seeing the beauty of Christ she felt free to approach any sort of creature, for she could see nothing that, compared with that beauty, was not ugly." How was it, then, that Christ and his beauty inspired such opposite reactions among people? The Pharisees, learned as they were, hated Christ. Their objection was that "he gives many signs," and for this reason alone was he put to death. Juana exclaims: "Good Heavens! The doing of excellent things is punishable by death!" Moreover, of all the virtues and achievements that elevate some above others, intelligence is the most resented. As Juana has observed, people may admit being less noble or rich or beautiful or even learned than others. But they never admit being less intelligent.

Juana meditates on the crowning of Jesus with thorns. The red cloak and the reed did not hurt, only the crown did. This was because

> the sacred head of Christ and his divine brain were depositories of wisdom; and it is not enough for a wise brain in the world to be an object of ridicule, it must be made pitiful and mistreated; the head that is a treasury of wisdom cannot hope to receive another crown than one of thorns. (P. 836.)

In Roman practice many different crowns were used to honor citizens and soldiers: the crown corresponded to the high deed that had been performed. Christ was given the most honorable one, the "obsidional crown," normally awarded to an officer who has successfully broken the siege of a city or camp. "It was not made of gold or silver, but of the grass or weeds growing in the area where the event had taken place." Precisely, Christ came "to break the siege of the Prince of Darkness, who was besieging all the earth." He was crowned with what grows on earth: "since the curse," earth "produces nothing other than thorns." Thus it was with a crown of thorns that "his mother the Synagogue crowned the courageous and wise conqueror." When Jesus went up to Judea for the resurrection of Lazarus, the apostle Thomas said "let us go with him and die with him" (John 11:16). He sensed that miracles and signs put Christ in great danger. For "it is less intolerable for pride to hear reproaches than for envy to see miracles" (p. 837).

Such reflections were of some comfort to Juana Inés when she found herself persecuted. The occasion of these persecutions was not even her extensive knowledge. It was "only that she loved wisdom and letters, not that she had achieved either." These reflections also suggest that Juana Inés gave paramount importance in her personal thought and piety to the events of the earthly life of Christ. A profound sense of the humanity of Jesus, the Word made flesh, lies behind the constructions of her symbolic imagination. If *Divino Narciso* becomes, at her hands, an effective Christian myth, she never forgets the gospels and their narratives of the life of Jesus.

The Twofold Purpose of the Incarnation: "Poems for the Incarnation"

Three "Poems for the Incarnation" will provide our conclusion, although they speak of Mary as much as of the child. Theologically, they make the point that "the loving Incarnation of the divine Love" has a twofold purpose: it is "the medium of Redemption, / the crown of Creation."[39] It aims at more than the forgiveness of sin in response to the *felix culpa* of Adam and Eve (the "happy fault" of the Easter Vigil liturgy). God pursues a higher design, to which Mary's beauty belongs: "in order for God to take flesh / Mary alone was enough." Juana insists: "The opposite I do not admit." Yet she is willing to join together two motives of the incarnation: the redemption of humanity and God's unique love for Mary of Nazareth. God was "compassionate with all, / and enamored of Her." The incarnation was due to "the sin of all / and the grace of Mary."

The second poem is more obscure. Its theme is the Word. The incarnation goes *de Verbo ad Verbum*, "from Word to Word."[40] The annunciation reverses the order of nature. "There was a Word first, / and then a Conception": this was the opposite of common human birthing. The voice resounds in the wilderness, "and thus among men / his Word goes passing." The written Law ceases; the law of Grace begins. "What is written no longer serves, / since God commands through his Word."

The last poem, a Latin hymn, chiefly sings the glories of the mother of God. The chief of these enshrines a neat summary of Juana's theology of the incarnation: "You show yourself as the Handmaid / in order to conceive the Servant."[41] This is the perspective of Isaiah chapter 53 as traditionally interpreted in Christian theology. The divine Word makes himself the Servant; only Mary, mother of God, can be the handmaid.

5

The Finesses of God

The tone of this chapter will vary considerably from the previous ones, for we are about to see Juana Inés doing theology in another medium than poetry. She had not passed through the exercises of academic studies. Excluded from the university because she was a woman, she was perforce self-taught in theological as in secular matters. As a result, she must have felt very little inclined to build a theological system or even to treat a theological question systematically. Yet, just as she made herself available to those who wished to obtain a poem, she accepted the invitation from the bishop of Puebla to theologize systematically when it came in 1690. Juana's only piece of systematic theological reflection was published against her wishes, in December of that year, by the bishop of Puebla de los Angeles, Don Manuel Fernández de Santa Cruz y Sahagún. The editor's somewhat pretentious title, *Carta atenagórica,* which was meant to evoke the intellectual glories of ancient Athens, indicated in what great regard he held the composition, which he equated with the achievements of the Greeks. He prefaced the publication with the letter that had accompanied the text when Sor Juana Inés sent it to him.

We need to look carefully at the circumstances in which she wrote this theological essay, at its theme—the finesses of God—which is related to typical concerns of her time and culture, at her treatment of the theme, and at some other works, notably *Neptuno alegórico,* where the same theme recurs in a less didactic and more symbolic mode. This will lead us to draw some conclusions regarding Sor Juana's experience of God.

Carta atenagórica: Occasion and Context

Bowing to the bishop of Puebla's wishes, Juana had put in writing ideas that she had expressed earlier in 1690 in a circle of visitors in the parlor of her convent. It is clear from the *Carta atena-górica* that the bishop of Puebla was present on that occasion. The group had discussed a sermon by a famous Portuguese Jesuit, Antonio de Vieira y Céspedes Meneses (1608–1697). Vieira, born in Lisbon, had been a distinguished missionary in Brazil and a determined defender of Indians and blacks. He had made three long sojourns in the Americas, where he died. In between, he had lived in Lisbon and Rome. From 1642 to 1652 he resided in Portugal. Preached in 1650 at the royal chapel of the College of Lisbon, the sermon in question had been composed for the celebration of Maundy Thursday, which includes the liturgy of the washing of feet, modeled on the Lord's action in John 13:1–20.[1]

Discussion of sermons must have been a typical parlor entertainment in a convent that laid claim to a degree of intellectual distinction. Certainly Vieira's Maundy Thursday sermon could have no direct impact in New Spain. By the time it was discussed in the parlor of St. Jerome's monastery, some thirty years after its composition, it was already somewhat out of date. It was, however, included in a collection of Vieira's sermons that appeared in Spanish translations in 1675 and 1678. The volume from 1678 contained the *mandatum* piece ("Maundy" derives from the Latin *mandatum,* taken from the words of Jesus in John 13:34: "*Mandatum novum do vobis,*" "I give you a new commandment.") The translations were dedicated to the current bishop of Michoacán, Don Francisco de Aguiar y Seijas, who became archbishop of Mexico in 1689. Presumably through this Spanish edition Juana became acquainted with the sermon.

There is no good reason to suppose, as have some authors, that Juana's critique had been suggested by the bishop of Puebla, who used her as a tool in a political game of his own.[2] Certainly a parlor conversation, even if it had been brilliant, would not have been transmitted to posterity had not the bishop of Puebla pursued a special purpose when he urged Juana to write it down, and when, without warning, he published her text. But the ideas expressed show every sign of being Juana's own. The bishop's purpose appears sufficiently clear from the letter to Juana Inés in which he drew his conclusions from reading the *Carta atenagórica,* conclusions that provoked her *Respuesta:* he wanted her to devote all her time and talents to what he considered to be a nun's vocation, namely, piety and the service of the Church. The bishop was himself a distinguished, if narrowly specialized, scholar, the author of an extensive concordance in two volumes of the biblical books of Genesis and Exodus.[3] He also must have been appreciated as a spiritual director, for he corresponded with a number of nuns. Obviously, he expected Sor Juana Inés de la Cruz to respond with gratitude to his advice and to stop wasting her time and talent with profane poetry. Even though he presumably knew Juana personally, he badly misjudged her character and the motivation behind her works.

The Concept of *Finesse*

Vieira, in his sermon, tried to identify the greatest finesse (*fineza*) of Christ. The word *finesse* is to be taken in a rather special sense that was more common in the seventeenth century than it is today. This sense is brought out well in the *New English Dictionary on a Historical Basis* of the Philological Society (London, 1884-1928): "delicacy or subtlety of manipulation or discrimination; refinement, refined grace." This meaning is "now rare" and is used "only as a foreign word." One instance of its use is taken from a text written in 1704, near to the time of Sor Juana: "The Perfection of an Operation shall depend upon a certain Finesse." This comes close to the meaning of *fineza* in the writings of Juana Inés and in Vieira's sermon.

The concept of finesse, however, is not primarily theological. Theologians borrowed it from human experience. In the writings of Sor Juana it is closely related to her understanding of love. As she sees it, love is universal, not only existing between humans, but also at work throughout creation. And since creation is modeled on the Creator, love is one of the keys for understanding God. The scope of love has no bounds. Juana was sufficiently influenced by Platonism to see love as Eros. But Eros, desire, nisus, need not be, as the Scholastics would have said, acquisitive. It can be totally self-abandoned. It can be love for the sake of loving, extended to another without concern for a reward or even a response. Juana makes it say of itself:

> I, because I am Love,
> am the soul of everything
> that shows being in what has life,
> and existence in the creaturely:
>
> I, who am among you
> with sweetest embraces

the bond that hems all in,
the union that holds all. . . .

_____

Y yo, que siendo el Amor,
soy alma de todo cuanto
ser ostenta en lo viviente,
y existencia en lo crïado:

yo, que soy entre vosotros,
con dulcísimos abrazos,
lazo que a todos os ciño,
unión que a todos ato. . . .[4]

But love cannot always come into the open. It may stay hidden, precisely in order to attract a suitable response. And this is where finesse comes in.

Fineza appears as an allegorical personage in the comedy *Los empeños de una casa,* which was shown in Mexico City on 4 October 1683. She is not featured in the three acts of the play itself but in a *sainete,* a "little scene," between acts one and two. Outside the action of the play, the sole purpose of such a scene was to praise the viceroy and his family, who attended the production. Five allegorical personages—Love, Respect, Courtesy, Finesse, and Hope—appear before a palace official. Each pleads his or her right to obtain the prize. But the prize in this case is a reversed prize, as in a game of *Qui-perd-gagne* (Loser wins): the prize is disfavor with the ladies in the palace. Because Love, Respect, and Courtesy lose, they are allowed to enter the palace and take their places in the distinguished company of the court.

Then Finesse takes her turn: "Finesse I am; / see if I have reason to claim" the prize. Asked on what she bases her claim, she answers

On what? On the delicate, the attentive,
on the humble, the obsequious,
on solicitude, vigilance,
and on loving for love's sake only.

_____

¿En qué? En lo fino, lo atento,
en lo humilde, en lo obsequioso,
en el cuidado, el desvelo,
y en amar por sólo amar.[5]

The official objects. If she truly were Finesse, she would not claim to be, for Finesse is nuanced, even conceited, knowing how to use deceit to a good purpose:

And the true lover
must have of the beloved
so high an idea
that he must think his love
does not come near meriting
the beauty that it serves:
and though loving her extremely
he must ever think his love
is less than its object,
and confess his failure to pay
despite all his ransoms;
for the fine point of love
lies in not showing itself.

And come, come inside;
for the greater Finesse
of a lover lies
in nonacknowledgment!

Y el amante verdadero
ha de tener de la amado
tan soberano concepto
que ha de pensar que no alcanza
su amor al merecimiento
de la beldad a quien sirve;
y aunque la ame con extremo,
ha de pensar siempre que es
su amor, menor que el objeto,
y confesar que no paga
con todos los rendimientos;

que lo fino del amor
está en no mostrar el serlo.

¡Y andad, andad adentro;
que la Fineza
mayor es, de un amante,
no conocerla!

As they come in, Love, Courtesy, and Respect sing a quatrain
that sums up the reason that they are admitted: "Love is courtesy, /
not contract." Courtesy "is paid" by the service she gives. Respect
is not paid: "No one is ever paid / what is his due." Since Finesse
has not won the negative prize, she too may enter the palace. "Nor
is Finesse," she declares, ever paid, "for, if rightly seen, / one cannot
in obligation / locate the fine point" (p. 656).

Finesse is that dimension of love in which love disguises itself
whenever disguise is necessary, for instance when self-disclosure
would expose love to rebuff, or when no response can be expected,
or when the purpose of love is better served by silence than by
openness. Implying a delicate sense of shades and nuances, finesse
is a subtle discernment of conditions and situations.

Finesse is also closely related to beauty. But what is beauty? In
the encomiastic poem celebrating the anniversary of the vicereine,
the countess de Galve, beauty is clearly defined:

The Beautiful is nothing other
than a proportion that orders
well some parts with others:
for it will not suffice to be beautiful
in the absolute, if
not also in the relative.

———————

No es otra cosa lo Hermoso
que una proporción que ordena
bien unas partes con otras:
pues no bastara ser bellas
absolutamente, si
relativa no lo fueran.[6]

In other words, beauty implies proportion, existing always in relationship. And relationships are not only perceived by the emotions; there is such a thing as intellectual beauty, especially in the Platonic view of the world that is dear to Juana Inés. As Intellect declares in the loa in honor of the anniversary of the queen of Spain, Doña María Luisa de Borbón:

> There is greater difficulty
> than in catching the will,
> in winning the Intellect;
> and this is the greater
> victory of its perfection;
> it keeps eternal the union
> of beauty and subtlety,
> and, for reason of Beauty,
> one beauty of Reason.

> que es mayor dificultad
> que prender la voluntad,
> vencer al Entendimiento;
> y pues es el vencimiento
> mayor de su perfección;
> conserve eterna la unión
> de hermosura y sutileza,
> y una, a razón de Belleza,
> belleza de la Razón.[7]

"The union of beauty and subtlety" could be another description of finesse. When beauty is aware of itself and its power, it may be led to conceal itself so as not to overwhelm anyone: such finesse is part of civilized living. For this reason, Juana's profane poetry often alludes to finesse in the singular or in the plural. For example, in the third act of *Amor es más laberinto,* Theseus acknowledges the "heroic finesses" of Ariadne, whom he does not love. He sees that Ariadne and her sister Phaedra, whom he loves, are both trying to "incite love with finesses." For his part, he can only serve Phaedra: "reduced to one single / action, the greater finesse / was to be unable to act otherwise."[8] Finesse discerns situations, sorts out possibilities, evaluates advisable approaches. It may be led to hide beauty and to conceal love for the sake of beauty and love. The fine point of beauty and love in their manifestations, finesse is at one extreme of human behavior tantamount to the art of flirtation, while at the opposite extreme it is the lover's renunciation of satisfaction for the sake of the beloved; between both extremes it is the ability to select appropriate symbols so that what is real will appear unreal and what is unreal, real.

In the context of baroque art, finesse would be that aspect of architecture and decoration that seeks to conceal the harsh lines of right angles. Devices were multiplied in baroque buildings, willingly incorporating in Spain the delicate finery of the plateresque and progressively bringing baroque to the threshold of rococo. Stones of contrasting colors, stucco figurines, trompe l'oeil painting resemble the soft brush strokes of an elegant woman applying makeup. Make-up transforms the visage without changing it; hides in order to reveal. Its method is to enhance and underline some features, to soften and shade others. Its purpose is to bring latent beauty to light. Thus does finesse act in relation to inner beauty and to love: finesse may conceal some feature or feeling; it may put on the guise of its contrary; it may follow a roundabout path, but for one purpose only— to bring love to fruition and beauty to recognition.

Finesse, the *Carta atenagórica,* and Juana's Response to Vieira

Given this understanding of *finesse,* it is not surprising that the concept found a place in the theology of the baroque era. The concept is theologically appropriate if Christ's relationship to humanity is one of love. If Christ plays the game of love, then he alternately hides and shows himself; he wears a mask and takes it off; he approaches and withdraws in a tantalizing ebb and flow of presence and absence.

The Jesuit preacher whose *mandatum* sermon occasioned Juana's *Carta atenagórica* devoted his oratory on the finesses of Christ during the solemn liturgy of Holy Week, a time when our modern liturgical sensitivity would least expect such subtlety. Vieira does not define *fineza,* nor does he need to do so: his topic belongs to the conventions of baroque preaching in the Iberian peninsula. As he declares at the beginning, the works of creation parallel the works of redemption: the greatest works of each are reserved to the end of the process. God "reserved for the end the greatest works of his love." Accordingly, Vieira wants to discover and reveal the finest point of Christ's love at the end of his life, when "the demonstrations, the extremes, the tenderness, and finally all the finesses pertaining to a love that is humanly divine and divinely human were the greatest: for in this final clause he joined finality with fineness: 'In finem dilexit eos.'"[9]

Precisely, Vieira discusses whether Jesus' washing of his disciples' feet, an act that embodied his humility, was his greatest finesse. The preacher asks: What was the greatest finesse of Christ? What was the greatest expression of his love? The sermon is in fact a respectable piece of eloquent sacred oratory. Once the genre is accepted, it is appropriate to the celebration of Holy Thursday; an audience that was familiar with the conceits of the baroque could be properly moved.

One has to face, however, a problem of method. How does one assess the finesses of Christ? Rather than making a directly biblical study, Vieira chose instead to examine the opinions of three doctors of the Church, St. Augustine, St. Thomas Aquinas, and St. John Chrysostom. In each case the Portuguese preacher discovered a greater finesse than these doctors had found, and he supported his contentions with examples from the Bible. Vieira announced at the start of his sermon that he would refute the three saints mentioned. In what still sounds like rhetorical arrogance, he even made a fantastic claim: whatever finesse of Christ they could put forward as the greatest, he, Vieira, would find a greater one! "And," he added for good measure, "as to the finesse of the love of Christ that I will state, no one will give me another equal to it!" Had Vieira said this in the peroration, little could be objected to his formulation. But since he said it at the start, he sounded as though a priori placing himself above the greatest doctors of the Church. Moreover, such an approach could only bring scandal in a community that was devoted to Augustine: the Hieronymites followed the Rule of St. Augustine; and it was commonly believed that Jerome, living as a hermit in Palestine, was a close friend of the bishop of Hippo, even though the two, who corresponded on occasion, never met.

The finesses of the love of Christ were a concern of the baroque age, and it was anachronistic and absurd to believe that Augustine, Chrysostom, and Thomas had spoken of such matters. The first two, in the patristic era, could not have practiced the kind of rhetoric that would have anticipated the subtleties of baroque imagination. In the high Middle Ages Thomas Aquinas had other aesthetic models to follow than those that were to be born out of the Renaissance, grow through Italian mannerism, and blossom in the churrigueresque style of the Iberian peninsula.[10] Juana Inés was probably no more sensitive to this historical problem than was the Portuguese preacher. She found too many of her symbols in the ancient world to be attentive to Vieira's anachronisms.

Juana had already discussed the question of Christ's greatest finesse in the introductory loa of her sacramental play, *San Hermenegildo,* a work that gives no hint of having been influenced by the sermon of the Portuguese preacher. In this loa Juana used a device that was not uncommon in the literary genre of the sacramental plays: three students hold a theological discussion that introduces the play's topic. They try to discover the greatest finesse of Christ's love. The first student opts for the authority of St. Augustine and concludes that the greatest finesse of Christ was his death. The second, opting for St. Thomas, affirms that it was Christ's presence in the sacrament of the eucharist. Pursing the sciences rather than theology, the third student serves as a neutral witness who urges the others to attain the clarity of thought and expression without which he would not be able to grasp what they mean. The problem of finesse remains unsolved. Since Hermenegild dies as a martyr who witnesses to the eucharist, it may well be that Juana Inés leaned at this time of her life to the side of Thomas Aquinas. This is by no means certain, however, for Hermenegild's fate does not directly answer the question concerning Christ's greatest finesse.

The idea of the finesse of Christ recurs in the *Poems of St. Bernard* of 1690. In poem 23, the greatest finesse is the death of Christ, which is memorialized in the sacrament. But the sacrament adds something to the finesse in that Christ remains in it as though dead:

> And I know that Christ
> in the Sacrament,
> being glorious,
> is as though dead.

> Y ya sé que Cristo
> en el Sacramento,
> estando glorioso,
> está como muerto.[11]

This is confirmed in the conceptist mode of poem 29:

Man arrived at a greatness
that the Seraph does not reach,
and in the finesse of the end
saw the end of the Finesse.

Llegó el Hombre a la grandeza
que no alcanza el Serafín,
y en la fineza del fin
vido el fin de la Fineza.[12]

That is, in the death of Christ the eucharistic presence could already
be discerned.

To judge from these various versions of the greatest finesse of
Christ, it would seem that Juana Inés did not ascribe any finality to
the discovery of finesses or even to the hypotheses that could be made
about the greatest finesse of Christ's love. A different context may
well suggest a different point of view, from which new light may be
thrown on the manifestations of Christ's love. Juana therefore did
not attempt to solve the problem in any final way until sometime in
1690, when, presumably after writing the *Letras de San Bernardo,* she
read Vieira's sermon. Profoundly scandalized by Vieira's claim, she
was shocked by the preacher's arrogance against three doctors of the
Church and by his unreasonable assertion that nothing could super-
sede his findings. For her part, she would take him at his word. She
would prove him wrong by discovering a higher finesse of Christ's
love than the one that he had acclaimed as the highest. Vieira's
contradiction of two venerable Fathers of the Church and of the
Common Doctor of scholastic theology ran contrary to one of her
fundamental principles, the respect of tradition.

Juana expressed herself clearly, if hyperbolically, on the matter
of tradition. In the substance of her theology she was a child of the
Council of Trent and the Counterreformation. This is manifest even
when her formulations were out of the ordinary. In *Neptuno Alegórico*
Sor Juana explains the symbols and inscriptions of the triumphal
arch that she devised at the request of the canons of the cathedral of
Mexico City for the official inauguration of the viceroy, Tomás de la
Cerda, marquis de la Laguna, on 30 September 1680. Most of her
symbols are borrowed from Greek and Latin antiquity; a few come
from the old religion of Mexico before the Spanish conquest. Such

borrowing is not only possible but also proper, for, as she states, "We never see a very noble reality (even in the Sacred Letters) that has not been preceded by several figures that represent it as though in outline."[13] A traditional kind of exegesis since the patristic era, this typological method searches Scripture for patterns of anticipation and fulfillment, for example by looking in the Old Testament for antecedent symbols (types) that prefigure a person or event in the New Testament.

Juana enlarges this principle as she applies it to the parables, images, comparisons, and metaphors of Scripture: not only is "this way of writing approved by usage," it also finds support "in the Divine Letters" with their "metaphors and apologues." Juana goes further. She extends the typological principle to nature: "For the things that are great, Nature behaves like a clever artisan, who, in order to make his work perfect under all lights, begins by making several models and copies in which he can alter and polish what is not yet perfect, so that later the work will have all the marks of consummate perfection."

But what is to be done if no antecedent models seem to emerge from nature? Juana Inés de la Cruz solves the difficulty through the ready availability of models in myth. Thus she has recourse to Neptune and other mythological figures to celebrate adequately the glories of the new viceroy. Neptune is a pagan god, but Juana accepts the theory that pagan gods were originally men and women who were later divinized by posterity: "Most myths have their origin in authentic happenings; and those that paganism called gods were actually excellent princes, to whom they attributed divinity on account of their rare virtues, or because they were inventors" (p. 789). Such a view of mythology was not unusual; for example, Juana's friend, Don Carlos de Sigüenza y Góngora, one of the intellectual lights of New Spain, applied the principle to Aztec mythology and even theorized that Quetzalcoatl, who was seen in Aztec tradition as both a priest and a god, was originally no other than St. Thomas the apostle, missionary to the Indies.

Juana's words in this context have far-reaching implications for her theological method and conceptions:

> It seems that Nature, lacking strength and capacity, dare not draw, even in shadows, what later, by the care of Providence, came to shine in the world in its most perfect original; and thus

it allowed thought to conceive an idea in which to delineate it; for in regard to what does not fall within natural limits one may give full scope to imagination.... (P. 779.)

This raises some critical questions that Juana Inés does not face at this point. Are there no limits to theological imagination? Are there criteria for assessing images and theories? Does not the opening of theological imagination run contrary to the principle of antecedent models? Does the principle of tradition always correspond to the principle of imagination? On the one hand, the search for models looks into the past for events and persons in whose lights one may both understand the recent past as well as the present and to some extent anticipate the future; in the present, it seeks among the inferior forms of nature for images of the higher levels of being. On the other hand, the freeing of imagination opens a hypothetical window into the unknown of an indefinite future, and it allows the mind to rise into higher mysteries that have no true mirrors in experience.

The first principle has been chiefly at work in scholastic theology. The second has been used by the Christian mystics of all times. When Juana Inés espoused the theology of the immaculate conception of the Virgin Mary, she disregarded the first principle: neither St. Augustine nor St. Jerome taught this doctrine, and St. Thomas Aquinas and St. Bernard refuted it. But the second principle liberated piety and imagination from precedent. Whether she ever felt herself caught between two ideas pulling in opposite directions, Juana gives no hint of it in *Neptuno alegórico*. And in the *Carta atenagórica,* she argues against Antonio de Vieira's feats of imagination regarding the greatest finesse of Christ's love. The principle of tradition predominates in her critique; the principle of imagination shapes her eventual reconstruction.

"In finem dilexit eos": "He loved them to the end" (John 13:1). Both Vieira and Juana Inés play on the word *finis* (end), letting it suggest the fine point of "the finesses of Christ at the end of his life."[14] Sor Juana spends more time with Augustine than with Thomas or Chrysostom. In part due to the Hieronymites' devotion to the bishop of Hippo, the focus on Augustine also reflects the assumption that, once his position has been successfully defended against Vieira, the defense of Aquinas and John Chrysostom is not so difficult; for their positions are based on the same principles as Augustine's. The ideas of the three doctors of the Church on the matter at hand are cumulatively, not historically, progressive. In terms of theology one can pass smoothly from the Augustinian conception of the death of Christ as the greatest finesse of his love, to the Thomist opinion that Christ's continuous sacramental presence is the greatest finesse, and hence to the view of John Chrysostom that the greatest finesse of Christ's love is the washing of his disciples' feet. In this sequence, Thomas builds on Augustine: the death of Christ makes the eucharist possible. And the opinion attributed to John Chrysostom adds an action that attests to the humility of Christ's death and the commitment to his disciples that is at the heart of his eucharistic presence.

As read by Vieira, Augustine placed the greatest finesse of Christ in his dying, in keeping with John 15:13. To this the orator objected that absence as a result of death is a greater finesse than death itself. He argued that Christ "loved men more than his own life"; that Mary Magdalen had wept at the sepulcher, when she found him gone, but not at the cross, where she saw him dead; that Jesus expressed more feeling in the garden of Olives, when he was away from the apostles, than at the cross; that he prolonged his absence up to three days when he could have resurrected immediately; that he had anticipated his absence when he created the sacrament of the eucharist; that his death needs only one remedy, the resurrection, whereas his absence to the end of time needs an infinity of remedies in eucharistic communion. In keeping with the theology of the eucharistic sacrifice that was generally favored in the Counterreformation, Vieira understood the eucharist as a repeated sacrificial dying of Christ: Christ "subjected himself to perpetual death in order not to suffer one instant of absence" (p. 813).

Juana refutes her adversary at length as she defends the position of Augustine. From the New Testament she infers that Christ, "the Good Shepherd who gives his life for the sheep" (John 10:11), "speaks of himself and qualifies his death as his finesse." Further, finesse, being an action, has a point of origin (*terminus a quo*) and an end (*terminus ad quem*). It is like a gift that the lover buys at a certain cost and the beloved receives and uses. Yet finesse need not always accrue at both ends. The many years of service given by Jacob (a great finesse of love on his part) were of no use to Rachel. In reverse, it was a great finesse for Esther to become the queen; but her becoming queen cost Assuerus nothing. The death of Christ, however, includes both terms: it both costs a price and gains a profit, so there is a finesse of love at each end. "The Word takes flesh, and for love of us measures the immense distance from God to man; he dies, and measures the limited distance from man to death" (p. 814). "A greater wonder, but not so great a finesse," the incarnation was "the means to death, since Christ made himself man in order to die for man."

Vieira believed that Christ "buys each presence with a sacramental death." Juana reverses the perspective: Christ "buys death with presence, since he is present in order to give us his death." Further, death is a greater finesse; for "the other finesses of Christ are told but not represented, whereas his death is told, is commended, and is represented. It is therefore not only the greatest finesse, but it is the compendium of all finesses." In the death of Christ Sor Juana Inés sees a renewal of creation, now restored "to the primitive state of grace"; a renewal of the conservation of the world, as Christ feeds us with his body and blood; and a renewal of the incarnation, since, already united to his mother's flesh, he now in death "unites himself to all." Indeed, if the sacrament is not represented in the death of Christ, that is because it is itself "the representation of his death."

Having defended Augustine, Juana proceeds to attack Vieira's own arguments. Her first point is based on Scripture: it is absurd and unscriptural to say that Christ chose absence as a greater finesse, for he is never absent. "It is true that he goes away, but it is false that he is absent. Let us not waste time: we know indeed the infinity of his presences" (p. 815). The rest of her refutation is based on experience. Experience ("the natural reason") shows that the greater sorrow is the one for which one cannot weep, for which no consolation is possible. Jesus wept for Lazarus but not for Judas, although he called each one his friend; Judas brought him the greater sorrow. The "Queen of Sorrows" did not weep at the cross: "For the lesser sorrow weeps; the supreme sorrow suspends tears and does not let one weep." The Magdalen wept at her brother's tomb but not at the cross because she loved Christ more than her brother, and her pain was greater when she could not weep (p. 816).

Vieira's treatment of Thomas Aquinas and John Chrysostom follows the same lines as his critique of Augustine. To Aquinas he objects that there is greater finesse in Christ's being in the sacrament without the use of his bodily senses than in the sacramental presence as such. This fine point is established by analogy: Absalom preferred death to exile! As though the substance of such an idea were not worth her attention, Juana faults the argument on logical grounds. When Augustine speaks of Christ "sacramenting himself" (a Spanish formula that has no equivalent in English), the bishop of Hippo includes in the sacrament "the infinite sorts of finesses that are contained in this most rich exchequer of Divine Love under the accidents of bread." The proposition is generic. Vieira refutes it with a specific proposition, as he focuses on one only of the many finesses of Christ that belong to the eucharist. He makes the mistake of confusing genus with species, passing illegitimately from the one to the other.

As for St. John Chrysostom, Vieira maintains that the greater finesse does not lie in washing the disciples' feet, but in the motivation for doing so. This argument, one must admit, is rather silly. For Juana, it is as illogical as Vieira's objection to Aquinas: "there" he argued "from species to genus; here, from effect to cause" (p. 817). One should not oppose the effect to the cause, since the effect is included in the cause. Furthermore, many causes are involved in Christ's actions, not just one. St. John Chrysostom includes all the causes of the washing of feet, all the motivations of Christ, in the action itself. Furthermore, there can be no greater finesse in the motive than in the action that is inspired by it.

Plainly, Juana points out, Antonio de Vieira does not understand the meaning of the word *finesse:* "What is finesse? Is finesse, perchance, loving? Certainly not; it is the demonstrations of love: these are called finesses. These external demonstrative signs, and the actions performed by the lover, his motive being love: that is called finesse" (p. 818).

To anyone who is acquainted with medieval theology, there is nothing of the Schools in this debate. Admittedly, some lingering Scholasticism was not alien to the Spanish mind of the Counterreformation. The university of Salamanca in the sixteenth and the early seventeenth centuries had given scholastic theology its last great period. Concern for the greatest finesse of Christ, alien to the scholastic mind, is typically baroque. At the time, the basic questions raised in Catholic thought seemed to have been solved. Creative minds needed no longer deal with them; they preferred to open up new areas of research. In France, new approaches to the history of doctrine were cultivated by the Jesuit Denys Petau (1583–1652) and the Oratorian Thomassin (1619–1695). Bossuet (1627–1704), bishop of Meaux, and Fénelon (1651–1715), archbishop of Cambrai, clashed as they investigated the nature of Christian holiness and "the

maxims of the saints."[15] Spain and Portugal favored more subtle
initiatives that were more germane to the exuberance of the Iberian
baroque than to the straight lines of the French classic. Suarez (1548–
1616) introduced considerable modifications of Thomism into a
renewed, post-Tridentine Scholasticism. Other, perhaps more com-
plicated, minds pursued a different kind of scholarship: an ethereal
search for the finesses of Christ's love. This is where both Vieira and
Juana Inés belong.

Vieira's refutation of the three doctors of the Church does not
give the measure of his theology. He has simply shown that what
they take to be the greatest finesse of Christ is not so great. It is now
his turn to tell the world about the truly greatest finesse of Christ.
Juana summarizes Vieira's conclusions: "Christ did not seek a re-
sponse to his love for himself, but for men; and this was the greatest
finesse: to love without response" (p. 818). Christ told the disciples
to wash one another's feet. In saying this, he indicated that he was
not seeking their love for himself but their love for one another. Such
finesse needs no proof. It has no model anywhere: "The greatest
proof of this finesse is that it has no proof, for it is peerless."

This, however, is the Achilles' heel of Vieira's position. His
contention is unbiblical, and Juana Inés can therefore easily void it:
"There is nothing else in the Sacred Letters than examples and
precepts ordering us to love God." She marshalls instances, with
quotations and comments, from both the Old and the New Testa-
ments showing that "God is very zealous for what touches this point
of the primacy of his love" (p. 820). Vieira's attempt to place his
interpretation beyond the need for proof is a patent absurdity.

Juana Inés de la Cruz concludes that she has fulfilled the task
assigned to her by her correspondent. She apologizes for being only
"a poor woman" who raises her voice against "the author's elevated
intellect" (p. 824). The preacher may well be mortified that this
refutation comes from "an ignorant woman, in whom this kind of
study is so alien and so distant from her sex," but there have been
notable precedents in Judith and Deborah. Juana, too, can be God's
instrument if God wants "to punish with so feeble an instrument
the apparent haughtiness of this proposition: 'that no one will put
forward another equal finesse.'"

The bishop of Puebla had asked Juana Inés to go further. He
wanted to know her own opinion on the substantive question: What
is "the greatest finesse of Divine Love"? Juana Inés intends to sep-

arate her refutation of Vieira and her positive exposition of Christ's greatest finesse, for her concern is quite different from the Portuguese preacher's. Vieira was interested in the greatest finesse at the end of Christ's life; Juana Inés favors another point of view that is not, in fact, contrary to the Jesuit's opinion. Being totally different, her view cannot be logically opposed to his; it is also not a part of the argument—it is other than what needed to be said—regarding Augustine, Thomas, and John Chrysostom. Juana's own conclusion about the greatest finesse of divine love is nonpolemical.

Her answer to the bishop's question is theocentric rather than christocentric. What she sees as the greatest finesse "is a finesse that God does as God, and one that continues for ever" (p. 825). This finesse has to do with two aspects of God's generosity: God wants to give us his graces in such a way that we will profit by them; it is therefore generous on God's part not to give us any favor when we are not prepared to respond as we ought. There, precisely, lies God's finesse: "I will say that the greatest finesse of God is, in my opinion, the negative favors; that is, the favors that God does not grant us because he knows how badly we would respond" (p. 825–26). And again, "The greatest finesse of the Divine Love, in my opinion, is the favors that it does not grant because of our ingratitude" (p. 825).

That this negative gift is God's greatest finesse in Juana's theology derives from her understanding of God. Being the "infinite bounty and supreme good," God is by nature "communicative and desirous of doing good to his creatures." In other words, God is by essence self-giving. This is in fact the nature of the Supreme Good in Platonic philosophy. Incorporated in Christian theology in a line of thinking that flowed from St. Augustine in the fifth century to Richard of St. Victor in the twelfth and to St. Bonaventure in the thirteenth, the idea implied that the divine nature had to be conceived in relational terms. And this was easily related in Christian theology to the doctrine of the Trinity. Thus Juana Inés de la Cruz belongs, in her conception of God, to a well-attested tradition.

As "infinite love," God is always prepared to give us infinite goods, and as "almighty," he is always able to do so. To grant favors to humans harmonizes with the natural orientation of the divine goodness, love, and power. It follows that when we receive no divine favors, God is "repressing the torrents of his immense liberality, containing the ocean of his infinite love, and checking the course of his absolute power." And God's reason to withhold gifts is that he "places the progress of humans before his own opinion and his own nature." Admittedly, Juana's choice of words is not at its best here; *opinion* is not a proper term to mean God's designs and purposes. But what the word conveys is quite clear, for it points up the divine condescension. God waits for men and women with a kind of transcendental humility until they are ready to receive the divine gifts. He holds his gifts for us; he shapes and moderates his giving according to human capacity to receive and respond; he restrains his generosity in the measure of human sinfulness. "It is to our benefit that he does not give us his gifts when we are about to misuse them" (p. 826). Then, abstention from giving is done out of love. Not giving becomes a negative form of giving.

Juana exclaims: "Oh! Lord and my God, how slow and blind are we when we do not recognize that sort of negative gift that you give us!" (p. 827). Even God's punishment is a gift: "God punishes those whom he loves." In this light Juana reads the episode in the synagogue of Nazareth, when Jesus wished to perform miracles in his home village and among his compatriots, but they did not welcome him; he did not do what he intended, "in order not to give them the occasion to be still worse" (p. 825).

Sor Juana is not expounding here a merely theoretical conception. She insists on conclusions that have a practical effect on piety and the spiritual life: "Let us appreciate the gift that God gives us in not giving us all the gifts we want. . . . Let us give thanks and let us contemplate this beauty of Divine Love, in which reward is a gift, punishment is a gift, suspending the gifts is the greatest gift, and not indulging in finesses is the greatest finesse" (p. 826). There is every sign that Juana speaks from experience. Her conclusion is eloquent and profoundly spiritual:

> And so I judge that this is the greatest finesse that God does to men. His Majesty gives us grace to know them [the graces], to respond to them, which is a better knowledge; and the contemplation of his gifts is not found in speculative discourses, but it passes into practical attitudes, so that his negative gifts turn positive when they find in us a good disposition that breaks the dam of the pent up torrents of the divine liberality, which restrains and checks our ingratitude. (P. 827.)

Why should Juana consider the negative expression of God's love—withdrawing grace from sinful humanity for the sake of hu-

manity—to be the highest finesse of love that God can show? Grant-
ed that, as she well explains, God's negativity is profoundly positive,
one may still be puzzled by the orientation of her solution of the
problem. She searches for God's favor in God's withdrawal, for
God's presence in God's absence, for God's love in what is experi-
enced in the spiritual life as aridity or dryness.

Presumably, this solution is generated by Juana Inés de la
Cruz's primary experience of God. As she struggles with Vieira's
treatment of Augustine, her tone is not that of a detached thinker.
The whole incident may have started as a conversation in the convent
parlor, but Juana is personally involved in the debate. Her profound
convictions have been shaken by the theological legerdemains of the
Portugese Jesuit. She reacts vividly. Even though, in keeping with
the proper form of such writing in the Spanish dominions, she duly
professes "to place all that has been said under the censure of our
Holy Mother the Catholic Church," she feels the intimate conviction
that Vieira is wrong and she is right. And in fact she has no fear
that the Church would condemn her position.

Symbolic Language, Beauty, and Silence in *Neptuno alegórico*

Juana's negative point of view in the *Carta atenagórica* fits what
she writes elsewhere about knowing God. We have already drawn
attention to her recourse to symbols in *Neptuno alegórico* and to her
fidelity to tradition in her selection of symbols. The recourse to
symbols, however, is justified not only because the human mind can
detect harmonies between the different orders of nature but also
because there is no way to speak directly about God. Symbols are
necessary. But once we understand that neither is the symbol God
nor is God the symbol, it becomes obvious that symbolic language
about God is not only indirect but also negative, a point made clear
in the introductory letter to *Neptuno alegórico*.

Presented as coming from "the Metropolitan Church of Mexi-
co,"[16] this letter has every chance of having been composed by Juana:
it explains the principles on which the poet conceived the triumphal
arch in honor of the new viceroy, its inscriptions, and their expla-
nations. Juana's archway illustrates a finesse that would be intoler-
able to the modern mind: the marquis and marchioness de la Laguna
are compared to divinities. The baroque mind could, however, easily
accommodate itself to this representation; this was the time when the

king of France, Louis XIV, and the rulers of England in the Stuart dynasty claimed to reign by divine law. And they were not contradicted by their theologians.

The letter appeals to the "custom of antiquity," the antiquity in question being Egyptian. Juana shares the taste of the baroque age for everything connected with ancient Egypt. Most of her scientific knowledge comes from the works of Kircher, an Egyptophile, as they were translated into Spanish. He attributed to Hermes Trismegistus the invention of the hieroglyphs. And these he understood, not as a mode of ordinary communication, but as a code revealing secret doctrines to those who could decipher it. With some major authors of the Renaissance, such as Pico della Mirandola,[17] he believed that these esoterica included the doctrines of the Trinity and the incarnation. Juana Inés followed Kircher's speculations about hermetism and egyptology no less than his scientific researches and inventions (such as the magic lantern, the remote ancestor of our cinema). This is clear in Juana's *Primero Sueño*, with its pyramids which are Egyptian as well as Aztec (verses 341 and 400) and its magic lantern (verse 873). Not blinded by her admiration for Kircher and her interest in Egyptian lore, however, she looks upon both with humor, as when, in a sonnet addressed to the marquis de la Laguna, she hispanizes Kircher's name as *Kirkero*, and when she creates the verb *kirkerizar* (to kircherize).[18]

In *Neptuno alegórico*, the religions of ancient Egypt, Greece, and Rome provided Juana with examples of negative symbolization of God. "It was the custom of antiquity," she writes, "and most especially of the Egyptians, to worship their deities under different hieroglyphs and various forms."[19] The circle, for example, signified the infinite. The hieroglyph *eneph* designated the creator of the universe. Mythic symbols also pointed to "all invisible things," such as units of time (days, weeks, months, and so forth) and elements of nature that are difficult to represent: the god Vulcan meant fire; the goddess Juno, the air; Neptune, water; Vesta, the earth. . . .

Why this symbolic language? The ancients did not use it, Juana explains,

> because they judged that the Deity, being infinite, could narrow itself to the figure and the condition of limited quantity; but because these were things that lack all visible form—and consequently it is impossible for them to appear to the eyes of men

(who, for the most part, only admit as an object for the will what is an object for the eyes)—it was necessary to assign to them hieroglyphs that would represent them by similitude, though not with a perfect image.

The purpose of symbolization is pedagogical, while the motive is awe before the holy, "reverence for the deities, so as not to vulgarize their mysteries to the level of common and ignorant folk." For this reason, our savior spoke in parables (Matthew 13:13).

Juana's symbols for the divine point to her doctrine of God. Like a mirror, as she explains at the beginning of *Neptuno alegórico*, a symbol "reflects as in a crystal the perfections that are inaccessible in the original."[20] Her choice of a divine model for the viceroy is Neptune—in one strand of Greco-Roman mythology the god of the sea and all its islands, brother of Jupiter, son of Saturn and Cybele. Cybele was also called Isis, the Egyptian goddess; and Isis was further identified with Io, who wandered about in the shape of a sacred cow—the symbol of wisdom. She also was associated with both the moon and the earth. As *magna mater*, Great Mother, she was the mother of all other gods. This made Neptune the son of the sun and the earth. He was also the god of good counsel. His altars were located in caves within the earth, both because counsel is given in secret and because he was equated with Harpocrates, "the great god of silence" (p. 780). Juana surmises that "the ancients venerated Neptune as the god of Silence" because he is the god of the waters, "whose sons, the fish, are silent."

Juana shares a basic humanistic optimism with most authors of the Society of Jesus, which was further developed in the controversies provoked by the Jansenist movement (Jansen's *Augustinus* was published in 1640); for this reason she has no difficulty looking for religious models in the pagan world. And she can declare: "Even in the blindness of paganism one finds many points of religion" (p. 802).

Neptune was the god of the sea, and "the sea was, in the mind of the ancient, the fount of the most celebrated and famous beauties." The sea was the mother of Venus, to whom she entrusted "the Empire of beauty" (p. 803). Beauty is precisely, for Juana, a major attribute of God. This line of thought had not been generally pursued by the scholastics, but it was quite at home in the baroque period. Baroque art wanted to beautify material and human realities, so that a church building would be experienced by worshippers as a mirror of heaven.

Moreover, that Neptune is the god of silence opens a path toward the true God that is not commonly traveled in Christian theology: Silence is a divine attribute. In the early second century, St. Ignatius of Antioch spoke of the divine Word "which proceeded from silence."[21] By considering silence as divine, Juana set herself in an authentic stream of the Christian theological tradition. By the same token, she opened to the faithful the contemplation of the divine silence; silence can be a way to God. At this point her conception of God found strength in the tradition of mystical prayer. The monastic tradition, shared by the Hieronymites, had made silence a fundamental factor in community life. The liturgy had always preserved moments of silence in the midst of its celebrations. All Christian mystics had stressed the importance both of exterior silence as a personal discipline and of interior silence as an essential factor in Christian prayer and contemplation: God dwells in the silence of the soul. St. John of the Cross had made the silence of the soul's faculties one of the marks of God's interior presence and action.

The Finesses of God in Juana's Theology

Juana Inés de la Cruz's concern about the finesses of "God as God" reveals several interesting aspects of her theology.

First, while the question raised by Vieira's sermons was christological, Juana's solution of the problem is theocentric. The finesse of divine love that she considers to be the highest pertains to "God as God."[22] In other words, her Christology belongs in the traditional line of what modern authors have called a Christology from above: Christ as the Word incarnate is the Second Person of the Trinity who has taken flesh from the Virgin Mary. This theocentric focus makes Juana's thought, eclectic though it undoubtedly is, germane to that of Thomas Aquinas, who had defined theology in the first question of the *Summa theologica* in relation to God as such.

Second, Juana's conception of God is remarkably open. She is not chary of seeking light in paganism and having recourse to pagan models. That she favors Greco-Roman paganism is naturally due to her reading and her self-education in the antecedents of the Hispanic tradition. Due to both the renewal of egyptology in her time and the example of her chief mentor in the study of science, Athanasius

Kircher, she is particularly fond of the strand in Greco-Roman paganism that derived from Egyptian religion. This use of the ancient mythology of Mediterranean cultures also derived, however, from a certain tactical prudence. On the occasion of her villancicos, Juana appeals similarly to the Aztec mythology of her own nation, thus introducing the entire culture of New Spain, including its Indian myths, into the theological arena. While she celebrates the viceroys in poems and relates to the vicereines in friendship, she neglects neither the black slaves, forcibly imported from Africa and now largely christianized, nor the American Indians, with their heritage of a highly civilized culture and a complex mythology. But she can integrate the native culture of old Mexico into her thought and works because she assimilated it under the broader and more familiar umbrella of Greco-Roman myths that were better known in the ecclesiastical world, where they had been explored theologically since the Renaissance.

Third, beauty and silence as attributes of God open new theological vistas. As we have seen on several occasions, beauty is one of Juana Inés's constant referents. Juana herself has told us that she was very interested in music. She owned a number of instruments which presumably she played; and she wrote a theoretical treatise on music entitled *El caracol* (a *caracol* is a shell with a spiraling shape). In the tradition of St. Augustine's *De musica*, the scientific study of music could be philosophical and theological rather than practical; indeed, the speculative study of music as propaedeutic to the study of philosophy assured its place as one of the seven liberal arts of traditional education. Thus Juana Inés was not divided in her interests, however many and diverse: as she made clear in the *Respuesta a Sor Filotea de la Cruz*, all her investigations of profane matters were intended to lead to the high ground of theology. Since the knowledge of God starts where we are, creation in all its aspects contributes to understanding the divine purpose in this world and thereby points to the nature of God. The nature of God, in turn, has been approached in Christian theology from two sides: from the attributes of the divine nature, its energies and the qualities of its actions; and from the inner structure of divine life, the holy Trinity. On the one hand, Juana accepts, and on occasion speaks of, the chief traditional attributes of God: oneness, power, knowledge, justice, and so forth. On the other hand, the doctrine of the Trinity provides the substance of her villancicos for Christmas as well as of *Divino Narciso* and of her encomia on the Virgin Mary.

In addition, Juana's dwelling on the divine attributes of beauty and silence is a rediscovery. In the course of the Middle Ages, the intellectual aspects of theology, developed in the Schools and explained in the tractates and commentaries of the doctors, had gradually separated from the discipline's aesthetic dimensions, embodied in church buildings and their decorations, in the illuminations of books of hours, in the melodies of plainchant, in the serene organization of life within the variety of monastic orders. The whole constitutes, as St. Bonaventure had said of holy Scripture, something "like a zither, and the lower string does not create harmony by itself, but in common with the others."[23]

To the eyes of Juana Inés, the beauty of the whole is reflected in all its parts. The image of the mirror, of which she is fond, is to the point: small as it may be, the mirror reflects everything. Every mirror is like the miraculous lighthouse in the harbor of Alexandria, in which all the ships of the sea can be seen. Likewise, the divine beauty is reflected in each one of the works of God as well as in their total harmony. The discerning person perceives a tight web of correspondences in the universe. The finesses of human love throw light on those of divine love, when God creates and orders the world and its inhabitants. Absence is presence:

> I approach and I withdraw:
> who but I can find
> in the absence before my eyes
> the presence in the distance?

> Me acerco y me retiro:
> quién sino yo hallar puedo
> a la ausencia de los ojos
> la presencia de los lejos?[24]

The eye hears and the ear sees: "Oyeme con los ojos" ("Hear me with your eyes").[25] What Juana likes to say of Laura, Lysi, Filis, or Elvira—or to Fabio, Silvio, or Feliciano—she says of God and to God. The sonnets that some authors have read as containing obscure allusions to Juana de Asbaje's passionate and secret personal love life read just as well, if not better, as the overflow of Juana's intense and not so secret love of God.

Fourth, the divine attribute of silence is less exploited and explained than that of beauty; there is, after all, no direct way to speak of silence, and Juana's approach is therefore largely symbolic. She stresses, for example, an aspect of the mythological accounts of Neptune that is not usually brought to the fore: Neptune as the god of silence. Not just abstention from speech, avoidance of noise, retiring in peace, silence is also interior quiet, inner stillness, a resting "at the still point" that lies at the center of all things as they swirl. The silence of God is not negative but, rather, is the interiority of the One who is the totality in which creatures participate. To the extent that human silence is a divine gift, it is also positive, for it participates in divine silence.

One may surmise that Sor Juana Inés de la Cruz had an unusually vivid experience of the silence of God. Some of her religious poetry explicitly describes the inner struggle between grace and the self:

> While Grace wakes me up
> to raise me to the Sphere,
> I am more deeply lowered
> by the weight of my miseries . . .

> I love God and I feel in God;
> and my own will makes
> of what is relief, a cross,
> of the haven itself, a storm.

> Mientras la Gracia me excita
> por elevarme a la Esfera,
> más me abate a lo profundo
> el peso de mis miserias . . .

> Amo a Dios y siento en Dios;
> y hace mi voluntad misma
> de lo que es alivio, cruz,
> del mismo puerto, tormenta.[26]

Juana knows spiritual struggle. God's love indeed "is quality without opposites,"[27] pure quality. Yet in human experience quality does not exist in a state of purity but is always compounded with quantity. She is well aware of the resulting ambiguity of feelings, even of religious feelings. Like her beloved Teresa and like John of the Cross, Juana perceives that life is death and that there is death that is life:

> I carry with me a concern,
> so elusive that I believe
> that, though I know I feel it so much,
> yet I myself do not feel it.

> It is love; but it is such love
> as, missing what is blinded,
> has eyes that are there
> to give it more torment.

> The point is not *a quo*
> that causes the weight I see;
> the other point being the Good,
> all the pain acts as the mean . . .

> Oh! our human frailty,
> in which the purest feeling
> cannot even denude itself
> of its natural sentiment! . .

> That he respond to my love
> adds nothing; but I cannot,
> however much I wish to,
> stop my desiring him . . .

> Thus, sadly feeding
> life with poison,
> the very death that I live
> is the life of which I die.

> But courage, O heart:
> for in such sweet torment,

in the midst of whatever fate,
I protest I will not cease loving.

Traigo conmigo un cuidado,
y tan esquivo, que creo
que, aunque sé sentirlo tanto,
aun yo misma no lo siento.

Es amor; pero es amor
que, faltándole lo ciego,
los ojos que tiene, son
para darle más tormento.

El término no es *a quo*
que causa el pesar que veo:
que siendo el término el Bien,
todo el dolor es el medio . . .

¡Oh humana flaquesa nuestra,
adonde el más puro afecto
aun no sabe desnudarse
del natural sentimiento! . .

Que corresponda a mi amor
nada añade; mas no puedo
par más que lo solicito,
dejar yo de apetercerlo . . .

Así alimentando, triste,
la vida con el veneno,
la misma muerte que vivo,
es la vida con que muero.

Pero valor, corazón;
porque en tan dulce tormento,
en medio de cualquier suerte,
no dejar de amar protesto.[28]

Juana's many pieces about the absence of the beloved may be
read in this light, even when they were composed on request and

they evoke a human love that was not her own. Given the correspon-
dences that Juana sensed in the universe, her love poetry may well
compress several levels of meaning—give voice to more than intel-
lectual imagination and sensitive empathy and echo what may have
been her own experience of interior abandonment. Her admirable
sonnet about love and tears acquires new connotations when it is
read in this light:

> This afternoon, my love, when I spoke with you,
> as on your face and in your acts I saw
> that my words did not persuade you,
> I wished you would see my heart;
>
> and Love, at the rescue of my intent,
> conquered what seemed impossible;
> for in the weeping that sorrow poured out,
> it distilled my heart undone.
>
> Enough hardships, my love, enough:
> let not tyrannic ardors torment you more,
> or ugly fear destroy your quiet
>
> with dark nonsense, with vain indices,
> for you have clearly seen and touched
> my heart undone between your hands.

> Esta tarde, mi bien, cuando te hablaba,
> como en tu restro y tus acciones vía
> que con palabras no te persuadía,
> que el corazon me vieses deseaba;
>
> y Amor, que mis intentos ayudaba,
> venció lo que imposible parecía:
> pues entre el llanto, que el dolor vertía,
> el corazón deshecho destilaba.
>
> Baste ya de rigores, mi bien, baste:
> no te atormenten más celos tiranos,
> ni el vil recelo tu quietud contraste

con sombras necias, con indicios vanos,
pues ya en líquido humor viste y tocaste
mi corazón deshecho entre tus manos.[29]

In 1691 Juana Inés composed her last piece of court poetry. The next year, she wrote a dedicatory poem addressed to "the reader" of the second volume of her poems, which was about to be published in Seville. In 1692 or 1693 she gave away her books, musical instruments, scientific devices. And she entered into total silence.

6

The Silence

Most of the authors who have studied the life and works of Sor Juana Inés de la Cruz have attempted to explain why she abandoned poetry, music, and science—or at least why she decided no longer to engage in these activities of the mind, the pursuit of which she had defended and justified in the *Respuesta a Sor Filotea de la Cruz*. Spirited as it was, Juana's *Response* was not printed during her lifetime; we cannot know to what extent her defense before Manuel Fernández de Santa Cruz y Sahagún was made public. But we can be sure that the *Carta atenagórica* was certainly well known. On 10 March 1691, a Spanish priest preached about Christ's greatest finesse at the Hieronymite monastery, in Juana's own church. While he praised Juana's talents, his allocating the dignity of the greatest finesse to the hiddenness of Jesus in the sacrament was tantamount to siding with Vieira against Juana. But, having stood up to the bishop of Puebla, Juana was not likely to be silenced by a rebuke like the Spanish preacher's, so we can assume that his remarks did not play a major role in her decision to enter silence.

In her response to the bishop of Puebla, she complained of persecutions originating both outside and inside the convent. Juana Inés had been victimized by jealousy, by envy of her talents, by prejudice about the proper place of women in society, by conservative views concerning the proper cloistering of nuns and about the social function of convents, even by fear of the Inquisition. In none of the criticisms, however, is there any hint that her theology might be at fault. Indeed, Santa Cruz was so impressed by her critique of Vieira's *mandatum* sermon that he reprimanded her for spending too much time on secular literary projects and on the accumulation of merely secular scientific knowledge.

The letter of Sor Filotea de la Cruz is dated 15 November 1690 and was written after the bishop had read Juana's critique of Vieira's sermon. The letter, however, was neither included in the *Carta atena-*

górica, nor did Juana append it to the *Respuesta.* Rather, it was first printed nearly three hundred years later as an appendix to the fourth volume of Méndez Plancarte's edition of Juana's works.[1] Filotea compares Juana to an eagle, lauds the clarity of her thought, even affirms that such clarity of thought is not acquired by work and effort but must be God given. Formal in tone, the letter honors Sor Juana Inés with the title "Your Mercy." The bishop does not condemn what Juana has accomplished so far: she has done well. Nor is he against women devoting time to arts and letters, for St. Jerome had approved of such pursuits. Yet he wishes that "from now on" she would do better. She ought to imitate "St. Teresa, Nazianzen, and other saints . . . not only in style but also in choice of topics." Furthermore, the religious life is one of self-sacrifice. It is well known that Sor Juana has written out of obedience (to the demands of her patrons). "If the other religious sacrifice their will through obedience, Your Mercy makes the intellect captive, which is the most difficult and most agreeable holocaust that may be offered on the altars of religion." In the bishop's eyes, she has not, however, made the greater sacrifice: curbing her taste for profane subjects. This urging is made particularly eloquent because Filotea's praise for Juana's achievements is so great. Repeated and reformulated several times throughout the letter, the conclusion is unmistakable: "Your Mercy has spent much time in the study of philosophers and poets; this is a reason for perfecting your examples and making your books better. . . . The science that does not give light for salvation—God, who knows all, calls it foolishness."

This point Juana Inés was bound to feel profoundly: the bishop was afraid for her soul's salvation if she did not desist from profane writing, for such literature was unworthy of her religious calling. Indeed, the bishop was not the only one of this opinion. Juana's own nephew, Miguel de Torres, included in his biography of the bishop Filotea's letter to Juana Inés. This letter, he stated, had the desired effect. From that time on, the Hieronymite sister devoted herself to things spiritual; "she lived setting a good example to the nuns, and she died with clear marks of her salvation."[2] It is doubtful that the letter alone would have been sufficient to bring about Juana's renunciation to her life's work. Its first effect was to provoke an answer, the *Respuesta a Sor Filotea de la Cruz.*

The attitude of the archbishop of Mexico City may have been influential in Juana's final decision to enter silence. Only two archbishops served in Mexico City during her years in the Hieronymite convent: Don Fray Payo Enríquez de Ribera, archbishop from 1668 to 1680 and viceroy from 1673 to 1680; and Francisco de Aguiar y Seijas, archbishop from 1680 to 1698. Obviously, her relationships with them could not be as close as her friendships with the vicereines.

After Juana had become a nun she applied to Payo Enríquez de Ribera, begging him to come to the convent and confirm her. She had not received the sacrament of confirmation in her youth, as was probably not unusual for children who lived at a distance from the seat of the bishopric (the dioceses of New Spain covered large territories, and confirmation was reserved strictly to a bishop). In our day, she would certainly be confirmed before being admitted to the convent;[3] in her time and place, the discipline regulating admissions to the convent was more lax. She even put her plea for the sacrament in the form of a romance.[4] But Payo Enríquez did not visit St. Paula's monastery to confirm Juana; rather, the sacrament was administered by a visiting bishop from Honduras, Don Martín de Espinosa.[5] Is this fact relevant? Does it attest to an estrangement between the sister and the archbishop? Unlikely. One may presume that few ordinaries would have gone in person to a convent for the belated confirmation of one sister.[6]

Years later, Juana might have come into conflict with the policy of Archbishop Francisco de Aguiar y Seijas in regard to the many convents of his diocese. The archbishop liked the sisters to maintain their traditional place and remain in the background. In 1680, when Aguiar y Seijas was promoted from Michoacán to Mexico City, his arrival coincided with the performance of the comedy, *Los empeños de una casa,* that Juana had composed in honor of the new viceroy, the marquis de la Laguna. A traditionalist, the new archbishop shared the negative attitude of most churchmen of his time to the theater. We cannot be certain, however, that he held Juana's dramatic works against her. Much later, Juana petitioned him for authorization to buy her cell from the convent, a peculiar practice that was acceptable to the Hieronymites and was not unknown in other religious orders. The archbishop granted the permission, and Juana bought her cell on 9 February 1692. One may surmise, albeit with no certainty, that just about that time he was urging her to model her religious life on a more traditional pattern than that of a fashionable authoress.

Certainly, Don Francisco could not be indifferent to the extravagant titles that were bestowed on Juana Inés in the publications of her works. As early as 1681 she was called "the Mexican Phoenix of Poetry" in a collected volume for the inauguration of a new convent of Poor Clares. By 1689, with the publication of *Inundación Castálida,* she had become "the tenth Muse," the title that had been given by Plato to the great poet Sappho; in 1663, a volume of religious poems, printed in Mexico, applied the same description to the Virgin Mary.[7] In either case, the title could not be properly transferred to a living nun. In 1690, when her villancicos on St. Joseph were printed, Juana was credited with "peerless erudition and ever acute intelligence." In 1691, her friend and admirer, Carlos de Sigüenza edited a compilation of works, *Epicinios congratulatorios . . . ,* in honor of the count de Galve and the so-called victory of Barlovento. Sigüenza's expanded title specifies that the authors count among "the most cultured Mexican intellects," and his introduction to Juana's poem—the first in the collection—calls her the "Phoenix of erudition in the line of all the sciences, emulation of the most delicate intellects, immortal glory of New Spain." In 1692, for the publication in Seville of her second volume of poetry, a number of Spanish priests and writers composed various pieces in her honor that are included in the preliminaries of the book; one of them declared that she had been assisted by the divine "Numen" and inspired by the Holy Spirit. Such encomia could not be mistaken as invitations to religious humility!

All this would be extravagant, were it not part of baroque convention and were Juana not in fact a truly great poet. Like Juana Inés herself, her literary-minded contemporaries liked to play with words and symbols. But what was accepted as an artistic style did not necessarily sound pleasant to ecclesiastics who were more concerned about modesty of life in the convent than about aesthetic fashion.

The *Respuesta* contains certain hints of Sor Juana Inés's state of mind at the moment of its composition. Reflecting on the reason why the doctors of Israel sought the death of Christ, she noted that it was "because this man does many signs" (John 11:48). The *signa* of the Latin Vulgate are, generally, miracles. Juana, however, gives them the broader meaning of "noteworthy things."[8] Yet, as she remarks, such a reason "does not seem worthy of learned men, as were the pharisees." She continues:

> But the fact is that when learned men become passionate they fall into such absurd conclusions. . . . Good heavens! doing

noteworthy things is cause for death! . . . A sign? Then let him die! Noteworthy? Then let him suffer, for this is the prize for one who excels!

Juana then borrows a parable from Greco-Roman practices. The "images of the Winds and of Fame" that used to be placed on the roof of temples needed to be protected from birds. Spikes were set in them so that birds could not approach. Juana sees this as a universal law of the human condition:

> She who is elevated cannot be without spikes that transpierce her. . . . O unfortunate height, exposed to such hazards! O sign that makes you a target of envy and an object of contradiction! Any kind of eminence, be it in dignity, in nobility, in wealth, in beauty, in knowledge, suffers this anxiety; but the one that feels it the most is that of the intellect.

Two reasons are given for this fate of intellectual achievement. First, unlike wealth and power, intelligence does not defend itself, "for, the greater it is, the more modest and patient is it." Second, "superiority in intellect is superiority in being." Their intellect makes angels ontologically superior to human beings, and human beings superior to animals. As no human being wishes to be inferior in being to another, no one will admit that another is more intelligent (p. 836).

In context, these remarks, as we saw in the previous chapter, lead to a reflection on the passion of Christ. We cannot exclude the possibility that Sor Juana Inés may have seen herself and her situation in that light. For twenty years, along with Don Carlos de Sigüenza y Góngora, she had occupied the peak of intellectual and literary life in New Spain. Several poems testify that she must have felt the hazards of such a position. The following sonnet is most explicit:

> In persecuting me, World, what is your point?
> Where is my offense, when I only wish
> to put beauties in my intellect,
> not my intellect in beauties?
>
> I do not value treasures or wealth;
> it always gives me more pleasure

to put wealth in my thought
than my thought in wealth.

I do not value beauty that, vanquished,
has been left politely by the years,
nor does perfidious wealth please me,

as I hold it better, in my verities,
to waste the vanities of life
than to waste life in vanities.

En perseguirme, Mundo, qué interesas?
En qué te ofendo, cuando sólo intento
poner bellezas en mi entendimiento,
y no mi entendimiento en las bellezas?

Yo no estimo tesoros ni riquezas;
y así, siempre me causa más contento
poner riquezas en mi pensamiento,
que mi pensamiento en las riquezas.

Y no estimo hermosura que, vencida,
es despojo civil de las edades,
ni riqueza me agrada fementida,

teniendo por mejor, en mis verdades,
consumir vanidades de la vida
que consumir la vida en vanidades.[9]

In this poem and in several others Sor Juana Inés opens a
window into her soul. She has a profound sense of the two dimen-
sions of life: divine grace and human sin. As she writes, "While
Grace excites me / to raise me to the Sphere, / I am drawn into the
depths / by the weight of my miseries."[10] Aware of the way to God,
she also knows that, as St. John of the Cross had taught, this way is
no way. In the following envoy she imagines her patron St. Jerome
as he meditates:

Following a silent Bugle
on the path that is no path,
to wise up to unwisdom,
seeking an end without end.

Siguiendo un mudo Clarín
por camino y sin camino,
por atinar, desatino,
a buscar un fin sin fin.[11]

These four lines recur separately as the end of the four stanzas of the poem. Juana does not simply play with the paradoxical contrasts of the silent bugle, the pathless path, the wisdom that is unwisdom, the end without end. She uses these images like a Zen master, hinting at an ineffable point, a point that she makes explicit in the *Respuesta:* "Gains in intellect are gains in being."[12] This principle Juana attributes to "Gracián," that is, Baltasar Gracián, S. J. (1601–1658), the theoretician of conceptism, whose *Art of Wit and Ingenuity* (1648) had considerable influence. That intellect and being belong together corresponds to the most profound inclination of the baroque mind. Thought and being are one. Since language expresses thought, language and being also are one. It follows that words and their use often suggest more than what they say explicitly. By dressing up the media it employs, art changes the experience of the visible into the experience of the invisible. What is seen and heard in this world opens a gate into another world. The baroque church, modeled on the heavenly Church, is the passageway to heaven.

A time may come, however, when speech becomes hindrance, when one no longer wishes to return to the visible. Then one is so caught up by the ineffable that silence offers the only open way, a way that is no way. Here, too, Jerome is Juana's model:

He travels to that City
where his spirit dwells
with an ardent Charity;
although the path is unknown,
God is the way indeed.

Camina a aquella Ciudad
donde su espíritu mora
con ardiente Caridad;
que aunque el camino se ignora,
Dios es vía de verdad.[13]

One may then say, with the Jerome of Juana's poem, that "the limit of my love / is the One without limit."

Earlier in her poetic career, Sor Juana Inés had written about the love of God. God, she declared, is the "sweet Lover of the soul, / sovereign Good, to which I aspire . . . / the Divine Magnet in which I adore."[14] This poem celebrates holy communion:

Today in loving union
it has seemed to your affection
that if you are not in me
it is not much to be with me.

———————

Hoy que en unión amorosa
pareció a vuestro cariño,
que si no estabais en mí,
era poco estar conmigo.

Yet, since before God all hearts are open, why sacramental communion? The poet puts this question in baroque terms:

Today, so as to examine
the love with which I serve you,
into my heart in person
you have yourself entered.

I ask: Is it love or suspicion
such a careful scrutiny?

———————

Hoy que para examinar
el afecto con que os sirvo,
al corazón en persona
habeis entrado Vos mismo.

Pregunto: Es amor o celos
tan cuidadoso scrutinio?

The obscurity of the human heart is no match for "the Divine Lynx,"
who sees all things everywhere:

In one intuition you hold
the presence in your register
of the infinite past
and of the finite present.

———————————

Con una intuición, presente
tenéis, en vuestro registro,
el infinito pasado
hasta el presente finito.

God has no need to enter the heart by communion in order to know
what is in it, Juana concludes, "Therefore it is love, not suspicion, /
that in You I see."

This is typical of the piety that pervades Juana's writings. The
conventions of the baroque imagination highlight a theological and
spiritual dilemma that was well known to the Scholastics: on the one
hand, God cannot be imagined, or thought of, or judged on a human
model; but on the other hand, we have no other vantage point than
human experience from which to imagine, or think of, or judge,
God. God's love is not human love; suspicion has no part in it, and
not by suspicion does God act in relation to creation and humanity.
Neither does the eucharistic presence somehow correct the incar-
nation, or the incarnation correct the Divinity, as though God,
through them, would come to discover what is not already seen by
the divine eyes.

Aware of the human condition, Juana knows that the only ob-
stacles to God are human will and freedom. She feels "the weight of
my miseries."[15] She leans in opposite directions:

I love and I feel in God:
and my very will makes
what is relief a cross,
the very haven, a storm.

———————————

Amo a Dios y siento en Dios:
y hace mi voluntad mesma
de lo que es alivio, cruz,
del mismo puerto, tormenta.

The awareness of such a duality lies of course at the heart of Martin Luther's concept of justification by faith alone.[16] Sor Juana Inés de la Cruz reached a point where the Counterreformation, anti-Lutheran as it wished to be, actually experienced and expressed Luther's insight, albeit in the new and different language of the baroque.

Seen on this background, Juana's selection of Neptune, "the god of Silence," for the triumphal arch erected at the inauguration of the marquis de la Laguna as viceroy of New Spain makes perfect sense. The silence of God is pregnant with meaning. And if silence is a divine attribute, participation in God implies sharing in the divine silence. As Luther, among others, had underlined, God is *Deus absconditus,* the "hidden God."[17] Precisely, when Juana Inés was searching for Christ's greatest finesse of love, she could not be fully satisfied with the positive determinations of Augustine, Thomas Aquinas, John Chrysostom, or Antonio de Vieira: the highest finesse is not what God does, whether in the death of Christ, or through the eucharistic presence, or at the washing of feet, or in inviting us to respond to his love by loving our neighbor. The highest finesse is what God does *not* do when we would spurn his graciousness and distort or refuse his gifts: at that moment, God's love is silence, and in that silence God is present.

Whatever incidental reasons for Sor Juan Inés de la Cruz may have had for putting her pen aside, for giving away her books and instruments, for no longer holding intellectual conversations in the parlor, she had long seen from afar a gate that opens on the silence of God. When she felt ready, she pushed the gate and entered. She did not gradually take her leave from her studies and writing, but, rather, she abruptly left them behind.

Juana Inés was at the height of her fame and powers when she chose silence. In fact, she gave us a hint in her last two poems that she was not giving up out of desperation. Before looking at these poems, however, we need to face an objection. At some time in the earlier part of her career, Juana composed two sonnets about hope that seem ambiguous enough to be also about despair. In the first, she addresses herself to the "long sickness of Hope"[18] that keeps her "tired years" as though in balance "on the needle between profits and frauds"; the "mistakes" of Hope do not stop "despair or trust." Indeed, Hope has been called a "murderess"; and this title is not unfair, for

> you keep in suspense the aspiring soul;
>
> and between bad and good fortune,
> you do not do so to prolong life
> but to bring in a slower death.

————————

> que suspendes el alma entretenida;
>
> y entre la infausta o la felice suerte,
> no lo haces tú por conservar la vida
> sino por dar más dilatada muerte.

The second sonnet is striking in its stark, dark beauty:

> Green fascination of human life,
> mad Hope, golden frenzy,
> confused dream of the awake,
> as of dreams, of treasures void;
>
> soul of the world, luxuriant old age,
> decrepit imagined greenness;
> the expected today of the happy,
> of the unhappy the tomorrow;
>
> let them follow your shadow in search of your day,
> those who, with green glass for spectacles,
> see all colored as they wish;
>
> but I, wiser in my fortune,
> hold my two eyes in my two hands
> and only what I touch I see.

————————

Verde embeleso de la vida humana,
loca Esperanze, frenesí dorado,
sueño de los despiertos intricado,
como de sueños, de tesoros vana;

alma del mundo, senectud lozana,
decrépito verdor imaginado;
el hoy de los dichosos esperado
y de los desdichados el mañana;

sigan tu sombra en busca de tu día
los que, con verdes vidrios por anteojos,
todo lo ven pintado a su deseo;

que yo, más cuerda en mi fortuna,
tengo en entrambas manos ambos ojos
y solamente lo que toco veo.[19]

Both poems are very personal. Quite possibly at some time or other Sor Juana Inés, deeply feeling the misunderstandings that she sensed around her, inside and outside the convent, touched the bottom of despair. Writing about it may have been good spiritual therapy: Juana Inés is never afraid of looking at reality. Furthermore, one cannot but be struck by the preoccupation with death in some other sonnets. Of a portrait of herself writes Sor Juana: "it is a corpse, dust, darkness, nothing."[20] The sight of a rose brings to her mind the oneness of "joyful cradle and sad burial"; and she speaks to the rose, "who with learned death and foolish life, / cause deceit in your life and teaching in your death."[21] From the rose, too, the beautiful woman that Juana de Asbaje undoubtedly is learns "that it is good to die beautiful / and not see the outrage of old age."[22] The religious with solemn vows feels sharply the risk of her chosen life: if one knew the dangers of the sea, one would never embark. Yet, evoking once more the myth of Phaëthon, she claims that a great soul, wishing to lead the carriage of the sun ("the fast chariot bathed in light"), "would do it all, and would not take only / a state that has to be for the whole life."[23] In spite of what she dreams of and would like, Juana knows that the chariot of the sun is not hers to lead.

Against such a backdrop, the two sonnets on hope acquire a meaning beyond the ambiguity of their images: hope dwells in the balance between two extremes. Juana's view approaches and suggests the classical ideals of moderation and self-control that characterize much of ancient Greek and Roman philosophy but her perspective is also profoundly Christian. When she writes of holding "her two eyes in her two hands" and of seeing only what she touches, Juana echoes the beginning of the first Epistle of John: "It was there from the beginning; we have heard it; we have seen it with our own eyes; we looked upon it and felt it with our own hands; and it is of this we tell" (1 John 1:1). Real and realistic, faith sees and touches both the Word and the world. Juana the woman wishes to die young and beautiful. Juana the nun chooses to embark on the sea with all its dangers. Juana the poet enters silence at the acme of her fame. She can do so because her eyes are in her hands. She has seen and touched the glory.

Juana's penultimate poem was composed to honor the viceroy, count de Galve, after his victory over the French forces in Hispaniola, the island of Haiti and Santo Domingo. This battle took place on 21 January 1691, at a spot named la Limonada. The French were vastly outnumbered by the twenty-six hundred Mexican soldiers that the viceroy had sent to reinforce the six hundred Spanish military already on the island. The French governor, Coussy, was killed in the battle, and his badly mauled force withdrew into the mountains of Haiti, where the Spanish army, itself in disarray, did not pursue. This incident ended the French occupation of Santo Domingo, which returned to the Spanish dominion. The viceroy, Gaspar de Sandoval Cerda Silva y Mendoza, count de Galve, had been ordered to recover Santo Domingo. To transport the Mexican reinforcements, he had used the five ships and one frigate that constituted the Armada de Barlovento, the fleet of the Windward Islands.[24]

The victory had little practical effect in Mexico, which was entering a period of catastophes. In June of the same year, the capital and the surrounding countryside were devastated by heavy rains and floods. The rains were followed by a blight that destroyed the crops of wheat and corn. Furthermore, on 23 August, a total eclipse of the sun spread terror among the Indians and other segments of the population. One year later, on 7 and 8 June 1692, desperate rioters set fire to several official buildings, including the viceregal palace. Heavy repression followed. Then when all the turmoil seemed to settle down, the population was decimated by the plague. Meanwhile, the security of the Spanish dominions in the Caribbean and in Mexico itself was threatened by both French and English enterprises.

One cannot rule out that these episodes and the general gloom of the period affected Juana Inés, who was friendly with the viceroy and vicereine, yet, as her villancicos show, was also emotionally close to the Indians and the poor. Her last writings make no allusions to such events, however, with the one exception of the battle of Barlovento.

News of the victory reached the capital of New Spain on 14 March 1691. Carlos de Sigüenza y Góngora, who was often consulted on scientific and other matters by the count de Galve, wrote a two-volume history of the war (one volume for the decisive battle on land, the other for the events at sea). To honor the viceroy's victory, he also organized a public homage, which took the form of a publication to which a number of authors contributed, among them Juana Inés. Don Carlos gave her the singular privilege of placing her poem first in the anthology. In Juana's poem, the episode has become a major naval battle. The ships are "white swans on the Western Sea." They well deserve their name, as they have mastered the winds (*Barlovento,* "Windward," that is, "against the wind"). A "winged Deity," Victory makes the "two distant poles one" under the "double Crown" of Castile and Aragon.

In form and style this last courtly poem of Juana's, of 142 lines, closely resembles *First Dream.* Allusions to Hippocrene at the beginning and to Mount Helicon at the end set it in a mythological framework. Two fountains on Mount Helicon, in the Greek province of Boeotia, were sacred to the Muses; one of them was called Hippocrene ("the horses' fountain"). Juana presents the viceroy's nobility. Then she builds up the poem to the point where, facing "Gallic arrogance," the Armada meets the enemy and wins. Juana's ascent to this point takes the form of a complaint about the insuperable difficulty of speaking of the ineffable. Granted the convention that the viceroy, who represents of course the Spanish monarchy, seems to be endowed with divine power, Juana Inés uses this device to speak of the shortcomings of human thought and speech before the divine.

Writing is a parturition in the mind. The poet compares it to a cloud, full of water, "perspiring the thick rains of its agony,"[25] and to the halting speech of the oracle at Delphi, when the people consulted Apollo through the Sybil, who was,

as though shaken by the high Numen,
yet virgin, pregnant
with divine concepts,
the young Pythia
of Delphi,
her mind inflamed. . . .

———————

O como de alto Numen agitada
la, aunque virgen, preñada
de conceptos divinos,
Pitonisa doncella
de Delfios, encendida,
inflamada la mente. . . .

Likewise,

. . . the human heart
—however cheerful, however, suave—
close to the divine flame
comes; and, uncontained,
sallies forth not only in hasty words
from the throat's narrow channel,
but, seeking ways of expression,
wishes to make, with wanton acts,
all limbs into tongues
at the service of such great wealth.

———————

. . . el humano pecho
—aunque gustoso sea, aunque süave—
a ardor divino estrecho
viene; y el que no cabe,
no sólo en voces sale atropelladas
del angosto arcaduz de la garganta,
pero, buscando de explicarse modos,
lenguas los miembros todos
quiere hacer, con acciones desmandadas,
que a copia sirven tanta.

These words may well be the key to the mind of Sor Juana Inés de
la Cruz as she is about to enter silence: the tongue is not enough;
words no longer suffice; there is too much wealth for speech. Now,
at last, through "wanton acts" she should give glory. As, practically
for the last time, she gives free rein to her taste for baroque poetry,
Juana Inés gives notice of her knowledge of another way that is not
a way of words, but of action.

Juana's other late work we owe to a request from Marchioness
Lysi, who was about to have a second volume of Juana's works
published. This was issued in 1692, and the dedication cannot be of
a much earlier date than the publication itself. Some four years had
passed since the marquis and marchioness de la Laguna left New
Spain for their home country. Perhaps there was a regular corre-
spondence between the marchioness and the nun and all such writing
has been lost. What remains is the romance of sixteen quatrains,
addressed to "my reader."[26]

Essentially, Juana invites her reader to choose freely between
liking and condemning the verses that she has "consecrated to his
pleasure." She herself holds that "the only good that is in them /
is that I know them to be bad." Her verses are of varied kinds, some
of which "so slay the meaning / that the word is a corpse." But they
were composed, if this is an excuse, "in the short space / left to
leisure by / the requirements of my state." Moreover, if they have
come "to light, it is only / in obedience to mandate." The tone
remains typically baroque; the meaning, purposely ambiguous. The
poet claims not to care what effect her verse will have: "either it
pleases you / or it does not please you"; in either case she will not
interfere. "There is nothing freer than / the human intellect; / since
God does it no violence, / why should I do it violence?" The last
quatrain formulates Juana's farewell:

And *a Dios*, this is no more than
to show you the cloth;
if you do not like the piece,
do not untie the parcel.

Y a Dios, que esto no es más de
darte la muestra del paño:
so no te agrada la pieza,
no desenvuelvas el fardo.

(P. 4.)

Juana's biographer, the Spanish Jesuit Diego Calleja, reports
that in the following year, 1693, she rid herself of her books and her
musical and scientific instruments.

- February 1694: Juana wrote a few lines, the last one in her
  own blood, reendorsing her religious profession and vows and
  promising "to believe and defend" the immaculate concep-
  tion of the Virgin Mary "for the love of her and of her Son."[27]
- 17 February 1694: Juana solemnly reiterated her vow to de-
  fend the immaculate conception of Mary.[28]
- 5 March 1694: Juana once more repeated this vow, and she
  signed the statement in her own blood.[29]

Such are, I presume, the "wanton acts" that Juana had foreseen in
her encomium of the count de Galve after the victory of Barlovento.
Through them she cried out with all her soul what she no longer said
through poetry. The great silence into which she entered was the
pregnant silence of action.

In her deeds during the last years of her life, Sor Juana Inés de
la Cruz was, no less than in her literary career, a child of the baroque
age and imagination. The vow that she signed with her blood was
taken, precisely in the seventeenth century, by innumerable confra-
ternities of the immaculate conception that flourished in the cities of
Spain. It was taken in 1617 by the universities of Granada, Alcala,
Baeza, Santiago, Toledo, and Saragossa; in 1618 by the university
of Salamanca, in 1619 by the university of Huesca; in 1646 by King
John IV of Portugal. The form of Sor Juana's self-renunciation and
of her consecration to the mother of God was borrowed from the
accepted piety of her times. What she abandoned was unique to
herself.

- 17 April 1694: Some time during the early months of 1694,
  Juana cared for some of her religious sisters who had fallen
  sick with the plague that was rampant in the city. She herself
  caught the disease and died.

7

The Theology of Beauty

One can learn a good deal from the theology of Sor Juana Inés de la Cruz in a number of areas. The modern mentality may particularly appreciate her insistence on the intellectual and spiritual equality of the sexes and its consequences for the social order of both the secular world and the Church. Presumably Juana does not herself draw all the logical implications of the fundamental idea that "sex is no essence in the intellect," that, as she writes to the marchioness de la Laguna, "souls / ignore both distance and sex."[1] She affirms the right of women to study, and to study theology; but she does not demand the right to teach. If she anticipates some aspects of women's emancipation, the question of the ordination of women does not come up. And she seems to have no basic problem about the subordinate place of religious women in the Church's structure. A number of conventions that would be questioned today she takes for granted. Juana is by no means a revolutionary.

It is of course conceivable that in some obscure way Juana was aware of these more questionable aspects of the feminine condition in her day and age. At any rate, her statements on sexuality have an undeniable theological dimension, for they directly affect the doctrine of creation. They suggest a certain relationship between the orders of creation and of the incarnation. This is hinted at in a verse that has been widely misinterpreted. A "gentleman from Peru," who was traveling in New Spain and who presumably had visited Juana in the convent, sent her a poem in which he wished that she would be changed into a man. She responded with two romances. In the second (n. 50), she reveals his identity as the count de la Granja. In the first (n. 48), she tackles the more basic question of her own identity:

> I am no expert in those things;
> I only know that I came here

so that, if I am female,
no one could verify it . . .

Therefore it is not well taken
that I be viewed as female,
since I am not a female who
could serve anyone as female;

I only know that my body,
not leaning to either side,
is neutral or abstract, in that
it only encloses my soul.

Yo no entiende de esas cosas;
sólo sé que aquí me vine
porque, si es que soy mujer,
ninguno lo verifique . . .

Con que a mí ni es bien mirado
que como a mujer me miren,
pues no soy mujer que a alguno
de mujer pueda servirle;

y sólo sé que mi cuerpo,
sin que a uno u otro se incline,
es neutro, o abstracto, cuanto
sólo el Alma deposite.[2]

The Platonist Tradition

This is of course a statement about Juana's self-understanding;
nevertheless, it reveals more about her conception of her vocation to
the religious life than it does about her experience of sexuality. Philo-
sophically, Juana Inés is much more inclined to a Platonic than to
an Aristotelian anthropology. As she shows in *Primero sueño,* she is
well acquainted with both traditions, and she is eager to treat them
as epistemological markers and to try them as ways of cognition.
When it comes, however, to a basic understanding of the self, she
squarely chooses Platonism. Juana defines herself by reference to her

soul, not to her body. Female in her body, she is simply and totally human in her soul. This had been, in substance, St. Augustine's anthropology.

Now there is a constant characteristic of Platonism: it always focuses attention on beauty. This is true of Plato's dialogues as well as of Plotinus's *Enneads*. For both philosophers, the elevation of the soul to God begins with the contemplation of earthly beauty, whence the soul ascends progressively to spiritual beauty, arriving finally at the beauty of the One who is also the Good and the Beautiful. In Christian theology, the traditions that have been more indebted to Plato than to Aristotle have had no difficulty integrating the notion and the experience of beauty into their theology.

One of the early writings of Augustine was a treatise on beauty, *De pulchro et apto* (*On the Beautiful and the Fitting*). This treatise has been lost, but Augustine mentions in the *Confessions* (397/401) that it made a distinction between what is beautiful in itself (*pulchrum*) and what is rendered beautiful by its harmonious setting in a wider context (*aptum*).[3] Augustine also wrote a treatise on order (*De ordine*, 386) and one on music (*De musica*, c. 387/390), both of which deal with aspects of the beautiful. The *Confessions* contain a famous passage in which Augustine expresses his longing for the beauty of God: "Too late have I loved you, Beauty so old and so new."[4] God's beauty is utterly attractive and, when perceived, totally satisfying. This desire for the beauty of God is related to Augustine's basic division of reality in two realms: the things that are to be used (*uti*); and the things that are to be enjoyed (*frui*).[5] Utility is a matter of technique; fruition is reached through contemplation. As supremely enjoyable Being, God alone can be contemplated as totally beautiful. Augustine could already have affirmed this when he was enthralled by "the books of the Platonicians" during his journey from Manichaeism to Christianity. As a Christian, he learned something more: God has brought his beauty near to us through his Word, especially in the incarnation; by grace, the beauty of Christ can be shared by the faithful. Therefore, Augustine's long inquiry into the nature of the City of God (413 to 426) could properly end on a discussion of the beauty of Christ and of the risen bodies of the saints.[6]

As has been shown by Hans Urs von Balthasar, the perception of the glory of God has inspired the Christian search for beauty. The history of Christian theology can be seen as a history of attempts to express the glory of God in successive styles and theories of beauty.[7]

Although Juana Inés is not mentioned by Urs von Balthasar, she deserves a prominent place among those who have seen the divine beauty in creation.

Juana Inés could have been acquainted with many instances of a theological interest in beauty. There was the example of the theologians who were also poets. Many theologians of the past, who devoted all their intellectual attention to the contemplation of being, oneness, and goodness in God, also pursued beauty, though as a sideline, in the occasional poetry that they wrote. From St. Gregory Nazianzen (327–390) in Greek and Boethius (c. 480–524) in Latin to St. Thomas Aquinas, through innumerable patristic and medieval authors, poetry expressed the sense of beauty that is inseparable from the perception of the divine. More importantly for understanding Juana, there were the poets who were also theologians, for instance— near in time to Juana Inés and in her own mother tongue, Luis de León and St. John of the Cross. With John of the Cross, the sense of the beauty of God is at the center, as appears in the *Spiritual Canticle* (stanza 35 in version A, stanza 36 in version B): "Let us rejoice , Beloved, / and let us go see ourselves in your beauty." At the same time a poet, a mystic, and a theologian, the Mystical Doctor gave a major place to the beauty of God both in his poems and in his theological commentaries.

Also among the mystics were those without systematic theological training. This was the background of most of the many women mystics who were influential in spirituality from the twelfth to the fifteenth centuries. St. Hildegard of Bingen (1109–1179) and St. Gertrude of Helfta (1256–1302) are the most well known,[8] but there were many others. More concerned with living the mystery of Christ and the Spirit than with thinking about it, they nonetheless had to formulate their insights in order to communicate them, making full use of imagination and inventing poetic or visionary theologies.

In the heyday of the Renaisance, which was closer than the Middle Ages to the baroque mind, Nicolas of Cusa (1401–1464), himself a distinguished philosopher and theologian, had recommended focusing attention on a picture of the holy face of Jesus as the initial step toward Christian contemplation;[9] the beauty of the picture acted like the mantras of Eastern religions, opening a gate to the garden of spiritual beauty. In the Orthodox church, a nonverbal theology—expressed, taught, and experienced through the icons— had reached official status. Although they never became similarly official, the Gothic art and architecture of the West were justified theologically, in the line of the great mystics and theologians of St. Victor, Hugh (1096–1140) and Richard (1104–1173), by the builder of the first Gothic church, Suger (c. 1081–1151), the abbot of St. Denys. Following St. Bernard's conception of spiritual aesthetics, a form of Gothic art that was bare of ornamentation came to characterize the constructions of the Cistercian order. In my own investigation of theological methodology, I have upheld the value of theologies that use languages and media other than the systematic or the academic.[10]

Certainly Juana Inés never saw a purely Gothic church. And to what extent she was acquainted with poets and mystics outside the Spanish and Latin languages is impossible to ascertain. Nevertheless, she probably was familiar with at least a few instances of the theological concern for beauty (the works of St. John of the Cross, St. Teresa, and perhaps, St. Bernard, for example). More importantly, her own work places her squarely within this long tradition.

Theology of Beauty

A theology of beauty turns around three related concepts. First there is an understanding of *beauty* itself. Second, since beauty, seen in a theological perspective, is spiritual, even when also physical, there is a certain understanding of what constitutes the relation between beauty and grace; for Juana Inés de la Cruz, this relation is identical with *love*. Third, there is a global perception of what beauty ultimately reveals, namely the *glory* of God, manifested in his creation.

Even the scholastic tradition that Juana Inés knew well could offer paradigms for an understanding of beauty. When related to ordinary human experience through the sense organs, the perception of beauty was commonly compared by theologians to hearing and to seeing. By way of hearing, beauty is associated with music. "The whole of Scripture," St. Bonaventure had written, "is like a zither, and the lower string does not create harmony by itself, but in common with the others."[11] By way of sight, beauty evokes architecture, painting, and sculpture. The description of the Temple in Ezechiel chapters 40–43 and of the walls of the New Jerusalem in Revelation 21:10–23 open biblical vistas in this direction. The traditional liturgy for the dedication of a church enlivens this approach to spiritual and divine beauty. Both as church ornamentation and as miniature illumination, painting had been employed by mystical visionaries, such as Hildegard and Julian of Norwich (who wrote c. 1373–1393, died after 1416). Sculpture, universally present in Gothic art, offered an obvious model for the spiritual denudation of the soul in search of God, as the sculptor chips away at the wood or the stone in order to bring out the latent image that has been haunting him.

The pursuit of beauty in the arts raised two basic problems in classical theology. The first related to the question whether beauty is, along with oneness, truth, and goodness, one of the inseparable dimensions of being that are called the *transcendentals*. The problem of transcendental qualities that are inherent in being as such had been mooted in medieval theology by Philip the Chancellor (d. 1236) in his *Summa de bono* and was discussed by the Scholastics through the thirteenth century. As transcendental qualities, oneness, truth, goodness, and beauty are no more definable than being itself. As coextensive to being, they are present in everything that God is and creates. That beauty is considered an attribute of God is patent in the scholastic theologies that argue from *convenientia* to *veritas*, from the harmony of doctrines to their truth. In fact, all the classical theologies were able to accommodate the fourth transcendental. While the question was philosophical, the doctrine of the Trinity was expected to throw light on it, as theologians tried to relate the transcendentals to the three Persons. But there was a specifically Christian difficulty, if the doctrine of the three Persons of God had to accommodate the existence of four transcendental qualities of the divine Being. The more common solution appropriates the first three as attributes to the three Persons: oneness to the Father, truth to the Word, goodness to the Spirit. Beauty may then be conceived as an attribute that is not appropriated to one Person but is affirmed jointly of the three. Or, beauty may be identified with one of the other transcendentals; goodness and truth have been the main choices here. Yet even if this identification may be philosophically acceptable, it is not artistically satisfactory. For if beauty is considered a general attribute of God, it is not distinguishable from other general attributes. And if seen as a secondary aspect of goodness or truth, beauty is the quality of a quality, and as such it becomes an abstraction. But when beauty is really perceived, it is always perceived as a quality of concrete being; it is not abstract, but has real existence.

The second problem concerned links between bodily and spiritual beauty. The existence of such links had always been taken for granted. It was essential, for example, for the renewal of the arts in the Renaissance. It was in harmony with an old idea that had been prevalent in the medieval conception and practice of church architecture and the decorative arts. The ideal proportions between parts that are conducive to the perception of the beauty of the whole are already set by the Creator in the form of the human body. The golden number of medieval architects ($\phi = 1.618$) corresponds to a proportion perceived in the human body.[12] The human microcosm is an effective symbol of the macrocosm, the entire cosmos of the created universe. There was also a trend of theological thought, beginning with Augustine in the West and Pseudo-Dionysius in the East, that took the "light" of Genesis 1:3 as the spiritual principle of the created beauty inscribed in the actual structure of the physical world with the creation of the "luminaries" of Genesis 1:14, the sun, the moon and the stars. Accordingly, in much of medieval theology, light is the central symbol for the transcendental and actual beauty of creaturely beings. The light as such is not seen; one only sees lighted objects. Likewise, it is not beauty that is seen, but a beautiful object. Given Aristotle's philosophy of hylomorphism, many authors understood beauty to be given to a created entity along with its form. And since the creed of Nicaea-Constantinople included the statement that the divine Word is *lumen de lumine*, "light from light," it was easy to use light further as a symbol for the divine beauty and for the radiation of the divine glory.

St. Bonaventure had made considerable use of the symbol of light in his theological approach to beauty. Always sober in his recourse to physical symbols, St. Thomas had simply made beauty a transcendental attribute of *ens commune*, the abstract "common being" that comes to concrete existence in individual created realities. At the concrete level of existence, "beauty" is experienced, noted Thomas in the *Summa theologica,* as "what is pleasing to the eyes."[13] It pertains to the order of the formal cause. As to bodily beauty, it resides, as Augustine had said, in "the proportion of the parts, along with some pleasant color."[14] Whatever the basic approach (beauty as form and light, or beauty as being), there remains the questions: Why is something pleasing to the eye? What is the aspect of concrete being that makes it beautiful? Here, everybody agreed that beauty has something to do with proportions.[15] The relationships of parts to one another and to the whole result, when they are properly ordered, in a perception of consonance and harmony. Beauty consists in "the right proportion." At the universal level, beauty is the cosmic order. At the individual level, it is both the internal order of a thing and its orderly place in the cosmos.

The baroque age did not depart either from the fundamental conviction that there is beauty in creation, that beauty is manifested as light, or from the logical inference that discernment of this beauty and this light opens a way to the hidden beauty of God. In fact, the typical baroque church is entirely suffused with light. The principles relating to light and beauty, to proportion and proportionality, were expounded and expanded in the books of Juana's intellectual mentor, Athanasius Kircher, notably in his *Musurgia Universalis* (1650),[16] an investigation, in two volumes, of musical harmony, taken as the key to a philosophy of the universe. The very title referred to "the great art of consonance and dissonance." And the philosophy that was envisaged by the author included, still according to the title, "philology, mathematics, physics, mechanics, medicine, politics, metaphysics, and theology." Extended to science, philosophy, and theology, the musical art of consonance becomes an art of combinations, that is, a discernment of correspondences. It is based on the principle of universal analogy and conveniently symbolized in numbers.

Despite her recourse to philosophy in *Primero sueño*, Juana Inés de la Cruz is not primarily inclined to the abstractions of philosophy or mathematics. In science it is physics that keeps her interest. Whatever she knows of the previous aesthetic tradition, she does not retain the philosophical discussions about the four transcendentals. But she fully shares the conclusion that beauty resides in harmony and is symbolized well by light. In fact she willingly admits that she practices the art of discerning relations and proportions, as when, with a humorous touch, she writes to the "gentleman from Peru":

> If the *Combinatoria*
> in which at time I *kircherize*,
> is not mistaken in counting
> or wrong in its tally. . . .

Pues si la Combinatoria
en que a veces *kirkerizo*,

en el cálculo no engaña
y no yerra en el guarismo. . . . [17]

This is a typically Augustinian principle: the science of numbers is at the service of music and thereby of beauty.

Undoubtedly, beauty is a major concern of Juana's thought. Her vocabulary in this area is varied and abundant. She uses all the Spanish terms that denote and connote the notion of beauty. *Hermosura* is the most frequent, but *beldad* and *belleza* are far from rare. *Primor* occurs also in the sense of beauty. Juana refers abundantly to human beauty in her poetic compositions. Indeed, she is not chary of describing Lysi's bodily beauty, which, in her eyes, reflects the marchioness's spiritual beauty. In an image, the beauty of the original is at the same time present and absent. The person who sees her picture, Juana tells Lysi, "will boldly contemplate you / seeing you without you."[18] Yet art does bring a contribution to the original, for it will not fade away as fast as human life. To "perfection of the Original," it adds "duration of the Portrait." In fact, Juana Inés conceives of bodily beauty as a coordinate of many lines. She "sings" Feliciana's beauty (Feliciana is Filis, alias Lysi, the countess de Paredes) in terms of music, finding in her beauty the keys, the notes, the spaces, the rules, the *re, mi, fa, sol* of a musical scale:

> Your body, caliper-wrought,
> from proportion to persistence,
> creates a divine harmony
> with its good organization.

> Tu cuerpo, a compás obrado,
> de proporción a porfía,
> hace divina harmonía
> por lo bien organizado.[19]

Fond of the comparison between beauty and music, Juana extends it to the Virgin Mary. Sheer music also is the Virgin's life. Mary, the most perfect choir-leader, passes "from the *ut* of *Ecce ancilla* . . . to the *la* of *Exaltata*."[20] In her we have heard the

> *Be-fa-be-mi*, which, joining
> different Natures,
> united the *mi* of the Divine
> with the low *fa* of ours.

> *Be-fa-be-mí,* que juntando
> diversas Naturalezas,
> unió el *mi* de la Divina
> al *bajo fa* de la nuestra.

Undeniably, the baroque age, indebted as it was to the Renaissance, had a much more developed sense of the beauty of nature than the Middle Ages. Not by accident does Juana compare the beauty of the Virgin to that of the sky and the stars, of the Zodiac's signs and the planets, of medicinal herbs, of flowers, and chiefly of the lily and the rose.[21]

The most subtle and delicate beauty of nature, however, is that of the human body. And like most artists, Juana Inés finds it chiefly in the female body. She is inspired by Lysi's body:

> Painting Lisarda's beauty,
> in which Nature has surpassed itself,
> with simple style,
> comes to my pen and my hand.

> El pintar de Lisarda la belleza
> en que a sí se excedió Naturaleza,
> con un estilo llano,
> se me viene a la pluma y a la mano.[22]

This long poem of 396 verses describes Lysi's body with a sense of humor—called a "burlesque" tone by her commentators—that helps to balance and tone down the suggestive familiarity of the images. Juana is one of many painters who have cast "a woman in an infusion of flowers." Many verses describe the hesitancies of the painter and the difficulties of such a painting. "The coral among the wise / was like berry between the lips" (p. 173). The teeth are "pearls." As the picture unfolds, the hair becomes a wood, and the

forehead, a clearing in the wood, is also a sky. In fact, Lysi has two
skies, "one in the mouth, one on the brow" (p. 176). Juana paints
the eyebrows, the nose, the cheeks that are "flesh and nothing else"
(p. 177), the hands, the waist so slim that "one line" of the brush is
enough (p. 179). Although the painter declares that she has not seen
the feet, she imagines that they must be small and light, in keeping
with the lightness of Lisarda's movements.

The theme recurs in a romance in which Juana Inés draws on
the Song of Songs for her description of Lysi's body: her forehead
forms "a circle divided in two arcs" by her eyebrows;[23] her eyes are
"lamps"; her nose, an umpire marking the limit between two pure
lights; her cheeks, "the seats of April"; her teeth, "pearls of dawn"
in her mouth; the dimple of her chin is a concavity of jasper "where
souls find repose"; her throat, "a passage to the gardens of Venus";
her arms, "vine branches made of crystal and snow"; her fingers,
"shells of alabaster"; her waist, "a Bosphorus of narrowness"; her
form, "a heap of beauties, / shading" the doric sculptures of her
legs; her feet, "moving wee bits."

What is beauty? Juana's conception is developed in the "En-
comiastic Poem for the Anniversary of the Countess de Galve."
Beauty is proportion: "in the proportions of parts / the beautiful
only consists."[24] It is to sight what harmony is to hearing:

> The Beautiful is nothing other
> than a proportion that orders
> well some parts with others;
> for it will not suffice to be beautiful
> in the absolute, if
> not also in the relative . . .

> Thus, Beauty is not
> only in that the parts are
> exceedingly beautiful,
> but in that to one another they have
> a relative proportion.

> No es otra cosa lo Hermoso
> que una proporción que ordena
> bien unas partes con otras;

pues no bastara ser bellas
absolutamente, si
relativa no lo fueran . . .

Así la Beldad no está
sólo en que las partes sean
excesivamente hermosas,
sino en que unas a otras tengan
relativa proporción.

(P. 607.)

The Creator has filled this world with beauty; the beauty of nature and of humanity is not closed upon itself, however, for it is enhanced by the new order of the incarnation. For this reason Juana Inés praises the Virgin Mary as God's new gift of beauty to this world:

To illumine the very light
to delight the very Glory,
to enrich the riches
and to crown the crowns,

to make Heaven, Heaven,
to make beauty beautiful,
to ennoble nobility,
to honor the very honors,

she ascends, being of the Heavens
honor, riches, and crown,
light, beauty, and nobility,
Heaven, Perfection, and Glory.

———————

A alumbrar la misma luz,
a alegrar la misma Gloria,
a enriquecer las riquezas
y a coronar las coronas;

a hacer Cielo al mismo Cielo,
a hacer la beldad hermosa,

a ennoblecer la nobleza
y a honrar a las mismas honras,

sube la que es de los Cielos
honra, riqueza, corona,
luz, hermosura y nobleza,
Cielo, Perfección y Gloria.[25]

The originality of Juana Inés de la Cruz in relation to aesthetics
and theology was that from her perception of natural and spiritual
beauty she drew a theological method. There have been theologies
centered on the oneness of God—Plotinus and Neoplatonism come
to mind. Neoplatonism had been adapted to the Christian faith in
the theology of Gaius Marius Victorinus (fourth century). A prom-
inent Neoplatonist before he asked for baptism and entered the
Christian Church, this older contemporary of Augustine had inter-
preted the doctrine of *homoousios* in several tractates on the Trinity
according to Plotinus's understanding of God as the One. Other
theologies have been centered on the good as the supreme paradigm
for the concept of God: such was the theology of St. Bonaventure
and of the Franciscan school in general. Still other theologies have
highlighted truth as the main focus for theological reflection because
it was identified as the most basic transcendental quality of being;
there is in this case a scale of being, of which God is the first ana-
logue. The system of St. Thomas Aquinas is entirely built on this
premise.

Theological Method

No one, however, before Juana Inés, had chosen beauty, the
fourth transcendental, as the chief attribute of God, as the focus of
thought, and as the point of view from which God should be, in the
words of St. Anselm, "that than which nothing greater can be
thought." As she made clear in the *Respuesta*, Juana fully endorsed
the contention of the Scholastics that theology must be the queen of
sciences. As she had before her eyes the model of the court of New
Spain she naturally saw the servants as necessary links in approach-
ing the queen. She therefore studied all the sciences as much as she
could in order to reach the high level of theology with a properly
prepared mind. Now, when the Scholastics called theology the queen

of sciences, they did not primarily affirm their own prominence in the organization of universities; most of the time, the other three faculties (Arts, Canon Law, and Medicine) that constituted, along with Theology, a university, did not recognize this prominence. The statement was essentially about the nature of theology. As "faith seeking understanding," to use the phrase of St. Anselm, theology cannot remain in a corner of the mind, isolated from other dimensions of self in general and of knowledge in particular. Insofar as faith, in the classical sense of the term—that is, as insight and acceptance, knowledge and trust—is to inform all life and thought, so theology is relevant to all life and thought. It shapes, and is shaped by, the totality of one's mind, of one's concerns, hopes, experiences. It learns from one's achievements and failures, as faith inspires a search for higher levels of awareness and articulation.

One may remark at this point that our own period, aware as it is of new methodologies in the sciences, human as well as technical, has paid attention to the methodology of theological knowledge, defining the theological method in integrative terms. In the language of Bernard Lonergan, theology applies to Christian faith the transcendental principles or injunctions: "Be attentive, be intelligent, be reasonable, be responsible."[26] In the perspective of some of my own writings, the search for method, which I called *general theology* to distinguish it from the special theology of each tractate or topic, draws on the entire realm of cognition and its expression in language. In the terms of David Tracy, the current theological task is largely one of "retrieval"; from the monuments of human imagination that are recognized as classic, theology should retrieve the elements that may provide insights into the diverse manifestations of the mystery of being. This amounts to saying that contemporary theology is in dire need of recovering elements of the tradition that have been lost or forgotten.

Generally standing between the scholastic stress on analysis and the modern concern for wholeness, the baroque age carried elements of previous methodologies. There were still theologians, especially in Spain, who practiced a form of Scholasticism. The Jesuit Francisco Suarez (1548–1616) had even produced an impressive scholastic synthesis, based on John Duns Scotus as much as on Thomas Aquinas and oriented toward a baroque restoration of theology, parallel to the ongoing restoration of the Church in the spirit of the Counterreformation. It was in Spain, too, that the Friar Preacher Domenico

Bañez (1528–1604) and the Jesuit Luis Molina (1536–1600), in defending opposite interpretations of Thomas Aquinas, had initiated a famous but rather sterile dispute *de auxiliis*, on the nature and effects of the means of grace for salvation. Juana Inés, in fact, shows no interest in this question, and no affinity to the contentious aspect of the scholastic mind as it survived into the Counterreformation.

The theology of the baroque age also put forward some fresh initiatives. When they wished to go beyond Scholasticism, the authors frequently distinguished between two theological methods. Theology could be done in what was sometimes called the Augustinian manner (*modo Augustiniano*), which proceeded historically from the early statements of Scripture, to the formulas of the patristic tradition, and then to the formulations of more recent times, whence it investigated possible applications to current problems. This method tried to do justice to the Protestant emphasis on Scripture while respecting the Catholic concern for the decisions of councils and the consensus of subsequent centuries.

Theology could also be done in what was called the geometric mode (*modo geometrico*). This proceeded step by step from a statement that was considered to be primitive to its ultimate consequences. Not proceeding in the scholastic manner shaped by Aristotle that relied on syllogisms, the geometric way imitated the new philosophical methodology of Descartes, who attempted to reconstruct the universe of knowledge, starting from the one point that escaped his methodic doubt, namely the certainty of being that emerges from the actuality of thinking (*Cogito ergo sum*). A contemporary of Sor Juana Inés, the Jansenist theologian Antoine Arnauld d'Andilly (1612–1694)—the "great Arnauld"—practiced both methods.[27] He also distinguished, in theological argumentation, between the "mode of discussion," in which each point is taken for a detailed examination; and the "mode of prescription," inspired by Tertullian, in which some key points are selected, from which to obtain a central or general view of the matter under study.

The *Carta atenagórica* follows the mode of discussion and comes close to the Augustinian mode. Generally, however, Juana's theological reflection does not fit any one of these precedents. She pioneers another way, which, for lack of an agreed term, I will call the *Hieronymian mode*. Juana of course is inspired by St. Jerome, who was officially considered the founder of her community. She honors St. Paula, herself a paragon of knowledge in her time, as the first member of this community and its model for life and scholarship. In his Letter 22, Jerome had asserted that he was renouncing literature. For he had had a dream in which Christ castigated him for being more Ciceronian than Christian. And so Jerome was giving up his Ciceronian concern for beauty of form. But he did so, as any Latinist can see, in highly Ciceronian prose! This is of course a parable: the one who has once perceived the beauty of God, be it only as it is reflected by creaturely beauty, will always remain haunted by the impression of divine beauty, even when it is hiding.

The situation of Juana Inés is close, though not identical, to the case of Jerome. Let us go back to her christological play, *Divino Narciso*. All her discourse about God and about Christ focuses on a profound sense of the beauty of God. The very idea of treating the theme of Jesus Christ as the shepherd Narcissus derives from a deep insight into the beauty of all the actions of God, including the eternal act of the procession of the Word. The beauty of Narcissus, the most beautiful of humans, is divine. In search of the perfect image of his beauty in human nature, he finds it in the pure fountain, and the image is none other than Human Nature transformed by Grace, their two reflections forming one composite picture in the pool of unsullied water. Between his divine beauty and that of the graced creatures, however, a barrier remains that cannot be overcome in the present life; total unity is not yet possible between them. We live at the time of espousals, not of consummated union. Hence the death of Jesus through love. Only by way of love-filled death can full oneness be reached between the divine beauty and its human image. Only beyond his own dying and rising can Narcissus truly be the bridegroom of the soul. Christ has sought human nature because he has been enamored of its beauty, of its beauty that is the image of his own. And his own beauty, as divine Narcissus, is God's uncreated beauty.

Juana's central idea emerges on the background of the medieval Augustinian theology of "divine exemplarism." In this line of thought, which reached its high point in the theology of St. Bonaventure, the Word or Logos of God is the eternal model of all that will be. But Juana Inés has left behind the scholastic debates concerning the status of the fourth transcendental in the framework of a trinitarian understanding of God. In her theology, God should be affirmed primarily as "that than which nothing more beautiful can be seen." By the same token, new dimensions are opened in the vision of Christ, in the understanding of grace, in the view of the Holy Spirit and its work, in the perspective on the new creation. Indeed, the theory of worship and the experience of liturgy would be transformed, were the participants truly convinced that only a thing of beauty is worth proclaiming, presenting, and preaching as a sacrament or sacramental of the divine presence. One would have to translate the *charis* of the New Testament as "beauty," so that the tidings brought to Mary—*Kairè, kecharitôménè* (Luke 1:28)—would be rendered as "Hail, beautiful one." As the paradigm for every authentic visitation from God, the annunciation would then introduce all the faithful to a new vision of God. Only the beautiful can receive beauty. Only the beautiful can perceive beauty. Only uncreated beauty can create beauty. Artistic activity is therefore always a graced participation in the divine act of creation. Aesthetic theory and reflection are always meditations on the divine attribute of beauty. Such is the vista that Juana Inés de la Cruz opens before us.

Beauty and Love

For Sor Juana, beauty is never an abstraction. This appears clearly from the ties that she sees between beauty and love. For beauty is first of all a gift, a gift that is given by God's creative love. Nature, who appears several times as an allegorical personage in Juana's liturgical theater, is the first work of God, responsible for all the beings that are in the world. As such, Nature is in charge of both life and death. In a sort of triumphal hymn to creation, Juana Inés makes Nature survey the process of dying and rising in the cosmos:

> Since the first Cause's
> Omnipotence ordered
> that I, as the second cause,
> have absolute dominion
>
> over all natural work
> (for I am Nature
> in general, to whose learned
> ever-operative idea
> is due the sweet union
> of form and matter),

I make sure that the World
has being, making sure, anxious
for the survival of the species,
that individuals die;

and so that to corruption
may succeed generation,
I bring things to corruption
for their rejuvenation.

———————

Ya que de la primer Causa
dispuso la Omnipotencia
que yo, como su segunda,
dominio absoluto tenga

en las obras naturales
(pues soy la Naturaleza
en común, a cuya docta
siempre operativa idea
se debe la dulce unión
de la forma y la materia),

yo soy quien hago que el Mundo
tenga ser, haciendo, atenta
a que las especies vivan
que los individuos mueran;

y porque a la corrupción
la generación suceda,
hago corromper las cosas
para que rejuvenezcan.[28]

    In the course of time, each species is a "Phoenix, which from dead / ashes is born." The "greatest wonder" is not that Nature is thus "fecund Mother" of so many living species but that all is properly ordered,

that in such plenty,
in such an immense machine,

in such a wide space,
and in so diverse a multitude,

all is so measured
all is so well ordered,
that Sea has not one more drop,
Earth loses not one point,

Air does not lack one atom,
and no spark is left by Fire;
but rather as in a concert
they form inseparable links,

for in the form of a sphere
the Sea surrounds the Earth,
the Air encircles Water,
and Air is contained by Fire,

making their qualities,
in sisterhood, or in opposition,
such a perfect circle
such a mysterious *Chain*. . . .

———————

sino el que entre tanta copia,
en fábrica tan inmensa,
en tan dilatado espacio,
y en multitud tan diversa,

todo esté con tal mensura
todo con tal orden sea,
que ni el Mar crezca una gota,
ni mengüe un punto la Tierra,

ni el Aire un átomo falte,
ni al Fuego sobre centella;
sino que con tal concierto
eslabonados se vean,

que con esférica forma
a la Tierra el Mar rodea,
al Agua el Aire circunde,
y al Aire el Fuego contenga,

haciendo sus cualidades
ya hermanadas, y ya opuestas,
un círculo tan perfecto,
tan misteriosa *Cadena*. . . .

(P. 616.)

This is the beauty of nature: a universal harmony, an order, in which all components are measured and organized in proper proportions. Nature is "the great Mother," the "fecund and beautiful / generous Mother of the Universe," the "beautiful Goddess of the World," the "great Queen." Obedience to her is a "loving action" that seeks to express itself in "finesse." In this universal harmony, all is related to all. Thus Tellus, that is, Earth, asks:

If the Sea burns, what of the Earth?
If water burns, what of the flowers?
If the fish burn, what of the beasts?
If waves burn, what of the mountains?
If the foam burns, what of the grass?
If the tides burn, what of the woods?

Si arde el Mar, ¿qué hará la Tierra?
Si el agua, ¿que harán las flores?
Si los peces, ¿qué los brutos?
Si las ondas, ¿qué los montes?
Si la espuma, ¿qué la hierba?
Si los flujos, ¿qué los bosques?[29]

The symbol of the Phoenix points to the natural works of love. Telluric Love celebrates each day's beauty:

I, who am Love, and the purpose
from which its beauty is born,
in whose beautiful parts

it burns in sweet fires;
as the universal union
that I am (for there is nothing
in Fire, Air, Earth, and Water,
outside my embrace) . . .

I come. . . .

Yo que soy Amor, y efecto
de que su belleza nace,
en cuyas partes hermosas
en dulces incendios arde;
como unión universal
que soy (pues no puede hallarse
en Fuego, Aire, Tierra y Agua,
cosa que yo no la enlace) . . .

vengo. . . .

(P. 602.)

Loving all the beings of the universe, Nature herself comes
from creative Love. And Love comes from Beauty; as Venus says,
"I and Love, whose Mother I am." The universal harmony includes
Nature, Love, and Beauty. In this harmony the roles of the good
and the bad, of pleasure and pain, are interchangeable:

> *Sun:* Listen, Tellus, listen;
> *Venus:* and you will see that your pains are glories,
> *Sun:* and you will see that your evils are goods.

> *Sol:* Atiende, Telus, atiende;
> *Venus:* y verás, que son glorias tus penas,
> *Sol:* y verás que tus males son bienes.

(P. 598.)

Because of this transcendental circle in her vision Juana Inés favors
the symbols of the sun and, related to it, the sphere. The last line of
First Dream, after the soul's nocturnal wanderings, leaves, the poet

says, "the World illuminated, and me awakened."[30] Holding a central place in the old religion of the Aztecs, the sun becomes the major symbol in Juana's glorious vision of the Virgin Mary. Likewise the sphere, tracing the sun's journey through the heavens, is also the circumference of the divine presence encircling all of reality.

It is against this background that Juana's delicate celebrations of human love ought to be read. Whether composed on request, as most of them were, or written for Juana's personal reasons, her love poems explore the mutual longing that is at work in the whole universe, and in which she sees the divine relationships of the three Persons reflected. Even when they complain of absence—the beloved being removed by distance or by death—these poems always celebrate joy given and received. Therefore Juana has no difficulty passing from human to divine love, for she follows only one paradigm. Whether she sings of divine Lysi's "sacred deity,"[31] or of "divina Maria,"[32] or "of divine Love's / loving Incarnation,"[33] Juana Inés always relates love, like beauty, to God, the author and giver of all love, and the model and paradigm of all beauty.

Juana's suggestive verses should not be misread. True love is no mere emotion. Juana distinguishes between "affective" and "rational" love.[34] The former "is more affectionate / because it is more natural, / and also more sensual." The latter is "elective" and more complete. One should "love with the intellect," for this is the only love in which "the entire soul" is engaged. Given her conception of the universal harmony of the created order, Juana shuns dividing the diverse activities of the soul according to the three faculties of intellect, will, and memory. In reality, "all three are the Soul, / and the Soul is each one, / being an indivisible essence."[35] But, in keeping with Juana's generally Platonic approach to reality, the nature of the human soul is expressed by the spiritual faculties; the body is no more than their mirror and their instrument of communication. As she praises bodily beauty, Juana sings of the soul's beauty, and as she sings of the soul's beauty, she worships the soul's Creator.

Theology of Glory

This is the precise point where the theology of Sor Juana Inés de la Cruz flourishes into a theology of glory, in the best conventions of the baroque mind. Juana was probably not acquainted with Martin Luther's condemnation, in the theses for the Heidelberg disputation (April 1518), of theologians of glory: "The theologian of glory calls the bad good and the good bad. The theologian of the cross says what a thing is" (thesis 21).[36] But even had she known of this, she would not have been impressed. To be sure, she does not say directly what a thing is. Rather, she says how a thing looks when the universe is perceived as radiating the glory of God. Only the soul can have such a vision. If it does not emerge immediately from the perception of reality, the vision may still surface in the process of reflection. According to the conceptism of Baltasar Gracián that influenced Juana, describing experience through the ensuing reflection is better than simply conveying what is seen and felt immediately.

A difficult problem of expression remains. Juana expresses her ideas through the baroque symbolism that the culture of seventeenth century Spain and New Spain gave her as her accepted medium. In this symbolism as Juana uses it, everything created becomes an image of the divine glory and majesty. This is the reason why Juana Inés so often makes extravagant comparisons, exalts the persons she speaks of, gives them divine titles and attributes. In fact, she does not see them as they see themselves or as they are seen by onlookers; she sees them as they secretly are in the diverse hidden modes and degrees to which creatures participate in God by nature and by grace. Her art—bringing to light hidden relationships with God— cannot be accomplished directly, since no human language can adequately depict God's essence and action. Therefore she uses symbols and the compressed, allusive language of poetry. More systematic theologians would have carefully distinguished between symbols with a foundation in the analogy of faith, and symbols that pertain only to the analogy of nature or of human culture. But she does not make these distinctions. She borrows symbols from nature (flowers, birds, stars and planets, sun, for example); from the natural beauty of women and men; from the beauty of human culture and its intellectual and artistic achievements (such as grammar, science, painting, music, dance . . .); from the insights of natural religions as expressed in the mythologies of Egypt, Greece, and Rome and in the religion of the Aztecs; from the inspired data of Scripture (especially the Song of Songs); and from the doctrines of the Catholic tradition (the glories of the Word made flesh, the radiation of divine glory in the Virgin Mary as it is reflected in the marian dogmas and tradition, especially in what is still in her days a pious opinion concerning the immaculate conception).

The glory of God shines in many forms, radiates directly and indirectly. Juana speaks of joys and sufferings. The Virgin Mary herself—the most glorious daughter, mother, and bride of God—is also "the Mother most anguished . . . , most afflicted . . . , most disconsolate . . . , most forsaken . . . , most sorrowful . . . , alive only to torments and dead to all consolation."[37] In this combination too, Juana Inés the poet has perceived the finesse of divine love. As the Virgin ascends to heaven at her assumption, she is indeed magnificent with the glory that God bestows on her. Yet as Juana writes in 1679,

> With beautiful opposites
> adorned, the Queen ascends today:
> much covered to be poor,
> to be nude, very free.

> De hermosas contradicciones
> sube hoy la Reina adornada:
> muy vestida para pobre,
> para desnuda, muy franca.[38]

Even what Teilhard de Chardin called "the passivities of our lives" radiate divine glory.[39] This follows the logic of the incarnation and of the cross. Sor Juana knows it well, and she says it in the language of the baroque. Cardinal de Bérulle (1575–1629), one of the great spiritual authors of the period, had spread among the French Carmelite sisters a vow of servitude to Mary that was popularized later by St. Grignion de Montfort (1673–1716). Juana thinks along similar lines when she calls herself "the smallest of the slaves of the Most Holy Mary, Our Lady,"[40] and she signs, "I, the worst of the world."[41] At her religious profession of 24 February 1669, she had added to her signature: "May God make me holy!"[42] This prayer too falls within the symbolic universe of the baroque. Holiness is the radiation of divine glory that comes to the soul from grace as God's next total gift after the first gift of being and life. Silence is an attribute of God, pregnant with glory; in the final silence of Juana Inés the divine silence radiates. Whatever its exact circumstances, its remote motivations, and its immediate occasion may have been, Juana entered it in homage to the beauty and the glory of God, in which all her life had bathed.

Beauty, love, and glory are the three mansions of Juana's theology. As a theology of glory, it is a theology of God's beauty and God's love. Now, something is at work here that is absent from more academic theologies, whether scholastic or more modern. For the brief moment of Juana Inés's life the experience of beauty was given a prominent place in the context of Catholic thought. The light of aesthetics, which had been generally extinguished in the theological schools toward the end of the thirteenth century, was rekindled and shone again.

Juana pointed to the beauty of God that radiates through all the beauty of this world. Ultimately, this is what the baroque style aimed at; if they ever looked for it, the professional theologians of the baroque age were impeded by the categories of the Schools that many of them still used. Moreover, engrossed as they were in theological controversies—against Protestantism, over grace (*de auxiliis*), against Quietism, against Jansenism—they did not enjoy the serenity of vision that is necessary to perceive and express beauty. Working in her cell, conversing in the convent parlors, Sor Juana, sheltered from sterile polemics, was serene. In fact, she felt her peace shatter when the bishop of Puebla revealed to the public her sharp critique of Vieira. Juana's forte did not lie in the realm of controversy. Yet there is more to her originality than a sense of, and a concern for, beauty. The great Scholastics had such a concern when they debated about the fourth transcendental. But Juana's goal is not to construct a theory of beauty but to depict the natural and supernatural beauty that emerges from the light of faith. In other words, she was deeply sensitive to the third dimension of faith, the mythopoetic dimension.

Dimensions of Faith

The first dimension of faith is that of revelation and belief. The revelation in Christ functions as an objective datum, and belief is the subjective recognition and acceptance of this. The given, objective, reality of the revealed and preached gospel and the subjective, personal, conviction of belief stand in a strictly bipolar relationship. Belief is correlative to what is known of the deposit of faith. This dimension was analyzed at length in the scholastic questions about faith as the first of the three theological virtues. The basic problem was to discover the origin and the interior structure of the given *habitus* of faith; the relative roles of the intellect and of the will in the act of faith; the relationships between faith and grace, faith and reason, faith and the virtues of Christian life, faith and the Church, between the preaching of the gospel and the interior strengthening of the soul by grace so that it will believe with certainty something that is not intellectually self-evident. When Juana was still a child, such problems came back to the fore among a few authors of the Counterreformation. In my investigation of the Catholic tradition in England in the seventeenth century, I drew attention to the remarkable work of Henry Holden (1596–1665), an English priest who worked in Paris, in his *Analysis Divinae Fidei* (1652).[43] Similar studies of the noetic structure of faith have continued into our own times. A danger lurks, however, in isolating this dimension of faith: it can easily breed a propositional conception of divine revelation and a fundamentalist reading of the Bible and of the conciliar and papal decisions regarding what is to be believed.

The second dimension of faith—assurance and trust—became prominent at the Reformation. The *Augsburg Confession* (1530) had stated:

> They teach that men cannot be justified before God by their own virtues, merits, or works, but are justified gratuitously for Christ's sake through faith, when they believe that they have been received into grace and that their sins have been remitted for the sake of Christ, who satisfied for our sins by his death. God imputes this faith as justice before himself (Romans chapters 3 and 4).[44]

Here the objective assurance that the word of Redemption is addressed to me is received with personal (subjective) gratitude and trust. The gospel remains an irreplaceable datum: it is the saving action of God through Christ as it is proclaimed in the Church. The reception of the gospel, however, is never the mere belief that the statement that formulates it is true; rather, the reception is the called response of the whole person. As the saving truth is received in the soul, it elicits total commitment. No faith exists without the believer's trust of being the recipient of God's favors, included in the redemptive purpose of God. Belief without trust is not saving; it is the faith of demons, who know, but reject, salvation. Catholic theology commonly connected this lived dimension of trust with the infused gift of love: saving faith is the faith that is "informed by love" and that proceeds "to act through love." Luther's language was simpler: faith itself does all this; the trust of faith is a certainty. Classical theology before the Reformation ascribed such a certainty to hope. But Luther's formulation comes closer than Scholasticism to St. Paul's understanding of *pistis,* faith.

The third dimension of faith, what I would call the mythopoetic dimension, was mostly overlooked both by the Scholastics and by the Reformers. The faith that is both belief in Christ's revelation and trust in God's gift of salvation is active. Most theologies have identified the locus of this activity chiefly as the pursuit of the virtues, the sanctification of life, the search for perfection, and the doing of good works. In fact, John Calvin in the *Institutes of the Christian Religion* (1559) and the Lutheran authors of the *Formula of Concord* (1578) saw active belief at work in "the third use of the law," when the God-given law is taken by the faithful as a discipline of purification and sanctification.[45] None of the contestants in the debates between the Reformation and the Counterreformation pursued this crucial point: as both belief and trust, faith can be active in ways other than the pursuit of holiness; it can also reconstruct the mental and artistic universe of the faithful, reshape their vision of the world, launch them along new ways of imagination.

This third dimension of faith was integral to the theology of St. Bonaventure. In *De reductione artium ad theologiam,* the Seraphic Doctor explained—but one could also say, imagined—how the diverse disciplines and sciences relate to Christ the center.[46] His discourse took its terms from the metaphor of the rays that come down from the "Father of lights" (James 1:17), illuminating the mind "in itself" in intellectual cognition, as it turns "below itself" in sensory perception, as it operates "outside itself" in the arts and crafts, and as "from above," by grace, it receives the light that steeps the saving truth expressed in Scripture. Dominating the work is the image of the circle, as the light of the sun follows its symbolic course through the sky of the soul. This is theology, at the level not of dry abstraction, but of aesthetic imagination. It is symbolic, rather than speculative, theology: speculation, as the word indicates (*speculum* means a mirror), reflects, sending back an image or doctrine that has been

received; symbolization constructs new images that accrue to, and
may come to replace, the image or doctrine that has been received.
When the symbolization takes account of aesthetic conceptions and
endeavors to inspire an experience of the beauty of God as perceived
from the radiation of the divine revelation in glory, the resulting
symbolic theology is also aesthetic or poetic.

The early Renaissance had seen a flourishing of aesthetic the-
ology in the monumental poem of Dante Alighieri (1265–1321), *La
divina commedia*. In a pilgrimage through hell and purgatory, Dante
is led—by the symbols of two levels of divine grace that are Virgil,
the pagan poet, and then Beatrice, the young Florentine girl with
whom Dante had once been in love—to paradise. There, having
reached the eighth heaven, or sky of the stars, he hears the song of
the glory of God:

> "To the Father and to the Son and Holy Ghost
> Glory!" burst forth from all the heavenly spheres
> So sweet, my spirit in ecstasy was lost.

> "Al Padre, al Figlio, allo Spirito Santo"
> cominciò "gloria!" tutto il paradiso,
> sí che m'inebriava il dolce canto.[47]

The sense of a theological aesthetic had not entirely disappeared
at the Reformation. In spite of his strictures on theologians of glory,
Martin Luther had not rejected it; in line with his personal tastes
and talents, he had focused it on music. "Next to the Word of God,"
he had declared, "music deserves the highest praise."[48] Choral sing-
ing was essential to worship, for worship is not only a matter of
reciting psalms and understanding them. "By adding the voice it
becomes a song, and the voice is the feeling. Therefore, as the word
is the understanding, so the voice is its feeling." Indeed, Luther had
nothing to do with the widespread destruction of religious art that
took place wherever the followers of Carlstadt gained the upper hand.

Be that as it may, the baroque age saw the rise of a new aesthetic
theology that was expressed chiefly in the decorated stone of its
churches, in the white light of its largely pictureless windows, and in
the scenes of its religious theater, especially, in Spain, in the villan-

cicos of Calderón, but also in the spiritual epic of Cervantés (1547–1616), *Don Quijote de la Mancha.*

Juana Inés's artistic constructions are in fact more symbolic than aesthetic. Aestheticism develops and follows theories of beauty. Pushed to the end of its logic, it is entirely focused on the medium and is correspondingly indifferent to content and meaning. "The medium is the message."[49] The form stands by itself independently of its matter. The container lacks content. Symbolism differs from this in that it seeks to express and signify something. Not only does it have a content and does it work on a matter to be presented and communicated, but also it entirely consists in establishing the links, in formulating (for the ear) and showing (for the eye) the *sym* (*cum,* "with") of *symbol,* by which what it tries to say is one with how it says it. Juana Inés is eclectic in regard to theories of beauty. Her focus changes from sight to hearing and back again; painting and music are equally favored. Unfortunately her own theoretical study of music, *El caracol,* is lost; in her extant writings, her preference goes to the power of language, to the dreams to which poets have given shape in myths, to the cosmic discourses of the great mythologies. And as she freely borrows from these myths, Juana herself starts mythbuilding. Christ is Narcissus.

Precisely at this level, however, Juana Inés runs into a fundamental difficulty. A theology in which beauty is perceived as the form taken by God's creative and redeeming love, and this love itself as the radiation of God's uncreated glory, has a special problem in regard to what Bernard Lonergan calls the functional specialty of "communications."[50] How can a personal vision of the divine glory be communicated? Given the deficiencies of human language and thought, the expression and formulation of such a vision can proceed only by way of symbols. One's particular choice of symbols will depend in part on personal imagination and taste, but it will also be deeply indebted to the predominant culture in which the theologian functions. This is precisely the point where many of Juana's symbols were, in her time, purely artificial and have now become totally obsolete and mostly ineffective. Borrowed to a great extent from the baroque cult of pagan antiquity, they presuppose a knowledge of mythological culture that is not shared by the modern world at large. Juana could justify her appeal to the Greco-Roman pantheon with the theory that pagan gods were originally great men and women. No one today would accept this hypothesis. But, even allowing for it, the argument is not persuasive, since the glory that Juana perceives and tries to express is that of the biblical God, manifested in Jesus Christ, the Word made flesh, dwelling in the hearts through the Holy Spirit, and leading the whole of humanity to the Heavenly Father.

Juana's Way

Within Juana's imagination and in the verbal pyrotechnics that so often burst in her sky, the Hieronymite sister holds onto the anchor of faith. As she conceives them, her myths are tested and controlled by the revelation given once and for all in Jesus Christ and known in the Scriptures through the Church. Narcissus is not Christ. Neptune is not God, nor is Lysi a goddess. There is an unbridgeable gap between Juana's vision and the means of its depiction. The medieval Scholastics were aware of the discrepancy between words and meaning; they still could speak of the ineffable, as long as their language was finely honed in the limits of the analogy of proper proportionality. But there is no way to stretch proper proportionality so that it can protect Juana's mythological borrowings and her myth-making from artificiality.

Undoubtedly, it is in the mythopoetic function of faith that are rooted Juana's baroque constructions, including her extravagant praises of the Virgin Mary, mother of God. In fact Mariology has been, and not only in baroque times, a favorite area for displays of the myth-making capacity of faith. The early hypotheses on the mode of Mary's death that are at the origin of the doctrine of the assumption were mythopoetic constructions. The progressive enlargement of early insights concerning Mary's sinless purity into the doctrine of the immaculate conception was the outcome of a long process of myth-building. And even the argument for the immaculate conception that John Duns Scotus proposed, and that proved to be finally persuasive, took the form of a hypothetical possibility: Could not God apply the future merits of redemption in advance? Raising a hypothetical possibility is tantamount to starting a myth.

Myth, of course, does not imply fallacy. Myth means that the poet (from Greek *poiein*, "to make") is in the process of enlarging a clue, an insight, an idea, to the cosmic scope of humankind and of the universe and even, beyond that, of projecting it into her vision of God. This is precisely the realm of glory where the glory of God's being is seen to radiate into God's creation. Then a human event, like the birth of a child, can shine with a glory that encompasses the whole world:

> His Nativity is applauded
> by all Oreads on the mountain,
> all Nymphs on the hillocks,
> all Dryads in the woods,
> all Naiads in the rivers,
> all Napeads in the flowers,
> all Nereids in the sea,
> where in ordered disorder
> they dwell, inhabit, preside,
> fertilize and combine!

> ¡Aplaudan su Natalicio
> cuantas Oréadas el monte,
> cuantas Ninfas los collados,
> cuantas Dríadas los bosques,
> cuantas Náyades los ríos,
> cuantas Napeas las flores,
> cuantas Nereidas el mar,
> con ordenado desorden
> habitan, pueblan, presiden,
> fertilizan y componen![51]

In context, this is not the commemoration of the nativity of Jesus but only the birthday of the viceroy. As she mythologizes the birth of the marquis de la Laguna, Sor Juana Inés follows a model that is given by her faith: the birth of the Son of God. The divine glory of the Word shines in the birth of a child. In reverse, the glory of nature that Juana has absorbed through all her senses inspires a symbolic depiction of the glory of Christ and of God. The glory of the mind that she experiences as she discovers and tests, through reading and observation, the theories of science and of philosophy Juana also turns into a symbolic model for understanding the internal and external glory of God.

There is, then, no cause for surprise in Juana's enthusiastic endorsement of the doctrine of the immaculate conception as she entered deeper into the silence that she had finally chosen. In signing her declaration with her own blood, Juana introduced her own body into the myth that her soul had sighted and that she had depicted, sung, and danced all her adult life: the myth of the glory of God embracing this world. At that moment, the mythopoetic function of faith was still at work, transforming the life of Sor Juana Inés de la Cruz.

*   *   *

Juana Inés de la Cruz explored the point where the physical and spiritual beauty of creatures that is a gift of God's love triggers a theophany through which the divine glory is perceived. The artist who is latent in all men and women need not go any further; for the perception and expression of beauty have their inherent justification. The theologian, however, may wish for some clarifications. Two points, it seems, call for theological reflection. First, one may wish for more light to be shed on the difference between the level of natural beauty and the special revelation that culminated in Jesus Christ and to which one has access only through faith. Second, if love and, to a lesser extent, beauty are at least intuitively understood by most, and have been analyzed theologically by some, glory is, ironically, a more obscure category, having all but vanished from Christian theology until Hans Urs von Balthasar began to retrieve the notion in his *Herrlichkeit*.[52]

Juana does not specify the distinctions between nature and grace that are familiar to Catholic theology. The art of the baroque was already modern in the sense that it wished to unite the two perspectives. Nature itself is God's gift. Yet grace is neither a substitute for nature nor an additional dimension artificially inserted in nature by the Creator's arbitrary will and power. The theology that serves as background to Juana Inés's writing is not that of the late nominalists, who focused the whole concept of the divine on the sovereign will of God. The theologians of Scholasticism and of modern times have explored the relationships between nature and grace in different ways; this is not the place to examine their theories. Yet the works of Juana Inés point in a certain direction of understanding.

Juana makes no sharp distinction between the human and the Christian, for the whole realm of human life is for her the theater of God's providential guidance. Nevertheless, a link exists in her works between grace and nature and between the data that constitute the stuff of the universe and the gifts that emerge in human life. This link is, precisely, the divine glory. The radiation of God's life and attributes unites the various gifts bestowed by God on creatures, for the same divine life and attributes are manifested in all of God's gifts. Among the recipients of these gifts an infinity of perceptions and of responses occur. Yet, whatever the kind of reception, the question still remains, "What is Glory?" Glory is itself neither one of the transcendentals nor a divine quality or attribute. The two stances that Juana takes in relation to glory are relevant. First, seeking in the sciences for the manifestations of God's wisdom, she bursts into admiration and praise; during most of her life, she expresses in poetry her sense of the beauty of God. Second, she closed her books and put aside her pen, choosing silence as a more eloquent context for inner praise.

This suggests a path down which our less spiritually sensitive culture may catch a glimpse of divine glory. Glory is not itself the radiation of the divine Being that the ancients liked to put in terms of light. Glory is the ineffable—the distance that always remains between what we perceive and imagine and what God is. To borrow Juana's words, glory is the *plus ultra* that stands like an untraveled ocean beyond what can be proclaimed positively about God by the Churches, a realm beyond the positive theology of the Scholastics. But it is equally beyond the negative theology of the mystics and the apophatic approaches that some theologies have incorporated. As our intimate knowledge of God may grow, glory may look like a receding aura; but it is always there, like the *ousia* of Greek theology, into which the human mind may not delve. Not a "species," as in the scholastic theories of cognition, glory may indeed be called, to borrow Urs von Balthasar's term, the *Gestalt,* or figure, of divine revelation—a figure or image that cannot be given a shape in human perception, the figure of the *mysterion* in St. Paul, the image of what seems like a void between our imagining and God's Being.

In the face of such a perspective, the contemporary mind may well say, with the younger Wittgenstein, "What we cannot speak about, we must consign to silence."[53] But silence is ambiguous, for its way can be a path of despair or of fullness. Confronted with this *plus ultra* of language, one may also write poetry, giving color and shape, not to the divine glory as such, but to its perception; this was the first and the main way of Juana Inés. Poetry, too, is ambiguous, for the reader may be so fascinated by the glitter of words and images that, going no further than the devices of decoration, attention lapses into aestheticism. One can also unite silence and expression, making silence the form and figure, and admiration the content and the inner fullness: this, as far as we know, was Juana's final way.

Whatever we say or do not say about it, whatever we do or do not do about it, the divine glory remains beyond human words and works. Juana sensed it remotely in the pageants of her country and more directly in the lives of the saints. She felt it closely in the traditional images of the Virgin Mary. She perceived it, in faith, as manifested in the love and beauty of Christ, the Word made flesh. She pursued it as she knew how, in loving her sisters and her friends, in dreaming of the divine Lysi, in taking care of the sick, and in adoring the Father, the Son, and the Spirit, whose love she experienced and whose beauty she discerned in the marks it leaves on this world.

Notes

Introduction

1. Alfonso Méndez Plancarte, ed., *Obras completas de Sor Juana Inés de la Cruz*, 4 vols. (vol. 4 completed by Alberto Salceda) (Mexico City: Fondo de Cultura Económica, 1950, 1952, 1955, 1957); Maria Esther Perez, *Lo Americano en el teatro de Sor Juana Inés de la Cruz* (New York: Torres, 1975); Marie-Cécile Bénassy-Berling, *Humanisme et religion chez Sor Juana Inés de la Cruz: La femme et la culture au XVIIe siècle* (Paris: Publications de la Sorbonne, 1982).

2. See Ermilo Abreu Gomez, *La ruta de Sor Juana* (Mexico City: D. A. P. P., 1938); Francisco de la Maza, *La ruta de Sor Juana, de Nepantla a San Jerónimo* (Mexico City: Dirección de Turismo, 1975).

3. N. 405, p. 831. I have used the convenient one-volume edition of Juana's works edited by Francisco Monterde, ed., *Sor Juana Inés de la Cruz: Obras completas* (Mexico City: Editorial Porrua, 1975). The text is the same as in the standard edition by Alfonso Méndez Plancarte cited in note 1, above. Monterde follows Méndez's ordering of material, so the numbers given in my references to Juana's writings (as at the opening of this note, the reference to work number 405, n. 405) applies to both editions; the page numbers refer only to Monterde's edition. One reference will apply until another is provided. When successive citations come from different pages of the same work, only the first will carry an endnote; for the others, the page number will be added in parentheses after the quotation. As I have tried to convey the baroque flavor of Juana's writing, I have purposely made my translations more literal than literary. All translations are my own unless otherwise indicated.

4. This is clearly stated by Juana herself in her letter to Antonio Núñez de Miranda. Before the discovery of this letter to the priest who had been her confessor (see below, note 5), it was generally assumed, following Juana's first biographer, that Núñez de Miranda had found the money. There may already have been a rumor to that effect at the time of the letter, which would explain why Juana asserted her financial independence from her confessor.

5. This is the main point in the letter mentioned in note 4. Aureliano Tapia Méndez, who discovered and identified the letter in the library of Monterrey Seminary, published it as *Autodefensa espiritual de Sor Juana* (Monterrey: Impresoria Monterrey, 1981). I have been unable to locate a copy of this publication, but I have the English translation in Nina M. Scott, "'If you are not pleased to favor me, put me out of your mind . . .': Gender and Authority in Sor Juana Inés de la Cruz and the Translation of Her Letter to the Reverend Father Maestro Antonio Núñez of the Society of Jesus," *Women's Studies International Forum*, vol. 11, n. 5, 1988, pp. 429-438; and a French translation by Marie-Cécile Bénassy, "Soeur Jeanne-Inés de la Croix: Lettre de la Mère Jeanne-Inés de la Croix au Révérend Père Antonio Núñez de Miranda de la Compagnie de Jésus," *La vie spirituelle*, Jan.-Feb. 1989, n. 683, pp. 87-100. Nina Scott's interpretation of Juana's position as a quasi-Protestant revolt against "the dictates of ecclesiastical authority" makes little sense. On the one hand, the point of the letter is that Núñez has no natural or canonical authority over her; on the other hand, what Nina Scott identifies as "Lutheran overtones" is no other than Thomas Aquinas's doctrine on the primacy of conscience. The commentary that accompanies the French translation is entirely more adequate.

6. The most persuasive recent supporter of the first interpretation is Octavio Paz, *Sor Juana Inés de la Cruz: O las trampas de la fe* (Barcelona: Editorial Seix Barral, 1982), tr. by Margaret S. Peden as *Sor Juana: Or, the traps of Faith* (Cambridge, Mass.: Harvard University Press, 1988). Bénassy, *Humanisme et religion*, leans to the second interpretation.

7. See Conor P. Reilly, *Athanasius Kircher, Master of a Hundred Arts* (Rome: Editioni del Mondo, 1974); Joscelyn Godwin, *Athanasius Kircher, Renaissance Man and the Quest for Lost Knowledge* (London: Thames and Hudson, 1979).

8. Georgina Sabat de Rivers, *Inundación Castalida* (Madrid: Castalia, 1982), pp. 26-71; this covers only the works included in the *Inundación*.

1. First Dream

1. Perez, *Lo Americano en el teatro de Sor Juana*, pp. 212-219.

2. N. 405, p. 845. Juana makes a similar point in her letter to Núñez: "The focus of Your Reverence's anger . . . has been none other than those unfortunate verses which Heaven . . . has bestowed on me. . . . I have always tried mightily to refrain from writing them" (Scott, "If you are not pleased," p. 433). In 1681-1682, the date of the letter, the *Sueño* had not yet been composed.

3. P. 839.

4. Alfonso Méndez Plancarte, *Juana Inés de la Cruz: El sueño* (Mexico City: Imprenta Universitaria, 1951), pp. 3-75; Ramón Xirau, *Genio y figura*

de Sor Juana Inés de la Cruz (Buenos Aires: Editorial Universitaria, 1967), pp. 144–155 (this is a summary of Méndez Plancarte's division); Georgina Sabat de Rivers, *El "Sueño" de Sor Juana Inés de la Cruz: Tradiciones literarias y originalidad* (London: Tamesis Books, 1976), pp. 129–130; Ludwig Pfandl, *Sor Juana Inés de la Cruz, la décima musa de México: Su vida, su poesía, su psique* (Mexico City: Instituto de Investigaciones Estéticas 1963), pp. 197–230; Luis Harss, *Sor Juana's Dream* (New York: Lumen Books, 1986), pp. 24–25; Elías Rivers and Emilio Carilla are cited in Georgina Sabat de Rivers, *El "Sueño"*, p. 129, note 3.

5. N. 216, p. 191. Compare Harss's translation: "over sublunar space reigning supreme, / with piercing sight / its intellectual eye / . . . " (*Sor Juana's Dream*, p. 46).

6. N. 218, p. 206.

7. N. 216, p. 196.

8. Méndez Plancarte, *El sueño*, p. 53.

9. Harss, *Sor Juana's Dream*, p. 106.

10. N. 405, p. 833.

11. Alanus de Insulis, *Regulae de sacra theologia*, reg. 7 (Migne, *Patrologia Latina* 210, 627). Méndez Plancarte erroneously renders the text of Alanus as "and the infinite circumference that contains . . . " (*El sueño*, p. 33). Bénassy makes another mistake: "at the same time center and circumference" (*Humanisme et religion*, p. 159).

12. N. 405, p. 196.

13. Méndez Plancarte, *El sueño*, p. 55.

14. Raúl Levia, *Introducción a Sor Juana: Sueño y realidad* (Mexico City: Universidad Nacional, 1975), p. 70.

15. George H. Tavard, *Poetry and Contemplation in St. John of the Cross* (Athens, Ohio: Ohio University Press, 1988), pp. 197–204.

16. Harss, *Sor Juana's Dream*, p. 121.

17. Teresa de Jesus, *The Interior Castle*, Mansion 7, ch. 2, tr. by Kieran Kavanaugh and Otilio Rodriguez, *The Collected Works of St. Teresa of Avila*, vol. 2 (Washington, D.C.: ICS Publications, 1980), pp. 432–438.

18. George H. Tavard, *Images of the Christ: An Enquiry into Christology* (Washington, D.C.: University Press of America, 1982), pp. 60–63.

19. N. 367, p. 390.

20. N. 405, p. 828.

21. P. 838. See St. Augustine, *Confessions*, bk. 10, 6, 9: "Ipse nos fecit"; see also Psalm 99:3 (Latin Vulgate): "Ipse fecit nos, et non ipsi nos."

22. N. 317, pp. 290–291.

23. As told by Juana Inés, respectively in her *Letter to Antonio Núñez* (see above, Introduction, note 5) and in the *Respuesta*.

24. The name of the prioress is given by Sor Juana in the *Letter to Antonio Núñez*.

2. The Baroque Edifice

1. Among these authors, see Irving A. Leonard, *Baroque Times in Old Mexico* (Ann Arbor: University of Michigan Press, 1959).

2. N. 54, p. 75 (St. Joseph); n. 55, p. 76 (St. Peter); n. 137, p. 128 (St. Joseph); n. 143, p. 133 (St. Jerome); n. 209, p. 165 (St. Joseph); n. 210, p. 166 (St. Juan de Sahagún); nn. 323–354, pp. 296–312 (St. Bernard). There are no separate poems for St. Paula and St. Eustochium.

3. N. 408, p. 872.

4. St. Teresa placed the first convent of the Carmelite reform under the patronage of St. Joseph (*The Autobiography of St. Teresa of Avila*, ch. 32–36, tr. by Kieran Kavanaugh and Otilio Rodriguez, *The Collected Works of St. Teresa of Avila*, vol. 1 [Washington, D.C.: ICS Publications, 1976], pp. 213–251) and always retained a great devotion to this saint.

5. Villancico 1, n. 242, pp. 226–227.

6. Villancico 2, n. 243, p. 227.

7. Villancico 3, n. 244, p. 228.

8. Villancico 4, n. 245, p. 229.

9. Villancico 5, n. 246, p. 230.

10. Villancico 6, n. 247, p. 231.

11. Villancico 7, n. 248, pp. 231–232.

12. Villancico 8, n. 249, p. 233.

13. Villancico 1, n. 259, p. 242.

14. Villancico 2, n. 260, p. 243.

15. Villancico 3, n. 261, p. 243.

16. Villancico 4, n. 262, p. 244.

17. Villancico 5, n. 263, p. 244.

18. Villancico 6, n. 264, p. 245.

19. Villancico 7, n. 265, pp. 245–246.

20. Villancico 8, n. 266, p. 246.

21. N. 233, p. 217.

22. Villancico 1, n. 234, p. 218.

23. Villancico 2, n. 235, p. 219.

24. Villancico 3, n. 236, p. 220.

25. Villancico 4, n. 237, p. 220.

26. Villancico 5, n. 238, p. 221.

27. Villancico 6, n. 239, p. 222. The image of God as Supreme Robber recurs in the writings of St. Thérèse de Lisieux, *J'Entre dans la vie. Derniers entretiens* (Paris: Le Cerf, 1973), p. 104.

28. Villancico 7, n. 204, pp. 222–223.

29. Villancico 8, n. 241, pp. 223–224.

30. N. 291, p. 270.

31. Villancico 1, n. 292, p. 271.

32. Villancico 2, n. 293, p. 271.

33. Villancico 3, n. 294, p. 272.

34. Villancico 4, n. 295, p. 273.

35. Villancico 5, n. 296, p. 273.

36. Villancico 6, n. 297, p. 274.

37. Villancico 7, n. 298, p. 275.

38. Villancico 8, n. 299, p. 275.

39. *Quimati* is Nahuatl for "I have known" (Méndez Plancarte, ed., *Obras completas*, vol. 2, p. 425). For the route followed to reach Mexico City, see Maza, *La ruta de Sor Juana*, pp. 68–69.

40. Villancico 9, n. 300, p. 277.

41. Villancico 10, n. 301, p. 278.

42. Villancico 11, n. 302, p. 279.

43. Villancico 12, n. 303, p. 279.

44. Villancico 1, n. 312, p. 287.

45. Villancico 3, n. 314, p. 288.

46. Villancico 4, n. 315, p. 289.

47. Villancico 5, n. 316, p. 290.

48. Villancico 6, n. 317, p. 290.

49. Villancico 7, n. 318, p. 292.

50. Villancico 8, n. 319, p. 293.

51. Villancico 9, n. 320, p. 293.

52. Villancico 10, n. 321, p. 294.

53. Villancico 11, n. 322, p. 295.

54. N. 369, loa, scene v, p. 428.

55. Scene vi, p. 428.

56. N. 370, scene xviii, p. 459.

57. Scene xxiii, pp. 462–463.

58. Scene xxiv, p. 463. That *St. Hermenegild* fails as a play is commonly recognized: "Her play lacks the comparatively intense unity of a sacramental play. There is a dichotomy in *St. Hermenegildo* that detracts from its hold on the audience. . . . Sor Juana's *The Martyr, St. Hermenegildo* is not so much a sacramental play as an inchoate three-act play about the life of a saint" (Flynn, *Sor Juana Inés de la Cruz,* p. 78). The failure, as I see it, comes from a conflict between the theme and the structure of the play.

59. N. 372, scene i, p. 471.

60. Scene iv, p. 476.

61. Scene xxii, p. 492.

62. Scene xxv, p. 498.

63. Letra 3, n. 365, p. 319.

64. Letra 4, n. 366, p. 320.

65. N. 268, p. 248.

66. Villancico 3, n. 227, p. 214.

67. N. 373, scene viii, p. 507.
68. N. 406, seventh day, p. 859.
69. Eighth day, p. 860.
70. Ninth day, p. 862.
71. N. 353, poem 31, p. 312. There are thirty-two poems in the series.
72. N. 354, poem 32, p. 312.

3. The Temple of God

1. N. 323, poem 1, p. 296.
2. N. 325, poem 3, p. 297.
3. N. 334, poem 12, p. 301.
4. N. 342, poem 20, p. 306.
5. N. 347, poem 25, p. 309.
6. N. 348, poem 26, p. 309.
7. N. 349, poem 27, p. 310.
8. N. 350, poem 28, p. 310.
9. N. 352, poem 30, p. 311.
10. N. 353, poem 31, p. 312. The monstrance is the container for the host that was used for benedictions of the blessed sacrament, which were popularized in the piety of the Counterreformation. Monstrances were often shaped like the sun, with the pix for the host at the center and rays all around.
11. For an overview of the doctrine of the immaculate conception and its history, see Michael O'Carroll, *Theotokos: A Theological Encyclopedia of the Blessed Virgin Mary* (Wilmington, Del.: Michael Glazier, 1982).
12. Villancico 1, n. 225, p. 212.
13. Villancico 2, n. 226, p. 213.
14. Villancico 3, n. 227, pp. 213–214.
15. Villancico 4, n. 228, p. 214.
16. Villancico 5, n. 229, p. 215.
17. Villancico 6, n. 230, p. 216.
18. Villancico 7, n. 231, p. 216.
19. Villancico 1, n. 275, p. 254.
20. Villancico 2, n. 276, p. 255.
21. Villancico 3, n. 277, p. 255.
22. Villancico 4, n. 278, p. 256.
23. Villancico 5, n. 279, p. 256.
24. Villancico 6, n. 280, p. 257.
25. Villancico 7, n. 281, p. 257.
26. Villancico 8, n. 282, p. 258.
27. P. 259 (*Juguetillo*).
28. N. 355, poem 1, p. 313. See above, note 11.

29. N. 356, poem 2, p. 313.

30. N. 357, poem 3, p. 314.

31. N. 311, poem 8, pp. 285–286.

32. See, in 1676, villancico 8, n. 224, p. 212; in 1679, villancico 8, n. 258, p. 241; in 1685, villancico 8, n. 274, pp. 253–254.

33. See villancico 8, n. 224, p. 212.

34. Villancico 8, n. 274, p. 254.

35. Villancico 2, n. 218, p. 206; villancico 5, n. 255, p. 238; villancico 8, n. 258, p. 242; villancico 8, n. 274, p. 253.

36. Villancico 2, n. 252, pp. 235–236.

37. Villancico 2, n. 305, p. 281.

38. Villancico 3, n. 219, p. 206.

39. Villancico 4, n. 220, p. 207.

40. Villancico 6, n. 223, p. 210.

41. Villancico 4, n. 254, p. 237.

42. Villancico 5, n. 271, p. 250.

43. Villancico 6, n. 272, p. 251.

44. Villancico 2, n. 305, p. 281.

45. Villancico 5, n. 221, p. 208.

46. Villancico 6, n. 309, p. 283.

47. Villancico 8, n. 311, p. 286.

48. Villancico 8, n. 274, p. 253.

49. Villancico 1, n. 304, p. 280.

50. Villancico 2, n. 305, p. 281.

51. Villancico 4, n. 307, p. 282.

52. Villancico 1, n. 267, p. 247.

53. Villancico 3, n. 269, p. 249.

54. Villancico 3, n. 306, p. 281.

55. Villancico 5, n. 308, p. 283.

56. N. 405, p. 847.

57. N. 406, p. 848. Written between 1655 and 1660 and published in Madrid in 1670, Maria d'Agreda's work, *Mística ciudad de Dios,* was placed on the Index of forbidden books by Pope Innocent XI (26 June 1681) but the decree was suspended (9 November 1681) on the intervention of the king of Spain, Charles III. In 1696 the book was condemned by the University of Paris, which was impervious to Spanish pressure. For an English translation, see Mary Coronel de Jesus, *City of God: The Divine History and Life of the Virgin Mary Mother of God, Manifested to Mary of Agreda for the Encouragement of Men* (Hammond, Ind.: Conkey, 1914).

58. N. 257, p. 240.

59. N. 206, p. 164. It seems that in Nahuatl, roses were called *castilan xochitl* (literally, Castilian flowers), presumably because they were not native to Mexico. Jacques Lafaye, who notes this point, also thinks that the word

maravilla (marvel), which recurs in the first and the last lines, alludes to a wildflower that abounds in Mexico, the *mirabilis jalapa;* this seems more far-fetched (Jacques Lafaye, *Quetzalcóatl and Guadalupe: The Formation of Mexican National Consiousness, 1531–1813* [Chicago: University of Chicago Press, 1976], pp. 74–75). On the origins of the Guadalupe legend, see Michael Carroll, *The Cult of the Virgin Mary* (Princeton: Princeton University Press, 1986) pp. 182–194; I have borrowed some details from this book.

60. N. 406, p. 853.

4. Narcissus

1. Villancico 1, n. 283, p. 260.
2. Villancico 2, n. 284, p. 261.
3. Villancico 6, n. 288, p. 267.
4. Villancico 7, n. 289, p. 268.
5. Villancico 8, n. 290, p. 269.
6. *Tres letras sueltas para cantar en la solemnidad del nacimiento,* poem 1, n. 361, p. 316.
7. Poem 2, n. 362, p. 317.
8. Tavard, *Poetry and Contemplation,* pp. 76–81, 160–167.
9. N. 53, p. 75.
10. N. 367, scene v, p. 390.
11. Scene i, p. 383.
12. Scene v, p. 389.
13. See the translation, Luis de León, *The Names of Christ,* Classics of Western Spirituality (New York: Paulist Press, 1984), pp. 88–103.
14. Tavard, *Poetry and Contemplation,* pp. 173–176. For the poem, *Un pastorcico,* see Kieran Kavanaugh and Otilio Rodriguez, *The Complete Works of St. John of the Cross* (Washington, D.C.: ICS Publications, 1873), pp. 722–723.
15. On the origins of the myth and the influences at work in Juana's play, see Méndez Plancarte, ed., *Obras completas,* vol. 3, pp. xii–lxxvii; see also Paz, *Sor Juana: Or, the Traps of Faith,* pp. 350–356.
16. N. 368, scene i, p. 391.
17. Scene ii, p. 395.
18. Scene iii, p. 396.
19. Scene iii, p. 395.
20. Scene iv, p. 399.
21. Scene xi, p. 412.
22. Scene xii, p. 413.
23. George H. Tavard, *Transiency and Permanence: The Nature of Theology According to St. Bonaventure* (St. Bonaventure, N.Y.: Franciscan Institute, 1974), p. 31.

24. Tavard, *Poetry and Contemplation,* pp. 28–29, 234–235. For the "Romance on the Incarnation," see Kavanaugh and Rodriguez, *Complete Works,* pp. 724–732.

25. N. 368, scene vi, p. 402.

26. Scene vii, p. 405.

27. Tavard, *Poetry and Contemplation,* p. 100.

28. The *improperia* were prayers in the style of lamentations, sung during the veneration of the cross. Preserved in the reform of the Holy Week liturgy by Pius XII, they were practically eliminated by the switch to the vernacular after Vatican II.

29. N. 368, scene viii, p. 407.

30. Scene ix, p. 408.

31. See above, note 14.

32. Scene x, pp. 409–410.

33. Scene xii, p. 412.

34. Scene xiii, p. 416.

35. Scene xiv, p. 418.

36. Scene xv, p. 420.

37. Scene xvi, p. 421.

38. N. 405, p. 834.

39. *Tres letras sueltas a la encarnación,* poem 1, n. 358, pp. 314–315.

40. Poem 2, n. 359, p. 315.

41. Poem 3, n. 360, p. 316: "te Ancillam ostendis / ut Servum concipias."

5. The Finesses of God

1. For the text of Vieira's sermon, see Méndez Plancarte, ed., *Obras completas,* vol. 4, pp. 673–694.

2. This is suggested by, among others, Levia, *Introducción a Sor Juana,* pp. 85–91.

3. Manuel Fernández de Santa Cruz y Sahagún, *Antilogiae Sacrae Scripturae,* vol. 1, 720 pages (Lyon, 1670); vol. 2, 800 pages (Lyon, 1685).

4. N. 374, p. 509.

5. N. 390, p. 655.

6. N. 384, p. 607.

7. N. 379, p. 563.

8. N. 399, p. 762.

9. Méndez Plancarte, ed., *Obras completas,* vol. 4, pp. 694–697; Juana's letter is dated 26 November 1690.

10. The architect of the cathedral of Santiago de Compostela, Juan de Herrera (c. 1500–1575) exaggerated previous forms of the plateresque and initiated a style of extremely refined baroque architecture. The style was

named for a family of architects: José Benito Churriguera (1650–1723), with his sons, Nicolas and Jerome, and his nephew, Alberto.

11. N. 345, p. 308.

12. N. 351, p. 311.

13. N. 401, p. 779.

14. N. 404, p. 812.

15. I have studied some of these authors in *La Tradition au XVIIe siècle en France et en Angleterre* (Paris: Le Cerf, 1969).

16. N. 400, p. 778; in the *Respuesta* Juana claims "the name of Catholic and obedient daughter of my Holy Mother the Church" (n. 405, p. 844).

17. Giovanni Pico della Mirandola (1463–1494) was a very influential lay theologian of northern Italy during the Renaissance; see Henri de Lubac, *Pic de la Mirandole* (Paris: Aubier Montaigne, 1974).

18. *Kirkero:* n. 193, p. 157; *kirkerisar:* n. 50, p. 72.

19. N. 400, p. 777.

20. N. 401, p. 779.

21. St. Ignatius of Antioch, *Letter to the Magnesians,* 8, 2, in *The Apostolic Fathers* (Washington, D.C.: The Catholic University of America Press, 1962), p. 98.

22. N. 404, p. 825.

23. St. Bonaventure, *Collationes in Hexaëmeron,* 19, 7 (*Obras de San Buenaventura,* vol. 3 [Madrid: Biblioteca de Auctores Cristianos, 1947], pp. 540–541); see George H. Tavard, *Transiency and Permanence,* pp. 31–55.

24. N. 77, p. 97.

25. N. 211, p. 167.

26. N. 57, p. 77.

27. N. 56, p. 76.

28. N. 56, pp. 76–77.

29. N. 164, p. 143.

6. The Silence

1. Méndez Plancarte, ed., *Obras completas,* vol. 4, pp. 694–697.

2. Quoted in Francisco de la Maza, *Sor Juana Inés de la Cruz ante la historia* (Mexico: Universidad Nacional Autónoma, 1980), p. 84.

3. The code of canon law of 1917, canon 782, summed up the previous Latin tradition. It specified that only a bishop is the ordinary minister of confirmation; the designation of a priest as extraordinary minister was reserved to the Holy See. In the code of 1983, canons 882, 883, and 884 recognize some priests as ministers of confirmation.

4. N. 11, pp. 16–18.

5. See Maza, *Sor Juana,* p. 76.

6. The *ordinary* is the bishop in the territory of his own diocese.

7. See Maza, *Sor Juana*, p. 46. Archbishop Aguiar's negative attitude to women in general is illustrated at length in Paz, *Sor Juana: Or, the Traps of Faith*. It is safe to assert that the archbishop looked no more favorably on Sor Juana, with all her achievements and the titles given her by others, than he did on any other woman. For Mirta Aguirre (*Del encausto a la sangre: Sor Juana Inés de la Cruz* [Havana: Casa de las Americas, 1975]), the archbishop's attitude truly reflected the cultural climate of New Spain. There may be some excesses in what these authors affirm, but the patriarchal context of Juana's experience is not to be denied.

8. N. 405, p. 835.

9. N. 146, pp. 134–135.

10. N. 57, p. 77.

11. N. 143, p. 133.

12. N. 405, p. 836.

13. N. 143, p. 133.

14. N. 58, p. 78.

15. N. 57, p. 77.

16. See George H. Tavard, *Justification: An Ecumenical Study* (New York: Paulist Press, 1983), pp. 49-69.

17. Martin Luther, *The Bondage of the Will*, V (John Dillenberger, *Martin Luther: Selections from His Writings* [New York: Doubleday, 1961], pp. 191–192). The counterpart of God's hiddenness is manifested in the Law, and above all in the Word. See Harry McSorley, *Luther: Right or Wrong?* (New York: Newman Press, 1969).

18. N. 151, p. 137.

19. N. 152, p. 137.

20. N. 145, p. 134.

21. N. 147, p. 135.

22. N. 148, p. 135.

23. N. 149, p. 136.

24. N. 215, p. 182. On this episode, see José Bravo Ugarte, *História de México*, vol. 2: *La Nueva España*, 4th ed. (Mexico City: Editorial Jus, 1960), pp. 229-293.

25. N. 215, p. 181.

26. N. 1, p. 3.

27. N. 412, p. 876.

28. N. 408, pp. 872–873.

29. N. 409, pp. 873–874.

7. The Theology of Beauty

1. N. 19, p. 26.

2. N. 48, p. 63.

3. St. Augustine, *Confessions,* bk. 4, ch. 15, 24. See George H. Tavard, *Les Jardins de saint Augustin: Lecture des Confessions* (Montreal: Bellarmin; Paris: Le Cerf, 1988).

4. St. Augustine, *Confessions,* bk. 10, ch. 27, 38.

5. St. Augustine, *De doctrina christiana,* bk. 1, ch. 2 (translated as *Christian Instruction,* in *Writings of St. Augustine,* The Fathers of the Church [New York: Cima Pub., 1947], pp. 28–29).

6. St. Augustine, *The City of God,* bk. 22, ch. 19, 2–20, 3.

7. Hans Urs von Balthasar, *Herrlichkeit,* 8 vols. (Einsiedeln: Johannes Verlag, 1961–1968). This is the first part of a trilogy; it is followed by a study of divine drama (*Theodramatik,* 4 vols. [Einsiedeln: Johannes Verlag, 1963–1983]) and of divine logic (*Theologik,* 3 vols. [Einsiedeln: Johannes Verlag, 1985–1987]). Some volumes of *Herrlichkeit* have been translated into English: *The Glory of the Lord: A Theological Aesthetics,* vol. 1: *Seeing the Form* (San Francisco: Ignatius Press, 1983); vol. 2: *Studies in Theological Styles: Clerical Styles* (San Francisco: Ignatius Press, 1984); vol. 3: *Studies in Theological Styles: Lay Styles* (San Francisco: Ignatius Press, 1986).

8. Jill Raitt, ed., *Christian Spirituality: High Middle Ages and Reformation* (New York: Crossroads, 1986), pp. 3–8, 121–139; A Benedictine Nun, ed., *The Exercises of Saint Gertrude* (Westminster, Md.: Newman Press, 1956); Columba Hart and Jane Bishop, eds., *Hildegard of Bingen: Scivias* (New York: Paulist Press, 1990).

9. Nicholas of Cusa, *The Vision of God* (New York: Ungar, 1960), pp. 1–6.

10. George H. Tavard, *La Théologie parmi les sciences humaines* (Paris: Le Cerf, 1975), pp. 91–94.

11. See above, chapter 5, note 23.

12. See Charles Ledit and Joseph Zeltz, *Les Chanoines de Pythagore* (Troyes: Editions Tetrakys, 1960), p. 23. The significance of numbers in Christian theology goes back to St. Augustine: "The perfection of the work [of creation] is indicated by the number six. For six is the first number that is the exact sum of its parts, that is, of its sixth and third parts and its half: one, two, and three, the sum of which is six" (*The City of God,* bk. 11, ch. 30).

13. St. Thomas Aquinas, *Summa theologica,* I, q. 5, a. 4, ad 1.

14. St. Augustine, *The City of God,* bk. 22, ch. 19, 2.

15. St. Thomas Aquinas, *Summa theologica,* I, q. 5, a. 4, ad 1.

16. See above, Introduction, note 7.

17. N. 20, p. 72.

18. N. 89, p. 106.

19. N. 87, p. 105.

20. N. 220, p. 207.

21. N. 222, p. 209 (stars); n. 254, pp. 237–238 (Zodiac); n. 228, pp. 214–215 (herbs); n. 270, p. 249 (flowers); n. 227, pp. 213–214 (lily); n. 209, p. 165 (rose).

22. N. 214, p. 172.

23. N. 61, pp. 79–81.

24. N. 384, p. 604.

25. N. 257, p. 240.

26. These correspond to "experience, judgement, understanding, decision"; see Bernard Lonergan, *Method in Theology* (New York: Herder and Herder, 1972), pp. 14–25; Joseph E. Kelly, ed., *Perspectives on Scripture and Tradition: Essays by Robert M. Grant, Robert E. McNally, George H. Tavard* (Notre Dame, Inc.: Fides, 1976), pp. 105–114; David Tracy, *The Analogical Imagination: Christian Theology and the Culture of Pluralism* (New York: Crossroad, 1981), pp. 99–135.

27. Tavard, *La Tradition au XVIIe siècle,* pp. 79–120.

28. N. 385, p. 615. In this poem, composed in honor of a priest, Fray Diego Velasquez de la Cadena, Juana includes his name, *Cadena* (chain), at three points, in close proximity to the "perfect circle" of creation. This is a delicate touch in the baroque style.

29. N. 383, p. 597.

30. N. 216, p. 201.

31. N. 83, p. 101.

32. N. 252, p. 235.

33. N. 358, p. 314.

34. N. 104, pp. 115–116.

35. N. 378, p. 556.

36. Dillenberger, *Martin Luther,* p. 503; see Alister E. McGrath, *Luther's Theology of the Cross: Martin Luther's Theological Breakthrough* (Oxford: Blackwell, 1985).

37. N. 407, pp. 867–872.

38. N. 253, p. 236.

39. Pierre Teilhard de Chardin, *The Divine Milieu* (New York: Harper, 1960), p. 46.

40. N. 408, p. 872.

41. N. 413, p. 876.

42. N. 411, p. 875.

43. George H. Tavard, *The Seventeenth-century Tradition* (Leiden: Brill, 1978), pp. 180–188.

44. *Augsburg Confession,* art. 4, in Theodore Tappert, ed., *The Book of Concord* (Philadelphia: Muhlenberg Press, 1959), p. 30; see the corresponding passage of the *Apology of the Augsburg Confession,* ch. 4, in Tappert, ed., *The Book of Concord,* pp. 107–168.

45. Tavard, *Justification,* p. 63.

46. Emma Thérèse Healy, *Saint Bonaventure's De reductione artium ad theologiam* (Saint Bonaventure, N.Y.: Franciscan Institute, 1955).

47. Dante Alighieri, *La divina commedia* (Milan: Bietti, 1977), canto 26, p. 584; the English translation is from Laurence Binyon, *The Portable Dante* (New York: Viking, 1976), p. 506.

48. Quoted in Eric Gritsch, *Martin—God's Court Jester: Luther in Retrospect* (Philadelphia: Fortress Press, 1983), p. 192–193.

49. As in the title of the book by Marshall McLuhan and Quentin Fiore, *The Medium and the Message* (New York: Bantam Books, 1967).

50. Lonergan, *Method in Theology,* pp. 132–133, 355–368.

51. N. 381, p. 573.

52. See above, note 7.

53. Ludwig Wittgenstein, *Tractatus Logico-philosophicus* (London: Routledge and Paul, 1961), n. 7, p. 151.

Further Reading

Except for the collected editions of Juana Inés's works, this short bibliography includes only books in English. Abundant material is available to readers in Spanish.

1. Collected Editions of Juana Inés's Works

Alfonso Méndez Plancarte, ed. *Obras completas de Sor Juana Inés de la Cruz.* 4 vols. (vol. 4 completed by Alberto Salceda). Mexico City: Fondo de Cultura Económica, 1950, 1952, 1955, 1957.

Francisco Monterde. *Sor Juana Inés de la Cruz: Obras completas.* Mexico City: Editorial Porrua, 1975.

2. Works of Juana Inés in Translation

John Campion. *El sueño: Sor Juana Inés de la Cruz.* Austin, Texas: Thorn Springs Press, 1983. [Includes an introduction that I find quite misleading.]

Pauline Cook. *The Pathless Grove: Sonnets.* Prairie City, Ill.: Decker Press, 1950. [Translation of a number of Juana's sonnets.]

Luis Harss. *Sor Juana's Dream.* New York: Lumen Books, 1986. [Includes an introduction and a commentary.]

Margaret Sayers Peden. *Sor Juana Inés de la Cruz: Poems, a Bilingual Anthology.* Binghamton, N.Y.: Bilingual Press, 1985. [Versified translation of selected passages from most of the poetic genres practiced by Juana Inés, including a long section from the beginning of *Primero sueño.*]

Margaret Sayers Peden. *A Woman of Genius: The Intellectual Autobiography of Sor Juana Inés de la Cruz.* Salisbury, Conn.: Lime Rock Press, 1982. [Translation of the *Respuesta a Sor Filotea de la Cruz.*]

Nina M. Scott. "'If you are not pleased to favor me, put me out of your mind . . .': Gender and Authority in Sor Juana Inés de la Cruz, and the Translation of Her Letter to the Reverend Father Maestro Antonio Núñez of the Society of Jesus." *Women's Studies International Forum,* vol. 11, n. 5, 1988, pp. 429–438.

Alan S. Trueblood. *A Sor Juana Anthology.* Cambridge, Mass.: Harvard University Press, 1988. [A good selection of Juana's works, generally bilingual, though not for *First Dream* and *Reply to Sor Philothea;* with a foreword by Octavio Paz and an introduction that follows Paz's interpretation.]

3. Works about Juana Inés and Her Era

Gerard C. Flynn. *Sor Juana Inés de la Cruz.* New York: Twayne Publishers, 1971.

Joscelyn Godwin. *Athanasius Kircher, Renaissance Man and the Quest for Lost Knowledge.* London: Thames and Hudson, 1979.

Irving A. Leonard. *Baroque Times in Old Mexico: Seventeenth-century Persons, Places, and Practices.* Ann Arbor, Mich.: University of Michigan Press, 1959.

Irving A. Leonard. *Don Carlos de Sigüenza y Góngora: A Mexican Savant of the Seventeenth Century.* Berkeley, Cal.: University of California Press, 1929.

Constance M. Montross. *Virtue or Vice? Sor Juana's Use of Thomistic Thought.* Washington, D.C.: University Press of America, 1981.

Octavio Paz. *Sor Juana: Or, the Traps of Faith.* Translated by Margaret S. Peden. Cambridge, Mass.: Harvard University Press, 1988.

Index